Hot & Spicy
CHILI

Also by Dave DeWitt

Hot & Spicy & Meatless (with Mary Jane Wilan and Melissa T. Stock)

Hot Spots

Texas Monthly Guidebook to New Mexico

The Fiery Cuisines (with Nancy Gerlach)

Fiery Appetizers (with Nancy Gerlach)

The Whole Chile Pepper Book (with Nancy Gerlach)

The Food Lover's Handbook to the Southwest (with Mary Jane Wilan)

Callaloo, Calypso, and Carnival (with Mary Jane Wilan)

The Pepper Garden (with Paul W. Bosland)

A World of Curries (with Arthur Pais)

How to Order:
Single copies of this book may be ordered from Prima Publishing, P.O. Box 1260BK, Rocklin, CA 95677; telephone (916) 632-4400. Quantity discounts are also available. On your letterhead, include information concerning the intended use of the books and the number of books you wish to purchase.

Hot & Spicy
CHILI

Dave DeWitt
Mary Jane Wilan
Melissa T. Stock

Prima Publishing
P.O. Box 1260BK
Rocklin, CA 95677
(916) 632-4400

Portions of this book first appeared in *Chile Pepper* magazine. Used by permission.

Chef Jim Heywood's chili recipe reprinted courtesy of *Taste,* vol. 21, no. 1 (Spring/Summer 1993), pp. 22–23. Copyright 1993 by The Culinary Institute of America. Used by permission.

Library of Congress Cataloging-in-Publication Data

DeWitt, Dave.
    Hot & spicy chili / Dave DeWitt, Mary Jane Wilan, Melissa T. Stock.
      p.   cm.
    Includes bibliographical references and index.
    ISBN 1-55958-420-3
    1. Chili con carne.   I. Wilan, Mary Jane.   II. Stock, Melissa T.
III. Title.   IV. Title: Hot and spicy chili.
TX749.D48 1994
641.8'23—dc20

                          94-2910
                           CIP

96 97 98 BB 10 9 8 7 6 5 4 3 2
Printed in the United States of America

*To all the chili cooks who believe, as did George Haddaway,
that chili can someday bring world peace.*

Acknowledgments

Thanks to all the chili chefs who provided recipes in this book—they are mentioned in their recipe introductions. Additionally, we appreciate the assistance of the following people: Bill Bridges, Red Caldwell, Phoebe Cude, Donald Downes, Nancy Gerlach, Ormly Gumfudgin, Jo Ann Horton, Andy Housholder, Sharon Hudgins, Sam Pendergrast, Mark Preston, Robert Spiegel, John Thorne, Harold Timber, John Vittal, Jim West, Betsy Wooten, and A. Vann York.

Contents

Introduction

As chile pepper aficionados, we naturally love chili con carne because the dish utilizes plenty of our favorite pungent pods. But beyond that, we love the spirit, enthusiasm, and just plain wackiness of chili cooks and those intrepid souls we call "chilosophers," who wax profound (and profane) on the subject.

Our purpose in this book is to present the widest possible range of information on chili. In addition to recipes, we have researched the origins, history, humor, ingredients, and techniques of chili and, additionally, the story of cooks, cookoffs, contests, and accompaniments. We predict that this book will be the source of much disputation from chili aficionados because many of them will disagree with everything we have written. But that's good because controversy is the true spirit of chili.

A word or two on the recipes. Because chili cooks are independent and often downright ornery, their recipes occasionally lack precise measurements of ingredients and exact instructions. Since cooking chili is an art as much as a science, such vagaries are to be expected. We have made every attempt to standardize the formats as much as possible without losing the charm of the recipes. While we have retained the humor inherent in many of them, we have, for example, placed all the ingredients in their order of use in the recipe instructions, which chili cooks often forget to do. We have also, in some cases, estimated amounts of ingredients because instructions like "chili powder—twice the amount in the package" are too vague for home cooks to follow. We hereby apologize in advance if we have tampered too much with any recipe.

There are no serving suggestions included in the recipes, but that problem is easy to solve. Accompany chili with any of the dishes in Chapter 6, or your own favorite accompaniments. Regarding the yield of the recipes, it is impossible to know exactly how many people each recipe will serve because we cannot predict the size of the servings. So we have made educated guesses for each recipe.

Finally, we should note for the record that the story of the chili organizations and their cookoffs is rather bizarre and confusing. So, for future reference, here are the organizations and the names of their ultimate championship cookoffs. The complete story is told in Chapters 3 and 4.

- Chili Appreciation Society, International (CASI): CASI Terlingua International Chili Championship
- "Behind the Store": The Original Viva Terlingua International Frank X. Tolbert–Wick Fowler Memorial Championship Chili Cookoff
- International Chili Society (ICS): World's Championship Chili Cookoff.

Now that you are totally befuddled, let's cook some chili!

1

The Evolution of Chili con Carne

Everything about chili con carne generates some sort of controversy—the spelling of the name, the origin and history of the dish, the proper ingredients for a great recipe, the awesome society and cookoff rivalries, and even what the future holds for the bowl o' red. Perhaps the fiery nature of the dish itself is responsible for such controversy, driving usually rational men and women into frenzies when their conception of the truth is challenged.

Name Games

As far as the spelling of the dish is concerned, etymologists tell us that there is enormous confusion about the terms that describe the Capsicums (chile peppers) and the recipes prepared with them. "For such a seemingly innocuous topic," wrote *Chile Pepper* contributing editor Sharon Hudgins, "a confusion of terms abounds. Take your pick of spellings: chile(s), chili(s,es), chille(s), chilli(s,es), chillie(s), chilley(s), chilly(s,ies). Then take your pick of meanings: a fruit, a berry, a vegetable, a spice, a specific dish (with many variations) of pureed mild or pungent peppers, a specific dish (with many variations) of mild or pungent peppers with meat, or a specific dish (with even more variations) of meat with peppers (usually hot ones)."

Debates about the spelling are endless, and this controversy has even made it into *The Congressional Record*. Senator Pete Domenici (R-N.M.) noted in 1983: "New Mexicans know that 'chili' is that inedible mixture of watery tomato soup, dried gristle, half-cooked kidney beans, and a myriad of silly ingredients that is passed off as food in Texas and Oklahoma." But at least Domenici allowed Texans to spell their chili with an *i* to differentiate it from the New Mexican versions of the dish.

Texans insist on spelling both the pod and the dish with an *i,* which is their prerogative. New Mexicans refuse to acknowledge that the word *chili* even exists, which is their right, and they spell the plant, pod, and dish with an *e*. In Illinois, for some strange reason, the dish is spelled *chilli*. In the end, say the true chiliheads, it really doesn't matter how you spell it—so long as you love it.

For the past decade or so, some writers who must use these terms quite often, such as ourselves, have reached an informal agreement on style. To avoid confusing the plant and pod with the bowl o' red, we use *chile,* the original Spanish-Mexican spelling, to refer to the plant and the pod. The word *chili* means the dish of meat and peppers. It is an abbreviated form of *chili con carne,* which is a curious combination of the Anglicized *chili* (from *chile*) and the Spanish *carne* (meat). Interestingly enough, some early California recipes were for *carne con chile,* which is actually a more accurate description, in Spanish, of the chili of today.

Carroll Shelby, founder of the International Chili Society.

Our style is not new. As early as 1949, Arthur and Bobbie Coleman, authors of *The Texas Cookbook,* noted: "The dish itself, the completed product, is chili with one 'l' and an 'i' on the end. . . . The word *chile* means a hot pepper, the fruit, not the powdered product. To spell the name of the dish *chile* would lead to confusing it with the main ingredients. . . ."

The Mexican Connection

Another endlessly debated controversy is the origin of the bowl o' red itself. Texans, New Mexicans, and Arizonans believe that the dish was invented in their state, and a chili historian, Bill Bridges, observed in *The Great American Chili Book:* "It has also been claimed that chili was invented by the army, the Texas Rangers, Confederate officers, American Indians, a Spanish nun, a Chinese chuckwagon cook, an Irish chuckwagon cook, Canary Islanders, Czechs, Greeks, Magyars, and the mountain people of the Caucasus."

Archaeological evidence indicates that chile peppers—and their culinary use—evolved in South America and were domesticated there and in Mexico. But despite evidence that reveals dozens of recipes combining meat and chiles, most writers on the subject state flatly that chili did not originate in Mexico. Even Mexico disclaims chili; the *Diccionario de Mejicanismos,* a Mexican dictionary, defined it in 1959 as: "A detestable dish sold from Texas to New York City and erroneously described as Mexican."

Despite such protestations, the combination of meat and chiles in stew-like concoctions appears frequently in Mexican cooking. Elizabeth Lambert Ortiz, in her book, *The Complete Book of Mexican Cooking* (1967), has a recipe for Chile con Carne made with ancho chiles, which she described as "an authentic northern Mexican style of cooking . . . as distinct from the version that developed in Texas." In *The Food and Drink of Mexico* (1964), George C. Booth commented: "In the United States, chili con carne is predominantly a bean dish, but in Mexico *chile con carne* is a generous meat dish."

Mexican *caldillos* and *pucheros* (thick soups or stews), *moles* (sauces made with a variety of chiles), and *adobos* (thick sauces) often resemble chili in both appearance and taste because they all sometimes use similar ingredients: various types of chiles combined with meat (usually beef), onions, garlic, cumin, and occasionally tomatoes. We have collected three such recipes from Mexico, Mole de Olla, Pork in Adobo Sauce, and Caldillo de Duranguense, to illustrate their fundamental similarity to chili.

There are even Texan chili purists who grudgingly—very grudgingly— admit a Mexican connection. As historian Charles Ramsdell noted, "It is true that in the northern part of Mexico, they serve what they call *chile con carne*. It is stewed meat with a kind of *salsa picante* (hot sauce) poured over it. This, no doubt, is akin to our chili, in about the same degree as the Neanderthal man or the orang-outang is akin to us. It may be a remote ancestor. But it is not chili."

Chili as we know it today may not have originated in Mexico, but it's there now. Since 1978, the Mexican National Championship Chili Cookoff has been held in various locations in that country. The Mexican cookoff is sanctioned by the International Chili Society—proving that the love of chili is indeed international.

Chili Conjectures

Chili con carne fanatics are not satisfied with a mundane theory holding that chili evolved from Mexican recipes. A strange tale about the possible origin of chili has appeared in several books, the first perhaps in George and Berthe Herter's 1960 book, *Bull Cook and Authentic Historical Recipes and Practices*. The story of the "lady in blue" tells of Sister Mary of Agreda, a Spanish nun in the early 1600s who never left her convent in Spain but nonetheless had out-of-body experiences during which her spirit was transported across the Atlantic to preach Christianity to the Indians. After one of the return trips, her spirit wrote down the first recipe for chili con carne, which the Indians gave her: chile peppers, venison, onions, and tomatoes.

Only slightly less fanciful is the theory that suggests that Canary Islanders, transplanted to San Antonio as early as 1731, used local peppers and wild onions combined with various meats to create early chili combinations. This theory, first advanced by H. Allen Smith, states that it was the Canary Islanders who first brought cumin—an essential spice in chili—to the United States. (Smith competed in the first chili cookoff against Wick Fowler—see Chapter 3 for that story.)

Everett Lee DeGolyer, a scholar, chili aficionado, and multimillionaire, believed that Texas chili con carne had its origins as the "pemmican of the Southwest" in the late 1840s. According to DeGolyer, Texans pounded together dried beef, beef fat, chiltepins (in Texas, "chilipiquins"), and salt to make trail food for the long ride out to San Francisco and the gold fields. The concentrated, dried mixture was then boiled in pots along the trail as sort of an "instant chili."

As Bill Bridges noted, "It seems obvious that chili would originate where there was an abundant supply of its two prime ingredients, meat and chile." Bridges quoted from *Mexican Gold Trail*, the journal of George W. B. Evans, who in the mid-1800s mentioned a chili-like concoction. "Beef is prepared for the long journey by pounding it together with lard and pepper," Evans wrote. "A small pinch of this . . . thrown into a pan or kettle of boiling water with a little flour or corn meal for thickening, will satisfy the wants of six men at any time; and it is a dish much relished by all."

This reference may be one of the first written mentions of chili—albeit not by name. This pemmican premise even has a modern incarnation: brick chili, a highly fat-laden concoction that—because of a pound of suet—solidifies into a brick when it cools.

A variation on the pemmican theory holds that cowboys invented chile while driving cattle along the lengthy and lonely trails. Supposedly, range cooks would plant oregano, chiles, and onions among patches of mesquite to protect the ingredients from cattle. The next time they passed along the same trail, they would collect the spices, combine them with beef (what else?) and make a dish called "trail drive chili."

According to another chili historian, Robert Stuart, large pots of this chili were stirred with a "chilistick," which had absorbed the flavors and spiciness of the chili and therefore could not be used to stir any other food. A further variation on the cowboy theory holds that chili descended from "son-of-a-bitch stew," a concoction made from the internal organs of a freshly killed calf or deer.

Some chili scholars believe that the ex–chuckwagon cooks, who knew that trail drives would soon be a phenomenon of the past, opened up the first chili joints in cow towns along the trails. John Henderson, a western historian, described an early chili joint as "about twenty-five feet wide, half that in length, with a small space in the rear partitioned off to screen the cook stove and hide the lack of sanitation."

Joe Cooper noted that "during the late years of the previous century, almost every Texas town had its quota of restaurants which placed stress on chili. An unbelievable number were proprietored by guys named Joe. They guarded recipes with a passionate jealousy."

Sam Pendergrast, the creator of "zen chili," was weaned on cafe chilis. He recalled in *Chile Pepper* magazine: "In Abilene, where I grew up in the 1940s, the best chili cafes were the Green Frog near Fourth and Pine, the wonderfully exotic Canton Cafe further south on Pine, the Grape Inn at Tenth and Grape, and the Dixie Pig at South 14th and Butternut. They all served the same chili—blood red, with an aroma of cominos that could be whiffed at least a block away, hefty chunks of meat you could get your teeth into (along with bits of gristle), and a rich sauce featuring at least an eighth of an inch of grease that would easily soak up a quarter's worth of crackers even at '40s prices." Sam's slightly zen version of cafe chili is presented in Chapter 5, along with more tales and recipes of cafe chilis.

The U.S. Army has often been given credit for originating chili, but these days that theory is generally discounted. According to chili scholar John Thorne, "Soldiers of the U.S. Army on the Western frontier had been eating chili since the war with Mexico (1846) but not necessarily in their messes. The first army publication to give a recipe for chili was published in 1896, the *Manual for Army Cooks* (War Department Document #18). By World War I, the army had added garlic and beans; by World War II, tomatoes."

The Devil's Soup

Probably the most likely explanation for the origin of chili con carne in Texas combines the heritage of Mexican food with the rigors of life on the Texas frontier. Most historians agree that the earliest written description of chili came from J. C. Clopper, who lived near Houston. He wrote of visiting San Antonio in 1828: "When they (poor families of San Antonio) have to pay for their meat in the market, a very little is made to suffice for the family; it is generally cut into a kind of hash with nearly as many peppers as there are pieces of meat—this is all stewed together."

Except for this one quote, which does not mention the dish by name, historians of heat can find no documented evidence of chili in Texas before 1880. Around that time in San Antonio, a municipal market—El Mercado—was operating in Military Plaza. Historian Charles Ramsdell noted that "the first rickety chili stands" were set up in this marketplace, with the bowls of red sold by women who were called 'chili queens.'

"The legendary chili queens," continued Ramsdell, "beautiful, bantering, but virtuous, made their first appearance. All night long they cooked, served, and flirted in the picturesque flare from hand-hammered tin lanterns, in the savory haze rising from clay vessels on charcoal braziers."

Alexander Sweet, a San Antonio newspaper columnist, described Military Plaza and the chili stands in 1885: "He will see an array of tables and benches, and he will be assailed by the smell of something cooking. At the fire are numerous pots and kettles, around which are dusky, female figures, and faces that are suggestive of 'the weird sisters' whose culinary proclivities were such a source of annoyance to MacBeth. These are the *chile con carne* stands, at which this toothsome viand is sold to all who have the money and inclination to patronize them."

A bowl o' red cost visitors like O. Henry and William Jennings Bryan a mere dime and was served with bread and a glass of water. O. Henry later wrote a short story about the chili stands entitled "The Enchanted Kiss." In it, a young San Antonio drugstore clerk eats chili in the mercado and hallucinates (another out-of-body experience) that he is the former captain of the Spanish army in Mexico who has remained immortal since 1519 by eating chili con

Betsy Wooten

The Cactus Jack & Co. Chili team in San Mateo, California.

carne! The alleged hallucinogenic (beer?) and life-lengthening properties (chile?) of chili are still much debated today at chili cookoffs.

Given the popularity of the dish, commercialization of it was inevitable. Somewhere between 1877 and 1882 (no chili historian seems to have figured this one out), William G. Tobin of San Antonio, Texas, produced (presumably in his home) the first canned chili, W.G. Tobin's Chili-Con-Carne. By 1884, he had constructed and was about to open the first chili canning factory, the Tobin Canning Company in San Antonio, but he died, and the factory project failed. Incidentally, the first printed chili recipe appeared in *Mrs. Owen's Cook Book* in 1880.

Chili became very popular in the Texas jail system between 1890 and 1900, giving some people the idea that the dish originated behind bars. Chili historian Floyd Cogan gives us the reason: "How else could you take bad or cheap cuts of meat, add chile peppers, spices, and herbs and make them taste first rate?" According to Cogan, inmates rated the jails according to the chili that was served, and after serving their time they wrote back to the jails for recipes. "Some, we are told," added Cogan, "missed it so bad that they committed crimes just to get back in jail so they could once again have their fill of real Texas jail chili."

The fame of chili con carne began to spread, and the dish soon became a major tourist attraction, making its appearance in Mexican restaurants all over Texas—and elsewhere. At the World's Fair in Chicago in 1893, a bowl o' red was available at the "San Antonio Chili Stand."

Around this time, commercial chili powder was created, but history is unclear about who actually invented it. Some chili historians credit the invention of the red dust to DeWitt Clinton Pendery of Fort Worth, who began selling his own brand of "Chiltomaline" powder to cafes and hotels in the early 1890s. It was Pendery who noted in his advertising: "The health giving properties of hot chile peppers have no equal. They give tone to the alimentary canal, regulating the functions, giving a natural appetite, and promoting healthy action of the kidneys, skin, and lymphatics." Pendery's company, first called The Mexican Chilley Supply Company, later changed its name to Pendery's, and it's still open and selling chili powder (and many other spices) today in Fort Worth.

Other sources insist that it was William Gebhardt of New Braunfels, Texas, who produced the first packaged chili powder in 1894. Two years before, Gebhardt had opened a cafe in back of Miller's Saloon and discovered that chili was the favorite food of his customers. But chili was a seasonal food because homegrown chiles were available only after the summer harvest. Gebhardt solved the problem by importing Mexican ancho chiles so that he could serve the dish year-round.

At first, Gebhardt ran the chiles three times through a home meat grinder. Later, according to a description of the time, Gebhardt "concocted a chili powder in a crude mill by grinding chile peppers, cumin seed, oregano, and black pepper through an old hammer mill, feeding a little of this and a little of that to the mill. What came out was put in little-necked bottles and then packed in a box for retail." At first he called the product "Tampico Dust," but he later changed the name to "Gebhardt's Eagle Chili Powder."

In 1896, Gebhardt opened a factory in San Antonio and was producing five cases of chili powder a week, which he sold from the back of his wagon as he drove through town. He was also an inventor, and eventually patented thirty-seven machines for his factory. By 1899, Gebhardt had received U.S. trademark number 32,329 for his Eagle Chili Powder. The Gebhardt brand is still in existence today.

The turn of the century witnessed a surge in the popularity of chili. Hodge Chili was canned in St. Louis, Missouri, in 1905, and in 1908, Ike's Chili House opened in Tulsa, Oklahoma. That establishment is still open at 712 South Boston Street. Lou Priebe, a regular customer there (and also a judge at the Blue Grass Chili Festival) commented on the establishment: "Chili was the 'soul food' of the Okies. During the Depression you could go into Ike's and get a bowl of chili for a quarter, and it was the main meal of the day."

William Gebhardt's own brand of chili was canned in San Antonio in 1908 (some say 1911), and "chile con carne" was first defined in an American dictionary in 1909, according to Joe Cooper. It was "a Mexican dish consisting of minced red peppers and meat." Another definition (not in a dictionary) referred to the bowl o' red as "the devil's soup," an allusion to the hot chiles in it.

By 1917, Walker's Red Hot Chile con Carne was being canned in Austin, Texas—note the *e* in *chile*. During the following year, Walker's was producing forty-five thousand cans of chili a day. In 1921, Wolf Brand Chili was being canned in Corsicana, Texas.

About this time, the popularity of the bowl o' red began to spread, and the first chili emporium opened in Cincinnati in 1922 (some say 1923), the Empress Chili Parlor. According to chili historian F. Starr, "Cincinnati chili was concocted in October, 1922, by a man who had never eaten a bit of Texas chili, and it has been made ever since by people immunized against it by geography and culture."

Indeed. The easterners began serving the chili in strange ways, which, of course, forever earned them the scorn of Texans. One-Way chili was straight, Cincinnati-style chili. Two-Way was served with spaghetti under the chili. Three-Way added cheese on top. Four-Way added onions to the spaghetti-and-cheese chili, and Five-Way added beans to the spaghetti base! The Empress Chili Parlor is still open today, serving the now-traditional Cincinnati chili.

Back in Texas, the chili queens were banned from selling in San Antonio in 1937 for health reasons—public officials objected to flies and poorly washed dishes. They were restored by Mayor Maury Maverick (a real name, folks— unbranded cattle were named after his dad) in 1939, but their stands were closed again shortly after the start of World War II.

Chili continued to be mentioned occasionally—and erroneously—as late as 1964, when William I. Kaufman, in his book *Recipes from the Caribbean and Latin America,* wrote in his recipe for Fiesta Chili con Carne: "The best known of all Mexican dishes, chili con carne, may also be eaten with rice instead of beans."

The Texans, however, never forgot their culinary heritage, and in 1977 the Texas Legislature proclaimed chili con carne to be the "Official Texas State Dish." Incidentally, in 1993, the Illinois State Senate passed a resolution proclaiming that Illinois was to be the "Chilli [*sic*] Capital of the Civilized World," a move that outraged Texans.

During the 1980s, San Antonio began staging what they call "historic re-enactments" of the chili queens, complete with some of the original queens, such as songstress Lydia Mendoza, who serenade the chili eaters. The "Return of the Chili Queens Festival," held each year in Market Square, recreates the era of the chili queens and celebrates the dish that, no matter what its origin, will live forever in the hearts, minds, and stomachs of Texans.

America's Official Food?

Chili lovers are never satisfied. Despite the fact that the bowl o' red is the Texas state dish, a movement has been growing for more than a decade to have Congress declare chili con carne to be America's "official food." In

1984, Congressman Manuel Lujan of New Mexico introduced House Joint Resolution 465 — the so-called "Chili Bill" — which contained ten instances of the word *whereas*. Here are four of them:

"Whereas chili enjoys a universal popularity throughout the width and breadth of this great land that is unequal to other American foods," Lujan wrote, "and whereas chili is a succulent, distinctive blending of meats and spices that has economically nourished countless millions of Americans since its historic inception in the nineteenth century; and whereas chili is a truly egalitarian cuisine whose vast popularity prevails with American people of every economic and social stratum, unifying gastronomes and those with more proletarian palates as its devotees; and whereas chili is a definitive food whose hearty, committed character embodies the robust and indomitable American spirit, be it Resolved by the Senate and House of Representatives in Congress Assembled, that chili be designated as the official food of this great Nation."

Since the Chili Bill's introduction, however, it has been simmering on Congress' back burner and has never been passed into law. But loyal chili fans try year after year with national publicity campaigns in hopes of getting the bill

Ormly Gumfudgin, historian of the International Chili Society.

Chel Beeson

passed. In 1988, a campaign led by self-proclaimed World Chili Ambassador Ormly Gumfudgin—and supported by the International Chili Society and Maximum Strength Pepto-Bismol—attempted to obtain the signatures of *one million* chiliheads on a petition to support passage of the bill, which had stalled in the House for four years. Because more than 750,000 people attend chili cookoffs each year, Gumfudgin believed that the goal was obtainable. The goal was not achieved, however, but the bill continued its long stewing in the House of Representatives.

Another publicity stunt was staged in 1993, when the International Chili Society and Hyundai Motor America co-sponsored the twenty-three–city "Chili Across America" tour. That motorcade, led by a motorized stagecoach with a three-hundred–pound copper chili pot mounted on top, was designed to begin at the Capitol building in Washington. The final stop in the tour— appropriately enough—was the ICS World Championship Chili Cookoff in Reno, with its $25,000 grand prize. It seems likely that the cantankerousness of Congress will match that of chili cooks all over the country, and that a final decision on our national dish will come long after this book is published.

Meanwhile, on January 23, 1993, a record crowd of thirty-five thousand chiliheads showed up in Greenway Plaza Park in Houston for the ninth annual *Houston Post* Go Texan Roundup Chili Cook-Off. And that was a local contest. So the public support for chili simply will not evaporate.

The recipes that follow in this chapter reveal the origins of chili con carne —and the nearly infinite combinations of ingredients and amounts.

Mole de Olla
(Kettle Stew)

Most people associate *mole* with the famous chocolate *mole*—*mole poblano*—but the word refers to both a mixture and a stew. No chocolate is used in this recipe, and with the exception of the potatoes and corn, this dish is quite similar to chili.

4   ancho chiles, seeds and stems removed (or substitute dried red New Mexican pods)
2   pounds sirloin steak, cut into ½-inch cubes
3   tablespoons vegetable oil
1   medium onion, chopped
2   cloves garlic, chopped
3   canned chipotle chiles

½   teaspoon ground cinnamon
¼   teaspoon ground cloves
4   black peppercorns
1   slice white bread
3   cups beef broth
1   cup cubed potatoes
1   cup fresh corn kernels
Salt and pepper to taste

Cover the anchos with water and simmer for 15 minutes until soft. Drain.

In a skillet, brown the steak in the oil, remove and drain.

Add the onion and garlic to the oil and sauté until the onion is soft. Remove the onion and garlic; reserve the oil in the skillet.

Place the anchos, chipotles, onion, garlic, and spices in a blender and puree into a smooth paste. Add the bread and 1 cup of broth and blend again.

Heat the oil and fry the chile paste, stirring constantly for 5 minutes.

Add the beef, potatoes, corn, and remaining broth to the chile mixture and simmer for an hour or more until the meat is tender and the potatoes are done. Add more water if necessary.

Serves: 6 to 8

Pork in Adobo Sauce

Mexican *adobos* usually contain vinegar—an ingredient not found in very many chilis. Nevertheless, could a recipe such as this be the ancestral origin of chili?

4   pasilla chiles, seeds and stems removed

4   dried red New Mexican chiles, seeds and stems removed

2   pounds pork, cut in 1-inch cubes

2   medium onions, chopped

3   cloves garlic, chopped

Water to cover

½   teaspoon dried oregano, crushed

½   teaspoon ground cumin

2   tablespoons red wine vinegar

3   tablespoons vegetable oil

Salt and pepper to taste

Cover the pasilla and New Mexican chiles with water and simmer for 15 minutes or until soft. Drain.

Cover the pork, half the onions, and half the garlic with water. Bring to a boil, reduce the heat, cover and simmer until the meat is tender, about 1½ hours. Remove the pork, strain the stock, and reserve both. Discard the onions and garlic.

Place the chiles, remaining onions and garlic, oregano, cumin, and vinegar in a blender and puree until smooth. Add some of the stock if necessary.

Sauté the chile mixture in the oil, stirring constantly for 5 minutes. Thin the mixture with 1½ cups of the reserved stock, add the pork to the sauce, and simmer over low heat for 30 minutes. The sauce should be very thick.

Serves: 6

Caldillo de Duranguense
(Durango Stew)

This thick and hearty stew from one of Mexico's northern states is another Mexican dish that closely resembles chili con carne. A very similar recipe, *carne guisada,* is given by Jim Peyton in his book, *El Norte: The Cuisine of Northern Mexico.* We use pork in our version, but beef (or even shredded beef) can be used.

8 ancho chiles, seeds and stems removed
1 cup water
2 to 3 pounds pork, cut into ½-inch cubes
3 tablespoons vegetable oil
1 large onion, chopped
2 cloves garlic, chopped

2 teaspoons flour
2 large tomatoes, peeled and chopped
2 to 3 cups beef stock
¼ teaspoon dried oregano
2 tablespoons lemon juice
Salt and pepper to taste

Cover the chiles with water and simmer for 15 minutes until they are soft. Puree them in a blender along with the water until smooth.

Brown the pork in the oil. Add the onion and garlic and sauté until soft. Add the flour and quickly brown, being careful that it does not burn.

Add the chile puree and tomatoes, bring to a boil, reduce the heat, and simmer for 15 minutes.

Add the beef stock and oregano. Cover the pan and simmer until the meat is tender, about 1½ hours. (The meat should be tender and the gravy quite soupy.)

Before serving, stir in the lemon juice.

Serves: 6 to 8

California Carne con Chile

This recipe is from Mark Preston, author of *California Mission Cookery*, who collected it from a turn-of-the-twentieth-century California cookbook. The original notes to the recipe called it: "Memorable."

½ cup salt pork, chopped

½ cup beef suet

½ cup chopped onion

1 teaspoon oregano

½ teaspoon saffron (Mexican *azafran*)

2 cups cooked beef, ground or chopped

2 cups kidney beans, cooked

2 cups red chile pulp (see method, page 37)

2 cups water

1 bottle beer

4 tablespoons New Mexican red chile powder

Salt to taste

Sauté the salt pork with the beef suet and the chopped onion and fry until tender. Add the oregano and saffron and fry all together. Add the cooked beef, kidney beans, red chile pulp, water, beer, and chile powder, and salt to taste. Cook for 40 minutes over low heat.

Variation: Use freshly ground cumin seed, say 1 tablespoon, for the above proportions.

Serves: 6

Original San Antonio Chili

According to legend, this is one of the chili queen's original recipes. Some changes have been made in order to take advantage of modern ingredients.

Flour for dredging
2 pounds beef shoulder, cut into ½-inch cubes
1 pound pork shoulder, cut into ½-inch cubes
¼ cup suet
¼ cup pork fat
3 medium onions, chopped
6 cloves garlic, minced
1 quart water
4 ancho chiles, seeds and stems removed, chopped fine

1 serrano chile, seeds and stems removed, chopped fine
6 dried red New Mexican chiles, seeds and stems removed, chopped fine
1 tablespoon cumin seeds, freshly ground
2 tablespoons Mexican oregano
Salt to taste

Lightly flour the beef and pork cubes. Quickly cook in the suet and pork fat, stirring often. Add the onions and garlic and sauté until they are tender and limp. Remove all pieces of fat. Add the water to the mixture and simmer for 1 hour.

Grind the chiles in a *molcajete* or blender. Add to the meat mixture. Add the remaining ingredients and simmer for an additional 2 hours.

Skim off any fat that rises, and serve.

Serves: 6 to 8

Mrs. Owen's Cook Book Chili

The original version of this recipe was first published in 1880. According to John Thorne, "This may be the earliest printed recipe for chili con carne and it is surprisingly authentic, save for the suspect addition of 'espagnole,' a white sauce seasoned with ham, carrot, onion, celery, and clove." Mrs. Owen wrote, incorrectly: "This might be called the national dish of Mexico. Literally, it means 'pepper with meat,' and when prepared to suit the taste of the average Mexican, is not misnamed." We have revised the recipe to add ingredient amounts, which, in the recipe-writing fashion of the day, Mrs. Owen omitted.

2	pounds lean beef, cut into ½-inch cubes	1	teaspoon ground Mexican oregano
2	tablespoons vegetable oil	1	teaspoon ground cumin
2	medium onions, chopped	1	teaspoon ground coriander
1	clove garlic, minced	5	New Mexican red chiles, seeds and stems removed
1	tablespoon flour		Salt to taste
	Water or beef stock to cover		
2	tablespoons white sauce (espagnole)		

Take the lean beef and put to cook with a little oil. When well braised, add the onions, a clove of garlic chopped fine and one tablespoon flour. Mix and cover with water or stock and two tablespoons espagnole, 1 teaspoon each of ground oregano, comino (cumin), and coriander. Take the dried whole peppers and remove the seeds, cover with water and put to boil. When thoroughly cooked (soft) pass through a fine strainer. Add sufficient puree to the stew to make it good and hot, and salt to taste.

To be served with a border of Mexican beans (frijoles), well cooked in salted water and refried.

Serves: 6

U.S. Army Chili

This recipe from 1896 was published in *Chile Pepper* magazine. For reasons of authenticity, we have not altered the original wording. The recipe is given "per soldier."

1	beefsteak (round)	1	cup boiling water
1	tablespoon hot drippings	Flour	
1	cup boiling water	Salt	
2	tablespoons rice	Onion (optional)	
2	large dried red chile pods		

Cut steak in small pieces. Put in frying pan with hot drippings, cup of hot water, and rice. Cover closely and cook slowly until tender. Remove seeds and parts of veins from chile pods. Cover with second cup of boiling water and let stand until cool. Then squeeze them in the hand until the water is thick and red. If not thick enough, add a little flour. Season with salt and a little onion, if desired. Pour sauce over meat-rice mixture and serve very hot.

Serves: 1

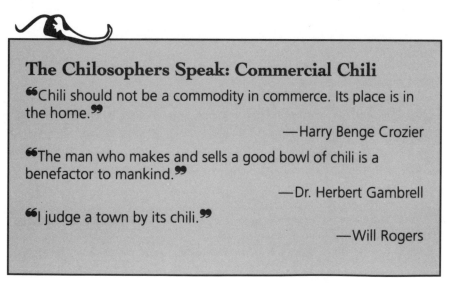

The Chilosophers Speak: Commercial Chili

"Chili should not be a commodity in commerce. Its place is in the home."

—Harry Benge Crozier

"The man who makes and sells a good bowl of chili is a benefactor to mankind."

—Dr. Herbert Gambrell

"I judge a town by its chili."

—Will Rogers

Walker's Red Hot Chile con Carne

The Walker Company was one of the first to can chili, and this is their recipe from around 1918. Note the fact that they spelled chili with an *e*, in the fashion of Mexico and New Mexico. Again, the wording has not been changed.

1 pound of beef cut in small pieces	2 tablespoons of Walker's Mexene (chili powder)
¼ pound beef suet, ground fine (or you can use lard)	1 medium onion, minced
	Water

Combine all; add water and boil until thoroughly cooked. The gravy from this chile con carne is fine for macaroni, spaghetti, and vegetables. If beans are wanted, use any good red bean. For instance—California Bayous, California Pinks, or Pinto Beans. When these are not convenient, use French Red Kidney Beans. Boil the beans separately and add beans when serving.

Serves: 3

Dallas County Jail Chili

John Thorne commented in *Chile Pepper* magazine: "Texas prison chili got its good reputation from Sheriff Smoot Schmid's truly fine recipe for the Dallas County Jail. Recently, however, a Texas prison chili contest was won by the Huntsville Penitentiary with a godawful recipe that called for twice as much cumin as chili powder and '2 handfuls' of monosodium glutamate. In Texas, this is called crime deterrence."

½ pound beef suet, ground
2 pounds coarse ground beef
3 garlic cloves, minced
1½ tablespoons paprika
3 tablespoons chili powder
1 tablespoon cumin seeds

1 tablespoon salt
1 teaspoon white pepper
1½ teaspoons ground dried sweet [mild] chile pods (or paprika)
3 cups water

Fry suet in a heavy kettle. Add meat, finely diced garlic and seasonings; cover. Cook slowly for 4 hours, stirring occasionally. Add the water and continue cooking until the chili has thickened slightly, about 1 hour. Serve plain or mixed with an equal portion of cooked pink or red beans.

Serves: 6

Chili DeGolyer

Chili historian Everett Lee DeGolyer was the owner of *The Saturday Review of Literature,* and was also, according to H. Allen Smith, "a world traveler, a gourmet, and the Solomon of the chili bowl." Here is the historian's recipe in his own words.

4   cloves garlic, chopped

1   onion, chopped

2½ cups fat rendered from beef suet

3   pounds center-cut steak (Trim and cut into cubes of less than ½-inch dimension. Lazy people grind meat in a food chopper using only the coarse knife.)

2   cups water, or the liquid in which the *chiles* have been boiled

2 to 12 pods of *chile colorado* [New Mexican], according to taste. If you are *muy fuerte,* use more.

1   teaspoon of *comino* seeds (cumin in English, or *kummel* if you understand it better)

1   teaspoon oregano (marjoram)

1   teaspoon salt

Brown the garlic and onion in the fat, add meat, and cook until gray (not brown) in color.

Add 2 cups of water and let simmer 1 hour.

Take pods of dried chile, wash, stem, and remove seeds. Put to boil in cold water and boil slowly until the skins slip easily, usually 45 minutes. Rub the pulp through a colander or sieve to make a smooth paste. You should now have ½ to ¾ cup of pulp. Chile powder, prepared commercially, may be substituted for the pulp at the equivalent of one heaping tablespoon of chile powder for 2 pods of chile.

Rub comino seeds and oregano to a powder, toasting if need be. Add chile pulp, comino, oregano, and salt to the meat and cook slowly for 1 hour.

Serves: 6 to 8

Chili H. Allen Smith

From the famous iconoclast and author of *The Great Chili Confrontation,* here's the recipe that infuriated Texans after it was published in *Holiday Magazine* in 1967. Smith had the gall to title his article "Nobody Knows More About Chili Than I Do." Once again, the directions are in Smith's own words.

3 pounds chuck, coarsely ground

2 or 3 medium onions, chopped

1 bell pepper, seeds and stems removed, chopped

1 or 2 cloves garlic

½ teaspoon oregano

¼ teaspoon cumin seed

2 small cans tomato paste

1 quart water

Salt and pepper to taste

3 tablespoons [New Mexican] chile powder

2 cans pinto or kidney beans

Get 3 pounds of chuck, coarse ground. Brown it in an iron kettle. (If you don't have an iron kettle you are not civilized. Go out and get one.) Chop two or three medium-sized onions and one bell pepper and add to the browned meat. Crush or mince one or two cloves of garlic and throw it into the pot, then add about a half a teaspoon of oregano and a quarter teaspoon of cumin seed. Now add two small cans of tomato paste; if you prefer canned tomatoes or fresh tomatoes, put them through a colander. Add about a quart of water. Salt liberally and grind in some black pepper, and, for a starter, two or three tablespoons of chile powder. (Some of us use chili pods, but chile powder is just as good.) Simmer for an hour and a half or longer, then add your beans. Pinto beans are best, but if they are not available, canned kidney beans will do—two 15–17 oz. cans will be adequate. Simmer another half hour. Throughout the cooking, do some tasting from time to time and, as the *Gourmet Cookbook* puts it, "correct seasoning." When you've got it right let it set for several hours. Later, you may heat it up as much as you want, and put the remainder in the refrigerator. It will taste better the second day, still better the third, and absolutely superb the fourth. You can't even begin to imagine the delights in store for you one week later.

Serves: 8

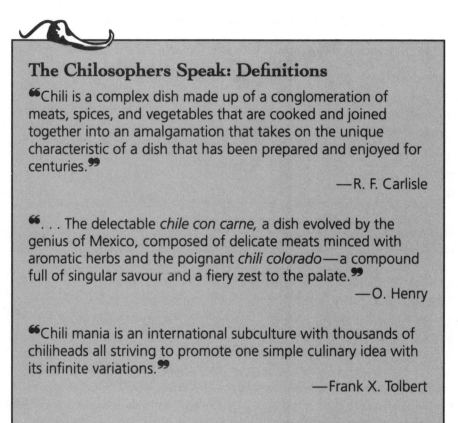

The Chilosophers Speak: Definitions

"Chili is a complex dish made up of a conglomeration of meats, spices, and vegetables that are cooked and joined together into an amalgamation that takes on the unique characteristic of a dish that has been prepared and enjoyed for centuries."

—R. F. Carlisle

". . . The delectable *chile con carne,* a dish evolved by the genius of Mexico, composed of delicate meats minced with aromatic herbs and the poignant *chili colorado*—a compound full of singular savour and a fiery zest to the palate."

—O. Henry

"Chili mania is an international subculture with thousands of chiliheads all striving to promote one simple culinary idea with its infinite variations."

—Frank X. Tolbert

Wick Fowler's Chili

Nowadays it's easy to re-create the chili that Wick used in the first cookoff against H. Allen Smith—just buy some of the famous Wick Fowler 2-Alarm Chili Mix. Or, you can follow the recipe below, which chili legend holds is Wick's original version that he cooked in Terlingua in 1967. Remember to remove the Japanese chiles and the chilipiquins before serving. If this chili is too hot, Wick recommended drinking a pint of buttermilk.

3   pounds chili-grind beef, mostly lean

1½ cups canned tomato sauce

Water as needed

1   teaspoon Tabasco sauce

3   heaping tablespoons chile powder

1   teaspoon oregano

1   teaspoon cumin seed or powder

2   onions, chopped

6   or more cloves garlic, chopped

1   teaspoon salt

1   teaspoon cayenne

1   tablespoon paprika

12 or more whole dried Japanese chiles (very hot)

6 to 8 chilipiquins (very, very hot)

3   tablespoons flour for thickener

Sear the meat in a large skillet until gray in color. Transfer the meat to a chili pot, along with the tomato sauce and enough water to cover the meat about ½ inch, mixing well. Stir in the Tabasco, chili powder, oregano, cumin, onions, garlic, salt, cayenne, and paprika. Add the Japanese chiles and chilipiquins, taking care not to break them open. Let simmer for 1 hour and 45 minutes, stirring gently at intervals.

About 30 minutes before the end of the cooking time, skim off any grease that has risen to the top. Mix the flour with a little water to make it liquid without lumps. Add this paste to ingredients in the pot and blend in thoroughly. Adjust salt and seasonings. Unless you are chili hungry at the moment, let the chili remain in the pot overnight, then reheat and serve. Freeze any chili left over. Serve with sliced or chopped onions and pinto beans on the side.

Serves: 8

Joe Cooper's Chili

Joe, the author of probably the best book ever written about chili, included his own recipe in *With or Without Beans.* "That which is to follow," he wrote, "represents many tedious, but gladdening, hours in the kitchen, not to mention countless pots of chili." Joe then presented three pages of description of his chili before revealing the recipe. He modestly stated that it should not be construed as the "best ever" chili, but rather one that satisfied the Coopers' appetites. "This recipe," concluded Cooper, "like most all worthwhile others, was conceived out of an uncertain past; born of a belief that no man can live long and prosper without good chili; reared in the confusion of trial and error; and now exists in maturity with the respect of neighbors and friends."

¼ cup olive oil

3 pounds lean beef (never veal), hand-chopped into bite-sized cubes

1 quart water

2 bay leaves (if desired)

8 dry [New Mexican] chile pods or 6 tablespoons chile powder

3 teaspoons salt

10 cloves garlic, finely chopped

1 teaspoon ground cumin

1 teaspoon oregano

1 teaspoon red pepper [hot chile powder]

½ teaspoon black pepper

1 tablespoon sugar

3 tablespoons paprika

¼ teaspoon cocoa (optional)

3 tablespoons flour

6 tablespoons corn meal

When the olive oil is hot, in a 6-quart pot, add meat and sear over high heat; stir constantly until gray—*not brown.* It then will have the consistency of whole-grain hominy. Add 1 quart water and cook (covered) at bubbling simmer 1½ to 2 hours.

Then add all ingredients, except thickening (flour and corn meal). Cook 30 minutes longer at same bubbling simmer. Further cooking will damage some of the spice flavors. Skim off the fat.

Now add thickening, previously mixed in cold water. Cook 5 minutes to determine if more water is necessary (likely) for your desired consistency. Stir to prevent sticking after thickening is added. A fairly hot chili.

Serves: 8

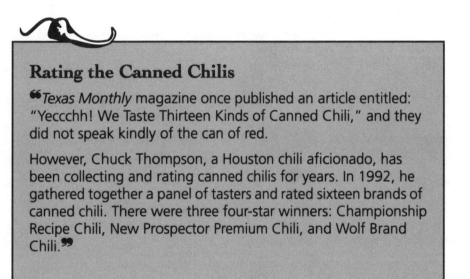

Rating the Canned Chilis

"*Texas Monthly* magazine once published an article entitled: "Yeccchh! We Taste Thirteen Kinds of Canned Chili," and they did not speak kindly of the can of red.

However, Chuck Thompson, a Houston chili aficionado, has been collecting and rating canned chilis for years. In 1992, he gathered together a panel of tasters and rated sixteen brands of canned chili. There were three four-star winners: Championship Recipe Chili, New Prospector Premium Chili, and Wolf Brand Chili.**"**

Cincinnati-Style Chili

This chili is often served over spaghetti and is then called chili-mac or Two-Way chili. According to Floyd Cogan, "The proper way to make chili-mac is to place cooked spaghetti (*al dente*) on a plate and cover it with chili, with grated parmesan cheese on top."

2	pounds coarsely ground chuck steak	3	tablespoons chili powder (or more for heat)
1	quart water	2	tablespoons cider vinegar
1	cup chopped onions	2	teaspoons Worcestershire sauce
2	8-ounce cans tomato sauce	½	teaspoon salt
4	cloves garlic, minced	1	teaspoon ground cumin
¼	teaspoon powdered allspice	1	teaspoon ground cinnamon
4	whole cloves, crushed	1½	teaspoons sugar
1	bay leaf, powdered	2	tablespoons flour mixed with ¼ cup water
½	ounce unsweetened chocolate		

Combine the chuck steak and the water and simmer for 30 minutes. Add the remaining ingredients except the flour mixed with water and simmer for 3 hours.

Add the flour mixed with water, bring to a boil, and cook for 5 minutes. Remove from the heat and serve.

Serves: 6

Whale Chili

In 1989, devoted *Chile Pepper* reader Sheldon P. Wimpfen, from Luray, Virginia, wrote that he had been a chili cook for fifty-five of his seventy-five years and that fact makes him an expert on the subject. He lambasted us for our "mistaken tales" about the origin of chili con carne. He enclosed as his evidence the first recipe ever used for chili con carne, dating from approximately 15,000 B.C. The ancient recipe which follows was invented by the Alaxsxaq Indians of the Valley of Ten Thousand Smokes on the Bering Land Bridge. He apologized in advance for any insult to whale lovers and wrote, "that's just the way they cook up there."

3   tons red chile pods
1   medium (50-foot) blue whale, cubed to fingertip size using razor-sharp *ulus* (a native knife)
60 *oogruk* (seals), cubed to fingertip size using razor-sharp *ulus*

30 tons onions, chopped fine using razor-sharp *ulus*
1   ton garlic, minced using razor-sharp *ulus*
100 pounds sea salt
600 pounds oregano
400 pounds cumin

Dig a bowl in the ice 40 feet long, 20 feet wide, and 10 feet deep. Place all ingredients in the ice bowl and mix well with dull *ulus*. Add water and fumarole-heated stones until the ice bowl is bubbling. Reduce heat and simmer for 2 weeks. Ladle leftovers into 5-gallon leather buckets and freeze in a glacier.

Serves: An entire tribe for a year

A Not Socially Correct Chili Prayer

This prayer was preached by Matthew "Bones" Hooks, a famous black range cook, who obviously felt honored to cook his favorite food.

"Lord, God," he shouted, "you know us old cowhands is forgetful. Sometimes, I can't even recollect what happened yestiddy. We *is* forgetful. We just know daylight and dark, summer, fall, winter, and spring. But I sure hope we don't never forget to thank You before we is to eat a mess of good chili.

"We don't know why in Your wisdom, You been so doggone good to us. The heathen Chinee don't have no chili ever. The Frenchmens is left out. The Rooshians don't know no more about chili than a hog knows about a side saddle. Even the Meskins don't get a good whiff of it unless they stay around here.

"Chili eaters is some of Your chosen people. We don't know why You so doggone good to us. But Lord, God, don't ever think we ain't grateful for this chili we about to eat. Amen."

2

A Chili Cookin' Pantry and Primer

This chapter examines the ingredients and techniques needed to produce the perfect bowl of chili. To achieve such an elusive goal, it is important first to deconstruct chili, to break it down into its component parts. The next step is to assemble the chili using the secrets of the experts.

Since there is no possible way any three authors can intuitively know everything there is to know about chili, we have appealed to various experts on the subject in the quest to produce the perfect bowl of chili. In this chapter, we are assisted by a top-notch team of chili historians, chili authors, chili cooks, an award-winning chili powder manufacturer, a chili chemist, a bean doctor—and, believe it or not, a chili systems engineering analyst!

This is an important chapter both for beginning cooks and those serious chili cooks who wish to win big bucks on the tournament circuit.

The Chile in Chili in General

We start with chile because without it, of course, carne would just be meat, not chili. Chile sets the course of chili much in the same way it directs famous hot and spicy dishes the world over—by dominating it with heat and flavor.

Any chili cook can look up heat levels of the various chiles and make a guestimate about the amount of any certain variety to use in a recipe, but such information will be useful only in a general sense. Chile peppers can vary in heat, even among pods from the same plant. "The only consistency in chile peppers and chili powders seems to be in their inconsistency," noted chili expert Floyd Cogan in his book, *The Devil's Sourcebook of Chili and Other Hellish Things*. To truly hone the heat, experimentation with different combinations of chiles is the only path to take.

But at least the heat in chili is linear and has exact parameters ranging from hot to not so hot. The flavors of the myriad chiles and their products, however, are a far more complicated story. R. F. Carlisle, a systems analyst who wrote a technical paper entitled "A Systems Engineering Analysis of a Process: How to Cook Winning Chili," detailed three reasons why there is a wide inconsistency in the flavor of various chilis: "There is no standard in the classification of chili powders; chili powders lose flavor with time; and different chiles affect taste and aftertaste differently."

Chef Mark Miller of the Coyote Cafe in Santa Fe has assembled a list of forty-one "Chile Flavor Descriptors," which he divides into the categories of "fruity" and "other" flavors. The fruity flavors included citrusy (particularly orange and lemon), which would apply to most varieties of habaneros and some of the yellow South American *ajís*, and raisin, which is the everpresent aroma of the anchos and pasillas. Other fruity descriptors were black cherry, fig, mango, and melon. In the other flavors category, Miller lists chocolate, tobacco, tannic, soapy, green tea, and—ironically—black pepper.

Unfortunately, the science of chile flavors is still in its infancy, and most of the hundreds of chile varieties have not yet been matched to their flavor descriptors. However, chili chefs on the edge will certainly do more research into this important facet of chili flavor.

Below is an overview of the chiles most commonly used in chili. For more detailed information, there are reference works available on the identification and the heat and taste qualities of the various chiles. Recommended sources are *Peppers: The Domesticated Capsicums,* by Jean Andrews; *The Whole Chile Pepper Book,* by Dave DeWitt and Nancy Gerlach; and *The Great Chile Book,* by Mark Miller.

Fresh Chiles in Chili

Fresh chiles are often used in chilis because they are easily available from the garden or market. The most ubiquitous peppers in the United States, are, of course, the familiar bells, which have no heat unless they are a variety called Mexi-Bell, which has a mild bite. Bells rarely appear in western chilis, although they sometimes show up in eastern restaurants and competition chilis.

The long, green New Mexican chiles are used fresh, frozen, or canned as an ingredient in Southwestern chilis. The fresh New Mexican chiles (available by mail order—see Appendix) must be roasted and peeled before using them in a recipe. Blistering or roasting the chile is the process of heating the chile to the point that the tough transparent skin is separated from the meat of the chile so it can be removed. The method is quite simple.

While processing the chiles, be sure to wear rubber gloves to protect yourself from the capsaicin that can burn your hands and any other part of your body that you touch. Before roasting, cut a small slit in the chiles close to the stem end so that the steam can escape. The chiles can then be placed on a baking sheet and put directly under the broiler or on a screen on the top of the stove. Or, place the pods on a charcoal grill about five to six inches from the coals. Blisters will soon indicate that the skin is separating, but be sure that the chiles are blistered all over or they will not peel properly. Immediately wrap the chiles in damp towels or place them in a plastic bag for ten to

The Armadillo Breath Chili team.

fifteen minutes—this "steams" them and loosens the skins. For crisper, less cooked chiles, plunge them into ice water to stop the cooking process.

The most readily available hot peppers in the produce sections of supermarkets are jalapeños and yellow wax peppers. Both are often floated whole in chilis to provide a little extra bite and are removed before serving. Some cooks remove the seeds and stems and mince them before adding them to the chili pot; others puree the peppers in a blender and then add them to the chili.

Other fresh chiles used in chili that are sometimes found in markets (especially farmer's markets) are serranos and habaneros. The serranos—smaller, thinner, and hotter than jalapeños—are the classic chiles of the Mexican *pico de gallo* fresh salsas. Habaneros, the world's hottest peppers, are lantern-shaped orange or red devils that have a unique, fruity aroma in addition to their powerful punch. Use them with caution. Generally speaking, any of the small fresh peppers may be substituted for each other in chilis.

All of the smaller chiles—habaneros, serranos, and jalapeños—can be frozen without processing. Wash the chiles, dry them, and put them one layer deep on a cookie sheet and freeze. After they are frozen solid, store them in a bag. Frozen chiles will keep for nine months to a year at 0°F. All of the small peppers can be frozen whole with no further processing needed, and their texture holds up surprisingly well in the freezer.

Dried Chiles in Chili

As is true with fresh peppers, the larger they are, the milder they are. The large dried peppers, such as ancho (a dried poblano) and the New Mexican varieties, are mild enough to add a lot of flavor to the chili without burning it up. They can be ground into powders (see the following section) or can be rehydrated and then pureed before adding them to the chili.

There are four main large peppers used as the base for chilis: ancho, pasilla, New Mexican, and guajillo. The ancho is a wide, dark pepper with a "raisiny" aroma. It is the only pepper that is commonly stuffed in its dried form (the pod is softened in water first). The pasilla is a long, thin, dark pepper that also has a raisiny or nutty aroma. Along with the ancho, it commonly appears in Mexican *mole* sauces.

The most common use of the red New Mexican chiles is to hang them in long strings, or *ristras,* until they are ready to be used in cooking. Then they are commonly rehydrated and combined with onions, garlic, oil, spices, and water and ground fine to make the classic New Mexican red chile sauce and stews. The guajillos, a shortened and hotter version of the New Mexican chiles, but grown in Mexico, are commonly used with anchos in chili-like stews in northern Mexico.

There are a bewildering number of small, hot pods used in chili, ranging in size from that of a little fingernail (the chiltepin) to the six-inch, skinny cayenne. Some varieties include piquin, Thai, santaka, de arbol, mirasol, and tabasco. These chiles also appear in stir-fry dishes, are floated in soups or stews, or are used to add heat to sauces that are too mild. A specialized dried chile that has become quite popular in chilis is the chipotle, a smoke-dried red jalapeño that adds a distinctive, smoky flavor. Another specialized dry chile is *chile pasado* (chile of the past), which is a New Mexican green chile that has been roasted, peeled, and dried in the sun. It is usually reconstituted in water, but some cooks add it directly to the chili pot.

Whichever chiles you choose for your chili, only practice will teach you how to use them. Red Caldwell, author of *Pit, Pot & Skillet,* advised: "You'll discover that the more you use them, the easier they are to use. But remember the old line about how porcupines make love . . . carefully!"

Powdered Chiles in Chili

All chiles can be dried and ground into powder—and most are, including the hottest of all, the habanero. Crushed chiles, or those coarsely ground with some of the seeds, are called *quebrajado*. Coarse powders are referred to as *caribe,* whereas the finer powders are termed *molido*. In our homes, we actually have more powders available than whole pods because the powders are concentrated and take up less storage space. We store them in small, airtight bottles. The fresher the powders, the better they taste, so don't grind up too many pods at once.

To grind the smaller chiles, first make certain they are completely dried. Use an electric spice mill and be sure to wear a painter's mask to protect your nose and throat from the pungent cloud of powder that you will create. The colors of the powders range from a bright, electric red-orange (chiltepins), to light green (dried jalapeños), to a dark brown that verges on black (ancho). Red pods can be made darker by dry-toasting them in a skillet on top of the stove, stirring constantly.

To grind the larger chiles, first place them on a cookie sheet in a 300°F oven until they are brittle and break when bent. Be sure to turn them often so they don't burn. Break the chiles into small pieces before grinding them. Occasionally, two steps are needed—a coarse grind in the blender and then a fine grind in the spice mill.

Some competition cooks grind their own secret blends of chiles that are added at the cookoff. John Thorne suggested that "an ideal blend would start with a base of New Mexican chiles, mixed with some dark and wrinkled ancho chiles, (for their deep, earthy flavor), and one or two pasillas (for their nuttier piquancy). To this combination, add a controlled amount of one of the truly fiery peppers—de arbol or piquin—to give the chili its true heat. The best powdered chile is made at home from a blend of different dried chiles—especially the milder ones. For while the fiery pods give chili myth and heat, the sweeter ones give it a depth of flavor."

Chili Powders in Chili

These chili blends take powdered chiles a step further by adding spices. John Thorne warned about the commercial blends: "Ordinary chili powder is a predetermined mixture of powdered chile and seasoning; its familiar stale flavor

Jack Curry (right) and associate at the San Mateo, California, cookoff.

Betsy Wooten

and musty odor summon nostalgia and indigestion in equal proportion. Use it only as a last resort."

Commercial chili powders are usually composed of 80 to 85 percent powdered chiles, but they can contain up to 40 percent salt! Some unexpected spices also crop up, such as ginger, saffron, cinnamon, allspice, and anise. Other unneeded ingredients are maltodextrin, monosodium glutamate, and tricalcium phosphate.

Certain chili experts, like Floyd Cogan, believe that some cooks will always use commercial blends. "If you are to have consistency in your attempts to make the perfect bowl of chili," Cogan advises, "you must take into account that no two chili powders are alike. Stick with one brand of chili powder if you can."

Many cooks grind their own blends of chiles and spice to make chili powder. The most common ingredients are chiles, paprika, garlic powder, ground oregano, salt, and cumin. Other occasional ingredients in home blends are turmeric, celery seed, cloves, coriander, sugar, and dried onion flakes. We have included in this chapter several typical recipes for chili powder—but cooks are encouraged to experiment.

Chile Pulp in Chili

Some of the older chili recipes call for chile pulp. To make the pulp, split New Mexican dried red chiles lengthwise, remove the stems and seeds, and soak in hot water for two hours. After rehydrating, the chile pulp can be scraped off the inside of the chiles with a dull knife and then strained. Another method is to tear up the chiles into small pieces, rehydrate them, and mash them through a sieve.

Hot Sauces in Chili

There are a bewildering number of hot sauces manufactured throughout the world, and many of them are used by chili cooks. In fact, in 1993 Chip Hearn of Dewey Beach, Delaware, was proclaimed to be the current hot sauce collector champion, with more than seventeen hundred different brands of sauces in his collection. The sauces are basically grouped into the following categories: Louisiana, Caribbean, Mexican, and Asian. The Louisiana hot sauces are made out of tabasco or cayenne chiles, whereas the Caribbean sauces usually contain the various pod types of the *Capsicum chinense* species

—commonly called habaneros. Mexican hot sauces contain a wide variety of chiles, from habaneros to de arbols to guajillos. Variations on them appear in the American Southwest and are often made with dried red New Mexican chiles. Asian hot sauces are made from the small, dried red pods grown in Southeast Asia, China, India, Malaysia, and Indonesia. Serranos, piquins, and cayennes are the American equivalents of the Asian chiles.

After hot sauce is added to chili, the taste of the concoction is affected to a limited degree by the type of chile used in the various sauces and more by the amount of vinegar the sauce contains. The vinegar gives the chili more acidity, which affects the flavor components. Chili chefs should exercise caution when using hot sauces by adding them in stages and by tasting the chili after each addition.

Meaty Matters: The Carne in Chili

The Chosen Meat

"Some Texans at a chili cookoff will make chili from any type of meat that isn't obvious poison," observed Texas food experts Phil Brittin and Joseph Daniel. "Riding high atop the whims of culinary inspiration, they will cook with wild boar, bear, rattlesnake, raccoon, armadillo, and nutria." Other animal meats that appear in chili are porcupine, javelina, jackrabbit, shrimp, and squirrel. Hunters believe that venison makes the best chili—or elk, or even moose— and restaurant chefs love pork or veal. It stikes us as odd that chicken chili is rarely mentioned.

Granted, there's no law prohibiting the use of such meat-bearing critters, but most competition cooks stick to beef. "The generally accepted *carne* is beef, mature beef," wrote Joe Cooper in *With or Without Beans* in 1952. After all, considering the possible origin of chili along cattle drives, it would be downright disloyal to put lamb or goat meat in chili. Given that the ideal meat in chili defaults to beef, the debate really begins to heat up.

Your Cut, Señor

There is a chili axiom that holds: Only Use the Poorest Cuts of Beef for Chili. One of the first chiliheads to formulate that axiom was Joe Cooper, who wrote, "It is not ever desirable, much less necessary, to buy expensive cuts of prime or choice beef for a pot of chili." The reasoning was that because of its long cooking time, chili needed meats that have worked the hardest on the steer and are therefore the toughest and least fatty: the neck, rump, and legs. Beef stew meat is composed of such cuts.

Cooper proclaimed that "the best *carne* is bull neck—normally the least desirable meat in the carcass of an animal which best should be three to five or six years old." Since such a cut was hard to find, he relented and suggested any chuck shoulder cut.

Bill Bridges reported in *The Great American Chili Book* that Merle Ellis, the syndicated butcher, recommended the center section of the beef shank. "With long, slow simmering, like a pot of chili gets," Ellis wrote in his column on chili, "the connective tissue in beef shank virtually dissolves and makes a rich, beefy pot liquor that is the very essence of a good pot of chili."

Floyd Cogan noted that cows and steers always lie down on the same side, and that the "beefy side" of a cow or steer is the side they don't lie down on. He suggested taking note of which side the steer lies on, and then selecting the other side for chili meat—a suggestion that our city-dwelling chili cooks will find a bit difficult to utilize.

Our chili chemist, Dr. John K. Crum, wrote in his paper, "A Small Dissertation Upon Chili con Carne," that a "good quality round steak" makes the best chili. Other steaks that commonly appear in chilis are chuck, flank, and even sirloin. John Thorne suggested brisket, which is certain to bring protests from the barbecue crowd. Andy Housholder, author of *How to Make a Championship Chili and Win!*, insists that London broil is the cut of choice. Whichever cut you select, Floyd Cogan suggests one with a little more fat than usually appears in round steak. Joe Cooper disagrees, suggesting lean meat, and wrote that the "fat will be added under its own entity." But more on fat later.

Battle of the Meats: Ground vs. Cubed

Finally, there is some minor agreement on one point in chili making: that hamburger meat makes lousy chili. John Thorne observed: "Ordinary ground meat turns to mush when subjected to long cooking. It also reminds some cooks of spaghetti sauce, with disastrous results . . . one-half inch cubes are the established norm."

Many chili cooks these days believe that only a stainless steel knife should be use to cut the cubes that size. Some purists disdain knives and prefer scissors because their cut supposedly retains the juiciness and flavor of the meat. Considering the fact that the meat breaks down during cooking no matter what cuts it, the fallacy of using scissors is obvious.

R. F. Carlisle analyzed that two sizes of cut meat were optimal: "Small pieces should be in the range of the size of a lima bean, large pieces in the range of the size of a purple grape." His theory held that in this combination, "the raw meat should have a coarser characteristic than desired in the final chili." Andy Housholder, who won fourteen out of eighteen chili cookoffs in eight years, wrote that cubed meats win 95 percent of chili competitions.

Abilene chili expert Sam Pendergrast vehemently disagreed with the cubed-meat concept. "The second and perhaps penultimate disaster for Texas Chili," he wrote in *Chile Pepper* magazine, "is the "Cubed Steak with Brown Gravy Syndrome" (CSWBG), and it probably started—as many bad things do for Texas—around Houston. I think the CSWBG movement might have evolved through a scenario rather like this: probably under the mistaken truism that more expensive is automatically better in all things, somebody started buying high-grade steak and carefully hand-slicing it into tiny, uniform, fat-free cubes, then sautéeing them into a rich gravy without too much of those old Mexican spices that have given chili such a good (or bad) name over the years. Eventually the cubed steak won a chili contest— probably sooner than later if the cook happened to be a judge. Eventually, lots of cooks started making the cubed steak 'chili,' and as more of it was made, more of it was likely to win contests—particularly since a preliminary judge who had cubed his steak might have an advantage in recognizing his own recipe."

Sam, of course, preferred his meat in the classic "chili grind" method, whereby butchers used three-eighths–inch or half-inch holes in the blades of the meat grinder. Chili grind is often not available in supermarkets, but it can be replicated by using an electric meat grinder with a coarse blade.

The purpose of cutting or grinding the meat is to, in effect, render it into smaller morsels that become tender more easily than larger pieces. "Tenderizing can also be effected chemically by using commercial products that contain papain or other enzymes that digest protein in muscles and connective tissue," suggested Dr. Crum. The chili meat of any cut or grind can be tenderized by marinating it in papaya juice or commercial tenderizing powder. Meat tenderized in such a fashion will not require the lengthy cooking time.

And with all due respect to championship chilis, we should point out that with quick chilis, made for lunch from commercial mixes in about an hour, hamburger meat works fine.

The Grease and the Browning

"Why is the meat not merely cut or ground and dumped into boiling water to cook?" posited Dr. Crum. He then went on to answer his own question: "The reason is that browning imparts a better flavor to the meat because of some interesting chemistry! Frying (or sautéing) with just enough fat or oil to prevent sticking at a relatively high temperature causes the meat to brown—in very simple terms, the proteins at the surface of the meat are converted to other proteins that result in a more intense flavor." And to achieve such a high temperature, Dr. Crum recommended using avocado oil, with its extremely high smoke point of 600°F. Such intense heat, according to food chemistry expert Harold McGee, triggers "browning reactions, exceedingly complex chemical changes that involve mostly proteins and carbohydrates."

Everyone knows that the crusty, browned portions of roasted and fried meats are more intensely flavored than the rest of the cut being cooked. The reason for this is that the interior of meats cannot be heated beyond the boiling point of water until all the water is removed—at which point the meat would be very tough. However, the outside of the meat can be extremely hot because moisture is being drawn from inside the meat. The extremely hot temperature

Tony Ochoa and Hank Wedenmeyer of Longhorn, Colorado.

accelerates the browning reaction, giving the meat much more flavor. It should be noted that Dr. Crum called for browning the meat thoroughly, whereas many of the early chili recipes recommended browning the meat just "until gray." It makes sense that chili meat that is more thoroughly browned will have more flavor than meat that is just gray.

There are quite a number of oils and fats used by chili cooks to brown the meat. The old-timers generally used beef suet, which is the fat that surrounds the kidneys. (Tallow is the fat around the muscles.) Butchers can still provide suet, which should be fresh and then ground or chopped. It is usually rendered before the meat is browned in it, but some cooks add the meat and suet together and leave the pieces of browned suet (cracklings) in their chili. One drawback to suet is that it is saturated fat and thus highly disreputable in this day and age. However, most of the fat can be removed later. Two other old-fashioned meat-browning agents are bacon fat and salt pork, which purists insist impart a unique flavor to the chili.

These days, vegetable oils are commonly used to brown the meat, with corn oil being the most popular. Interestingly enough, olive oil crops up often in some of the early recipes, including those from turn-of-the-century California. Safflower oil and peanut oil are also popular, as are margarine and butter. Before moving on, we should point out that some chili cooks brown the meat not by sautéing it in fat but by grilling the meat over wood or charcoal before it is ground or chopped for the pot.

Garlic, Onions, and Tomatoes

Chili purists often preach that garlic is necessary to good chili, but that onions and tomatoes are worthless. "Garlic sweetens and deepens the pungent flavor of chili without adding liquid (as do onions)," observed John Thorne. "It is a necessary part of the true 'grease and gladness' bowl of Texas red." As usual, a chorus of protests will rise from other cooks, such as Floyd Cogan, who noted that "although you can make good chili from garlic alone, adding a good-sized onion does wonders for it."

Besides the argument over garlic versus onions, some cooks even debate whether or not these ingredients should be sautéed first before adding them to the chili pot. The consensus seems to be that it makes no difference at all. All cooks seem to agree that fresh garlic and onions are mandatory and that garlic or onion powder, salt, flakes, or liquid are forbidden. "The flavors and aromas of onions and garlic are generally attributable to allyl sulfides," remarked our chili chemist, Dr. Crum.

"With the possible exception of beans," wrote Bill Bridges, "no ingredient provokes more controversy among chili cooks than the tomato." Indeed, Everett DeGolyer noted that "many cooks add ripe or canned tomatoes. We regard this as effeminate." John Thorne believes that: "Tomatoes and onions worked their way into chili from a familiar Southwestern dish called *chile colorado* ('red chile') which at one time referred both to a sauce of fresh red chile peppers and a stew made from them, usually of chicken, which often included tomatoes and onions. Since then, chili-makers who interpret chili as a bowl of grease and gladness eschew them while those more in sympathy with the dish's indigenous heritage embrace them." Some cooks, particularly Texans, take exception to the very idea of tomatoes in chili, although Wick Fowler used them both privately and in his commercial concoctions.

Cooks should remember that tomatoes add acidity to chili, but not with the sharpness of vinegar or lemon juice. Tomatoes used fresh should be peeled and seeded. Peel the tomatoes by plunging them in rapidly boiling water for a minute or so. When you see the skin split, remove the tomato and the skin will slip off easily. The seeds can be removed by cutting the tomatoes into quarters and gently squeezing out the liquid and seeds. If you are a lazy chili maker, you might use canned tomatoes, tomato juice, or even tomato sauce—just don't tell anyone.

We Do Know Beans About It

Beans are the biggest controversy in chili cookery—so big, in fact, that Joe Cooper named his book *With or Without Beans.* Cooper spent nine pages discussing the debate and concluded that "an assay of all material accumulated indicates a preference for with beans." That was in 1952. In 1981, when Bill Bridges wrote on chili, he cited Ray Shockley of Wolf Brand Chili as the source of the following statement: "In Texas, the preference for straight chili runs about three to one, while almost everywhere else in the country, chili *with* beans is preferred by the same majority." Nowadays, as we all know, beans are eschewed rather than chewed in competition chilis. In the rules of the Iowa Chili Appreciation Society, a member of CASI, "Anybody who knows beans about chili knows there ain't no beans in chili. The addition of beans, macaroni or other fillers will cause disqualification."

There are some pretty good reasons for cooking "straight" chili, or that without the beans. The most basic reason is that once beans are in the chili, they cannot be removed. At a dinner party, some guests will understandably be upset to find beans in their chili. However, beans can always be added to chili when it's served at the table, which is considered to be proper chili etiquette in the Southwest.

John Thorne detailed another good reason for keeping the beans out of the bowl of red: "Chili made with beans can't be reheated, since the beans get sour and turn to mush. But real (no bean) chili requires reheating to reach its final patina of perfection. If you are served beans in your chili, however, you should show forbearance—simply pick them out and quietly slip them under the table."

Let's assume for the moment that we take the side of the chili-with-beans contingent. Now, what kind of beans to use? Red kidney beans and pinto beans seem to run neck and neck in the home stretch, with some competition from Louisiana red beans and, according to Joe Cooper, pink bayou beans. He wrote, though, that "chili is no place for limas, navys, and black-eyed peas."

Luckenbach Mayor Hondo Crouch helps the women demonstrate at the Men's State Chili Cookoff in San Marcos, Texas, where women were not allowed to compete.

Some modern chili recipes call for black beans, which your authors love. They are not authentic, but are probably the best-tasting beans.

George C. Booth, author of *The Food and Drink of Mexico,* observed, with a sexist slant: "Making a good *chile con carne* is like making a good marriage; you give the same narrow eyed scrutiny to finding the right type of bean that you would to choosing a wife. Look for sturdy character, consistent quality, and recognized breeding." He suggested the Mexican red bean.

Whatever beans are chosen, they must be cooked in some manner. Everyone agrees (a miracle in itself) that raw beans cannot be added to chili, and even beans that have been soaked in water overnight take longer to cook than the chili itself—up to six hours. So beans are definitely cooked first, and don't make two crucial mistakes. First, never cook the beans in salted water, because they will be tough—add salt only after the beans are cooked. And second, never add partially cooked beans to the other chili fixings and expect the beans to be done when the chili is. The half-cooked beans will never soften.

"The bean cell wall hemicelluloses," explained Dr. Crum, "are more soluble in alkaline conditions, and the experienced chili cook knows that partially cooked beans, when added to the acidic conditions in partially cooked chili, will simply not get any softer as you continue the cooking process." The solution, of course, is to precook the beans to their desired softness. We have included a basic bean recipe in this chapter, which is designed to be combined with chili during its final serving—if the cook is daring enough to face the cookoff experts in the crowd.

Of course, one inherent problem with beans is that they are, indeed, the "musical fruit." Richard L. Potts, M.D., addressed this problem in an article for *Chile Pepper* magazine. "The combination of beans and beer tastes good to me—way too good," he wrote. "The problem is, a couple of hours later, it's rumble time, usually followed by eructation (belching), distention, and, eventually, dreaded flatulence. It's only a matter of time before the enzymes in my small intestine reject my beans and beer. They are unable to digest, chemically, all that I have consumed. A little further along, two nonabsorbable carbohydrates face off against the intestinal bacteria down there in my large intestine. The resulting chemical clash produces various gasses in quantities large enough to inflate the Goodyear Blimp. Ever so slowly, the gas accumulates. It pushes outward. It meets resistance. The skin covering my belly stretches. My colon is swollen. The expansion continues as the gas seeks the path of least resistance, and with various embarrassing sounds, vents my body." His description is enough to ban beans forever from chili!

One final word on beans from Floyd Cogan: "Please! Never used canned pork and beans or Boston baked beans in your chili—use them only when you are desperate or faced with an extreme emergency. Even then don't let anyone see you."

Cumin and Oregano

Cumin is the principal spice in chili, and its distinctive taste reminds people of both Mexican and Indian foods, which often contain quite a bit of it. Since cumin is also an ingredient in chili powder, some recipes give a double dose of this spice. "If you note a vaguely sweaty aftertaste to your bowl of red," John Thorne wrote in *Chile Pepper* magazine, "someone had an over-eager hand with the cumin. It is undeniably popular with Texas chili-makers, who sometimes use more of it than they do chile itself." Indeed they do, for in Sam Pendergrast's Zen Chili recipe in Chapter 5, he calls for an astounding one-half cup of cumin seed!

The best cumin is fresh cumin seeds, which should be kept in an airtight container in the freezer. For recipes that do not call for the whole seeds, the cumin seeds must be ground—but first, toast them. Place the cumin seeds in a dry, clean skillet and apply heat. Stir the seeds constantly until they release their aroma and turn a light brown color. Grind them with a mortar and pestle or use a spice mill.

Not all oregano is oregano. The European, or Greek, oregano is actually wild marjoram (*Origanum vulgare*) that was also called oregano. The Caribbean oregano of Cuba, Trinidad, and Yucatán is really a coleus known as borage, which is also called Spanish thyme. The Mexican oregano (*Lippia graveolens*), which is stronger, is the true oregano for chili. Mexican oregano is usually sold in its dry form, but cooks can easily raise their own in herb gardens. If you can't find Mexican oregano, use marjoram.

Other Herbs, Spices, and Ingredients

Floyd Cogan lists twenty-eight additional herbs and spices used in chili recipes (nearly everything on the spice shelf at the supermarket), and Bill Bridges lists twenty-two such ingredients. The most popular seem to be black pepper, basil, coriander seed, cilantro (fresh coriander leaf), bay leaf, thyme, sage, anise seed, cloves, nutmeg, and caraway. Cinnamon and allspice are common ingredients in Cincinnati-style chili. Some far-out herbal additives in other chilis range from turmeric to cardamom to fennel to mustard seed to mace to even woodruff and Texas farkleberries. The amounts and combinations of such ingredients are part of the mystique of chili and are always determined by trial and error by each individual cook.

Chocolate has long been used in its various forms; Joe Cooper used cocoa in his 1952 recipes, and unsweetened chocolate appears commonly in Cincinnati-style chilis.

Salt and sugar are ubiquitous in chilis—always to the cook's taste. However, as usual, it's not as simple as that. Arizona chili expert Andy Housholder devotes several pages to the subject in his technical treatise on championship chili. "A slight sweet and a tad oversalted chili is more important to pick up judges' points than the correct blend of other chili flavors," he wrote. Housholder advised using only dark brown sugar and then only during the last forty-five minutes of cooking. If it is to be added during the last ten minutes, it should be liquid brown sugar. He also recommended using only uniodized salt.

Weird Stuff: Ingredients That Do Not Appear in the Authors' Chili Pantries

Here is a list of ingredients appearing in some nefarious chilis (but not ours): almonds, aquavit, avocados, barley, bitters, carrots, celery, Coca Cola, coffee grounds, corned beef, currant jelly, curry powder, goose grease, horseradish, molasses, mushrooms, olives, Parmesan cheese, peanuts, peanut butter, pea pods, raisins, sake, spinach, water chestnuts, vinegar, and Worcestershire sauce.

Chili Liquidity and Cooking

Chili needs a liquid as its final cooking medium, and whatever you choose will either be water or water-based. Some of the more interesting liquids used by chili cooks are broths such as beef or chicken bouillon—or in some extreme cases, the broth the beans were cooked in. Beer is commonly used in recipes, but we suspect this practice has a lot to do with the drinking habits of the cooks. The alcohol doesn't do as much for the chili as for the cook, however, because the heat causes it to evaporate. Recommended brands are Lone Star and Coors, and chili cooks generally stay away from dark beers. Wine is occasionally used, and we suppose this connotes a more gourmet aspect to the chili. We have heard of tequila or scotch being added to chili, but we don't recommend them. Coffee also turns up in chili recipes from time to time, but again, that could reflect on the habits of the cook or the time of the day he or she started cooking the chili.

Most chili recipes call for simmering chili, usually uncovered, for two or three hours. But Dr. Crum advised a higher heat: "Inasmuch as the connective tissue of meat is comprised of three proteins—elastin, reticulin, and collagen—it is possible to make meat more tender by maintaining the cooking temperature near the boiling point of water. This has the effect of transforming the collagen into gelatin, which is a gummy solution that has the effect of making tougher meats more tender, and this is especially important if one decides to use a lower quality of meat for chili."

Tight Chili

The consistency (meaning texture) of chili is extremely important. When there is a great separation between the solids in chili and the liquids, the consistency of the chili is generally inferior. Slowly simmering (or even boiling) the chili can reduce the amount of liquid, but often not enough. Chili should cling evenly to the wooden stirring spoon when it is removed from the pot; some say that the spoon should stand straight up when placed in properly thickened chili. When a small spoonful of chili is placed on a saucer, no liquid should run out of it. This is called "tight" chili.

Often, a thickener is needed to bind the solids and liquids together into a homogenous mass. "The addition of thickeners blends liquid and fat into a rich, clinging gravy," noted John Thorne. "The two favorites are flour and masa harina, the corn flour used to make tortillas. The advantage of the latter is that it adds a hint of sweet corn flavor to the chili and can also be sprinkled in pinch by pinch during the cooking without fear of lumps. Since finer cut meats absorb much more liquid, some cooks grind about a third of their beef to use as a thickener. Others use cracker meal or—such as the U.S. Army—ground cooked beans."

Perhaps the most common thickener is white flour, which is premixed with an equal amount of water to avoid lumps, and is then added to the chili. An approximate amount is one-fourth cup flour to two quarts of chili. The pot is removed from the heat, the flour-water mixture is added, and then the pot is returned to the heat and is brought to a slow boil for about two minutes, or until the chili thickens to the desired consistency. If the chili is too thin, add more of the flour-water mixture; if it is too thick, add more liquid.

Cooks should remember that although there are quite a few thickeners, some are more efficient than others. For example, arrowroot is twice as efficient as flour, so use less of it. Also, some thickeners, such as corn meal or ground nuts, will change both the flavor and texture of the chili, making it "grainy." The list of possible thickeners includes: arrowroot, bread crumbs, corn flour (masa harina), corn meal, corn starch, flour, ground almonds (or other nuts), ground crackers, ground beans, ground pumpkin seeds, instant grits, oatmeal, potato flour or starch, potato flakes, rice flour, and tapioca.

Joe Cooper noted that thickeners should be the finishing touch to chili. "Thickened chili must be stirred almost constantly to avoid scorching," he wrote, "or at least sticking to the bottom of the pot."

Prizewinning Techniques

"It can be observed that you only have a random chance of ever winning a prize," cautioned systems analyst R. F. Carlisle, "until you can learn to be consistent and understand what you do, and what you expect to find when you taste your chili." It was Carlisle's theory that cooks should try to cook not their best chili, but rather the winning chili. To accomplish this task, they must first determine which chilis win over and over again and then attempt to duplicate them. Once duplicated, Carlisle advised, the chilis must be cooked in the same manner every time. Andy Housholder, the author of a guide to making winning chili, emphasizes: "You must please the judges, not yourself. You must cook what the judges will like best."

Some chili cooks have shared their chili-cooking techniques in print. John Thorne wrote that he sears his chili meat over mesquite wood to give it a "haunting hint of smoke." Floyd Cogan suggested not adding herbs and spices directly to the chili, but rather mixing them together first with a cup of boiling water. "This technique," he wrote, "blends and fixes your flavors more effectively than adding your spices and herbs one at a time to your chili pot." He also advised that the herbs and spices be added late in the cooking process so as not to overcook them.

Linda West Eckhardt, author of *The Only Texas Cookbook,* advised: "Remember that chili just doesn't taste right if you don't cook it in an iron pot. I suppose just a little of the iron leaches out in the chili and provides that little extra push it needs." However, not only are iron pots difficult to find these days, it is hard to keep them properly seasoned when acid ingredients such as tomatoes and vinegar are added to chili. Some cooks complain that an iron pot gives chili an unappealing metallic taste. A more reasonable cooking vessel is a heavy, metal Dutch oven that has been enameled.

In addition to the suggestion of using an iron pot, most chili cooks insist that a wooden spoon be the only kitchen utensil used to stir chili. Floyd Cogan pontificated: "A wooden spoon impresses your guests and adds to the important mystique that all good chili makers use. Besides, if you leave the spoon in the chili pot, it does not get hot like a metal one does." Call us conservative, but we fail to see how a simple wooden spoon will impress anyone. Perhaps Floyd was writing about a wooden spoon elaborately carved with chile pepper motifs by the Indians of Tiburon Island in Mexico.

Other techniques for winning chili include some "fixes" for chilis. To brighten the color of the chili from brown to red, for example, many cooks use paprika because it is extremely high in carotene, which gives it the bright red color without adding extra heat. For chili that is too salty, try adding some brown sugar and vinegar that have been mixed together. Add some vinegar or lime juice to chili that is too flat, and, conversely, add honey to chili that is too sour. Not enough flavor? Some cooks add monosodium glutamate (MSG) because it really does intensify the flavors of savory foods. This additive is extremely unpopular in some circles, however, because it is reputed to cause headaches and dizziness—symptoms which most chili cooks prefer to get from alcoholic beverages rather than from food additives.

Andy Housholder, author of *How to Make a Championship Chili and Win!,* has page after page of hints in his how-to guide designed for chili cookoff enthusiasts. He wrote that one of the biggest mistakes chili cooks make is "I like it, so I'll put it in." He advised: "When in doubt, leave it out." Another error is using spices that he says are "foreign to Championship Chili. No cinnamon, no curry, no parsley, or mint—they are not chili cousins." Andy also eschewed oregano, calling it a "spaghetti spice." Here are a few of Andy's championship hints at-a-glance: Freeze your competition spices; double-grind your spices; marinate the meat in your spice mixture (this is not allowed at some cookoffs); season the judging cup with your chili to remove the styrofoam aroma; add brown sugar and uniodized salt to taste forty-five minutes prior to judging, but add just a tad more salt because judges' tongues tire from all the tasting and they tend to like "a slightly oversalted chili."

From the "less is more" chili contingent, there is an old saw that goes: "To improve your chili, remove an ingredient." And here is some final advice on competition chilis from R. F. Carlisle: "If you improve your winning ratio, it will provide only a small extra reward over and above the rewards of participating in a fun-loving afternoon with chili cooks."

Serving Chili

The first step in serving any chili you prepare is to skim the fat off it. Although fat adds flavor to chili, too much of it tends to give your chili a reputation for being greasy. Since fat rises to the top of the chili, at least it's easy to find. A large shallow spoon can be used by keeping it parallel to the top of the pot and gently inserting it until just the fat runs into it. Another method is to wrap ice cubes in cheesecloth and skim them across the top of the chili—but this method is awkward and messy. By far, the best method is to place the chili in the refrigerator or freezer until the fat congeals on top and turns white. Then it can be easily removed with a spoon.

Select attractive bowls in which to serve the chili because presentation is part of the process of making and serving chili. "Use showmanship and style when cooking your chili," Cogan advised. Make sure you prewarm the bowls in the oven, so the chili will retain most of its heat during serving.

Many sources suggest that chili tastes best if it's not served right away. "You know, chili is better the second day," noted Linda West Eckhardt, author of *The Only Texas Cookbook.* "And the third day it's perfect." The problem with leftovers, according to Harold McGee, author of *On Food and Cooking,* is that "fats are the principal source of off-flavors in cooked meats"—even more reason to skim the fat before reheating chili. However, McGee noted that leftovers containing poultry and pork, which have a greater proportion of unsaturated fats, are more likely to have off-flavors than those containing beef and lamb.

Our chili chemist, Dr. Crum, believes that capsaicin, the heat ingredient in chile peppers, which is an antioxidant, minimizes fat oxidation in the cooking process, thus improving the flavor of chili. "Release of phospholipids and unsaturated fat from meat muscles," he wrote, "may actually be slowed during the heating process, leading to better flavor and a more palatable 'left-over' flavor. This is in fact suspected to be the case, because most chili lovers claim that it improves after one or two days, whereas beef fat normally deteriorates on standing."

Garnishes and Variations

We have already seen in Chapter 1 that Cincinnati-style chili is commonly served with pasta, cheese, onions, and beans, but these additions are just a few of the garnishes that can be served with the bowl o' red. Other toppings include chopped olives, bell peppers, hard-boiled eggs, cilantro, parsley, grated jalapeño (or other) cheese, crushed chile pods, croutons, tortilla chips, popcorn, avocado slices, a fried egg, or sour cream.

Side dishes to accompany chili can include steamed rice (strictly family fare), corn bread, bread or bread sticks, tortillas, biscuits or rolls, garlic bread, salads, pickles, fruits, and just about anything your imagination can think of. See Chapter 6 for our suggestions.

John Thorne, a chili purist, considers soda crackers to be the only acceptable accompaniment. "A true chilihead," he wrote, "considers soda crackers (or at least tortillas) as essential an ingredient with a bowl of red as the meat itself. The crackers, by the way, should be large enough to give diners the pleasure of crumbling them into their bowls—and that means no stupid little oyster crackers."

The recipes that follow are basic to the preparation of a great bowl of chili, plus a chili recipe from our chili chemist.

Pods to Chili Powder

This fresh chili powder should be ground immediately before adding it to the chili.

4   ancho chiles, ground (see grinding instructions, p. 35)

4   piquins or other small hot chiles, ground

2   tablespoons ground cumin seed

1   teaspoon oregano

1   teaspoon garlic powder

Place all ingredients in a spice mill and process until well mixed. Use immediately or store in a small, airtight jar.

Yield: ⅓ cup

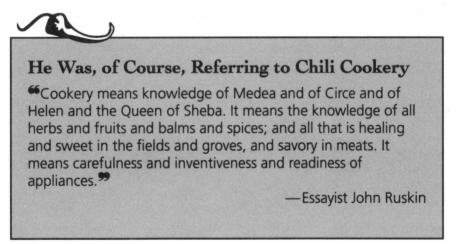

He Was, of Course, Referring to Chili Cookery

❝Cookery means knowledge of Medea and of Circe and of Helen and the Queen of Sheba. It means the knowledge of all herbs and fruits and balms and spices; and all that is healing and sweet in the fields and groves, and savory in meats. It means carefulness and inventiveness and readiness of appliances.❞

—Essayist John Ruskin

Hot Chili Powder

Substitute ground piquin, santaka, or even habanero for the cayenne in this recipe.

1 tablespoon ground cayenne	1 teaspoon garlic powder
1 tablespoon ground oregano	1 teaspoon salt
1 tablespoon paprika	1 teaspoon ground cumin

Place all ingredients in a spice mill and process until well mixed. Use immediately or store in a small, airtight jar.

Yield: ¼ cup

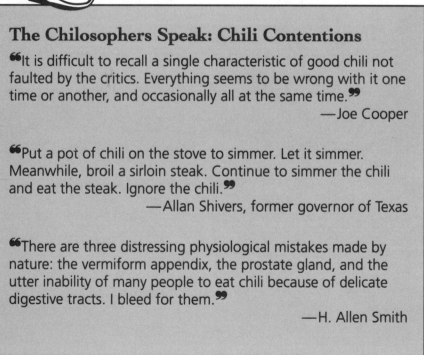

The Chilosophers Speak: Chili Contentions

"It is difficult to recall a single characteristic of good chili not faulted by the critics. Everything seems to be wrong with it one time or another, and occasionally all at the same time.**"**

—Joe Cooper

"Put a pot of chili on the stove to simmer. Let it simmer. Meanwhile, broil a sirloin steak. Continue to simmer the chili and eat the steak. Ignore the chili.**"**

—Allan Shivers, former governor of Texas

"There are three distressing physiological mistakes made by nature: the vermiform appendix, the prostate gland, and the utter inability of many people to eat chili because of delicate digestive tracts. I bleed for them.**"**

—H. Allen Smith

Beans for Chili!

This recipe is considered to be the basic one for beans that will be added to chili when it's served—assuming, of course, that you are a "with beans" aficionado. There is a great debate about whether or not to soak the beans overnight. The only simple answer is that if the beans are soaked overnight, they will take about half as long to cook the next day.

1   pound dried pinto or kidney beans, cleaned and soaked overnight in 3 quarts cold water

3   more quarts cold water
Salt to taste

Remove any beans that float, then drain the beans and replace the water with 3 quarts of fresh cold water.

Bring to a boil, reduce the heat and simmer, uncovered, for 2 to 3 hours or until the beans are tender and easily pierced with a fork. If additional water must be added, use only hot water.

Drain the beans and add salt to taste.

Yield: 6 cups

A Chili Embarrassment

Jack Curry of the Chili Darters team tells of the time he was fixin' his bowl o' red at the Malibu cookoff when TV star Larry Hagman sampled his chili. "While he was letting it cool off," Curry explained, "I tried to engage in conversation by asking where the ranch that was featured on his large belt buckle was located. I was quickly told that it was the Southfork Ranch on the *Dallas* television show—thus letting him know I had never seen his popular television series!"

Homemade Hot Sauce

Many chili cooks like to adjust the heat in their chili by adding various kinds of hot sauces. For the purists in the crowd who insist on making everything from scratch, here is our recipe for a homemade hot sauce. Any chiles of choice can be used. When subsituting dry chiles for fresh ones, soak them in warm water for ½ hour to reconstitute them. For more body in this sauce, add the carrots.

¾ cup chopped onion

2 cloves garlic, minced

1 tablespoon vegetable oil

½ cup chopped carrots (optional)

15 fresh hot chiles such as tabascos or piquins, chopped (or substitute 8 habaneros)

½ cup distilled vinegar

¼ cup lime juice

Pinch salt

Sauté the onion and garlic in the oil until soft. Add the carrots (if used) with a small amount of water. Bring to a boil, reduce the heat, and simmer until the carrots are soft.

Place the mixture and the fresh chiles in a blender and puree the mixture until smooth.

Combine the puree with the vinegar, lime juice, and salt, and simmer for 5 minutes to combine the flavors.

Strain the mixture into sterilized bottles and seal.

Yield: 1½ to 2 cups

Old Buffalo Breath

This recipe, from chili scholar John Thorne, was published in a slightly different format in *Chile Pepper* magazine. John commented: "On the Texas range, firewood meant mesquite. Not only did the trail cook use it for his open pit cooking, but the ranch cook used it to fire his wood stove. Until it was replaced with gas and electric, mesquite-flavored grilling dominated rural Texas cooking with its distinctive sweet savor. The meat for this chili is seared over charcoal where mesquite chips have been set to flame (the taste of mesquite charcoal is indistinguishable from that of any other hardwood), which gives the resulting chili a haunting hint of smoke—and without tasting a bit like barbecue, since there is no onion or tomato in it, none at all."

For the fire

Mesquite wood chips and
    hardwood charcoal

For the rub

2 or 3 cloves of crushed garlic, salt,
    and chili powder

For the chili

1   5-pound chuck roast
¼   cup olive oil

8   cloves garlic, crushed
1   cup or more beef broth
Juice of 1 lime
2   tablespoons each mild and hot
    chile powder
2   teaspoons Mexican oregano
1   tablespoon cumin seeds,
    toasted and ground
Small whole dried piquin chiles
Masa harina
Salt to taste

The chuck roast should be as lean as possible and cut at least 3 inches thick. Two or three hours before you plan to make the chili, rub the meat all over with a mash of crushed garlic and salt, then sprinkle it with chile powder to coat it lightly. Loosely cover it with plastic and set it aside.

    Fire up enough hardwood charcoal to sear the meat on an outdoor grill, preferably one with a cover. At the same time, soak a few handfuls of the mesquite chips in the water. When the coals are covered with gray ash, spread them out evenly, and scatter the soaked mesquite chips over them. Then immediately set the meat on a grill over the smoke, about an inch from the coals. Cover the grill and adjust the dampers to maintain a slow, steady heat. Let the meat sear for about 12 minutes (this process is meant to flavor, not to cook the meat) and turn over to sear the other side for the same amount of time. Remove it from the heat, saving any juices on its surface, and transfer to the refrigerator. Let it cool thoroughly, about 1 hour.

After the meat has cooled, trim away any surface fat or cartilage. With a sharp knife, cube the meat into the smallest pieces you have patience for, saving all juices. Heat the olive oil in a large, heavy pot over moderate heat. Stir in the garlic and sauté until it turns translucent. Stir in the meat and all reserved meat juices, adding just enough beef broth to cover, or about 1 cup. Pour in the lime juice and sprinkle in the chile powders, oregano, and cumin, stirring and tasting as you go. Crumble in a few piquins or other fiery chiles to bring the heat up to taste. However, do not try to adjust the seasoning to perfection right now; it's easy to ruin a chili by correcting the flavors too soon—the long cooking will smooth and sweeten it.

Reduce the heat to as low as possible. If the pot is left to boil, the meat will toughen. Every half hour or so after the first hour, taste for seasoning, adjusting and thickening with the masa harina a teaspoonful at a time. The chili should be about ready to eat in 3 hours, although it will benefit from a night's aging in the refrigerator.

Serve it simmering in large, heavy bowls with an ample supply of soda crackers and a side of beans, but not much else except, maybe, hot black coffee or quart-sized glasses of iced tea or a few frosty bottles of your favorite beer. And, after a good long while, push things aside, lean back in your chair, and start arguing.

Serves: 12

National Chemistry Day Chili

Our chili chemist, Dr. John Crum, culminated his paper on chili con carne by proposing the following "decent" recipe. He is obviously a "with beans" chili cook; however, he does note that the chili can be cooked just with the bean liquid and the beans can be removed and used "for other purposes."

1   recipe Beans for Chili! (see page 55), beans and cooking liquid reserved together
4   tablespoons avocado oil
6   pounds lean beef, preferably round steak, either cubed into ½-inch pieces or ground with the coarse blade of a food chopper (Dr. Crum recommends 2 pounds ground beef and 4 pounds cubed beef)
1½ pounds lean pork, cut into ½-inch cubes
6   small scallions (green onions), trimmed and cut into small cylinders
2   large yellow onions, chopped

1   red serrano chile, seeds and stem removed, chopped
2   green jalapeños, seeds and stems removed, chopped
3   ounces (1 bottle) Gebhardt Chili Powder
2   teaspoons powdered cumin
3   large cloves garlic, chopped
2   large tomatoes, peeled and chopped
2   cups strong black coffee
1   can beer
1   tablespoon brown sugar
½   cup masa harina
Water

In a heavy skillet, heat the avocado oil until very hot (more than 500°F) and thoroughly brown the beef, pork, and scallions.

Add the browned meat and scallions to the beans and bean liquid and bring to a boil. Add the remaining ingredients except the masa harina and water, and cook over low heat, covered, for about 2 hours. Remove the cover and cook until the chili thickens. If it is still not thick enough, add the masa harina (mixed with water to a thick paste).

Serves: 14 to 16

3

Cookoff Chilis

T he history of chili cookoffs begins with the Chili Appreciation Society International, which was the first organization to support the notion that chili is more than just meat and chiles — it's a way of life. Despite controversy and warring factions, CASI has been enormously successful. According to the ChiliHeads of Arizona, in 1992 there were fifty CASI "pods" or clubs in the United States and Canada. That year CASI had more than eight hundred members, and some nine thousand cooks competed in 420 sanctioned cookoffs that raised $471,291 for charity. In 1993, CASI affiliates raised more than $600,000 for charity. But here's how it all began.

CASI — A History, Sorta

Chilihead Jo Ann Horton, who is the editor of the *Goat Gap Gazette,* a publication devoted to chili, wrote the following "history" of CASI in 1989 for *Chile Pepper* magazine:

The Chili Appreciation Society was formed in 1951 by George Haddaway and Jim Fuller to "improve the quality of chili in restaurants and broadcast Texas-style recipes all over the earth." When chapters began to form in other countries, the word *International* was added to the name.

It was a non–dues-paying organization and members did their own secretarial work. Their bible was *With or Without Beans* by Joe Cooper of Dallas, which is now out of print. The Society slogan was: "The aroma of good chili should generate rapture akin to a lover's kiss." The organization was head-quartered in Dallas.

The Society's chapters had luncheon or dinner meetings about once a month over steaming bowls of red. Their "missionary endeavors" would be discussed, and members spent a lot of time answering letters from all over the world and sending out "approved" recipes to those who requested them. Vats of chili were even packed in dry ice and shipped to chili-starved members in Europe.

Haddaway—as Chief Chilihead—and a crew of Society members traveled to Mexico City to help start a new chapter. They signed up more than fifty new members there, all of whom raved enthusiastically about Chief Chili Cook Wick Fowler's chili.

By 1964 Haddaway and his honchos loaded up on Texas chili ingredients and headed for Los Angeles to establish a California chapter, which was duly installed at the Airport Marina Hotel. The Californians liked the chili and the Society, but warned the inexperienced: "Real chili con carne is not for sissies. Fowler's Four-Alarm Chili is reputed to open eighteen sinus cavities unknown to the medical profession."

Fowler went even further afield in his missionary work when, as a war correspondent, he took along a big supply of chile peppers and spices to Vietnam. There he prepared and served the fiery brew to frontline troops. He said later that water-buffalo meat made great chili.

The first Terlingua cookoff, held in 1967, was a fun promotion for Frank X. Tolbert's book, *A Bowl of Red,* and for land sales in that area for David Witts and Carroll Shelby. Tom Tierney, a public-relations man, and Frank Tolbert dreamed up the idea and chose Wick Fowler (inventor of Two-Alarm Chili Mix), and Dave Chasen of Beverly Hills as the combatants. Chasen became ill, and humorist H. Allen Smith was chosen to replace him after Smith wrote an article entitled "Nobody Knows More About Chili Than I Do," which was published in a 1967 issue of *Holiday Magazine*.

Because of the remoteness of the location, nobody thought spectators would come, but 209 chapters of CASI were represented. They flew into Chiricahua Ranch and came in school buses to Terlingua. Judges for the first event were Hallie Stillwell, who voted for "Soupy" Smith; Floyd Schneider of Lone Star Beer, who voted for Fowler's chili; and attorney David Witts. Witts tasted Smith's chili, and said his taste buds were paralyzed and declared he could not

Jo Ann Horton

Master of Ceremonies
Malcolm Fox interviews the
legendary judge Hallie
Stillwell (now 93 years young)
at Terlingua.

break the tie. The contest was called a draw by the referee, Frank Tolbert. More
than a thousand spectators attended.

In 1968, the second cookoff at Terlingua was also declared a draw by Tolbert. He had no choice—the ballot box was stolen by masked men with guns
who threw it into an outhouse located over a mine shaft.

The third world championship saw C. V. Wood of California declared the
winner over Wick Fowler. The third contestant, Wino Woody DeSilva, fell into
his huge "chili wok," and the judges didn't want to taste his chili. Judges were
said to be influenced by the bevy of starlets Wood had imported from California.

Wick Fowler finally won in 1970. C. V. Wood brought more girls and a
double-decker bus, wore a crown of chile peppers and robes with fur, but
declined to cook. That year marked the first time women were allowed to compete, and H. Allen Smith had Janice Constantine of Midland, Texas, arrested
for "trying to cook chili while then and there being a female person." It didn't
work. More than five thousand spectators were on hand.

In 1972, Fred McMurry of Houston attended a CASI meeting in Dallas
and then returned to Houston determined to form a CASI "pod," as he called
it. His friends Allegani Jani and Tex Shofield assisted in signing up members
and getting Fred elected "Great Pepper."

From that moment on, CASI changed forever. Things began to get organized. Other pods were formed, but for a while there were so few cookoffs

that people flocked to every announced event, no matter how far away they lived. But the number of cookoff contests grew, and eventually "chiliheads," as they were called, developed such a listing of cookoffs that competition cooking is now akin to a professional sports circuit.

Cooks in today's cookoffs might be termed "professionals." They know a great deal about cooking competition chili, about herbs, spices, pots, stoves, cooking temperatures, the weather, and other factors affecting the outdoor cooking of chili. Although cooks are allowed to bring meat and vegetables such as onions already cut up, and spices mixed in advance, they must still cook the pot of chili on the spot.

Most members of CASI belong to pods and compete for points to get to the big cookoff, Terlingua. Cooks are given points for placing at sanctioned cookoffs throughout the year: four points for winning, three for second, two for third, and one for fourth. At the end of the year, all cooks having enough points to qualify are invited to cook at Terlingua, always held the first Saturday in November.

Unfortunately, Terlingua can no longer legally be called "World Championship" because that phrase has been trademarked by the International Chili Society—it is now called "CASI Terlingua International Chili Championship." But such legalities don't matter to CASI members, who still view Terlingua as the "big one." Even if they can't cook there, they will likely go anyway and volunteer to judge or help in some manner. Nobody wants to be left out when it comes to Terlingua!

The Tale of Two Terlinguas

In addition to the rivalry between CASI and ICS, there has been a further dispute between CASI and some of its original members. When H. Allen Smith said that "the chief ingredients of all chili are fiery envy, scalding jealousy, scorching contempt, and sizzling scorn," he summed up the most overcooked and underhanded argument between the two "Original Terlingua Chili Championships." *Two* original cookoffs, you say? How could that be? Well, here's the lowdown on the lore, litigation, and love lost at Texas' most famous cookoff.

It all started out so innocently. Let's flash back to the Baker Hotel in Dallas in 1967. *Dallas Morning News* columnist Frank X. Tolbert and friends are musing over an article in *Holiday* magazine titled "Nobody Knows More

About Chili Than I Do," written by New York humorist H. Allen Smith. While feasting on bowls of Wick Fowler's famous red chili, Tolbert, who also authored the Texas sacred scripture, *A Bowl of Red,* thinks up the perfect scheme to let that New Yorker find out who really knows about chili: a chili cookoff challenge featuring Wick Fowler's chili versus H. Allen Smith's red.

The Great Chili Confrontation, as it was to become known, was scheduled to happen in the Texas ghost town of Terlingua. After much hype, the first Terlingua cookoff attracted more than a thousand people, most of whom indulged in the shameless (and fun) debauchery that still exists to this day. Fowler and Smith cooked their chili, but there was no winner named. The contest was called off after a tie-breaking judge supposedly gagged on a spoonful of that New York chili. But great fun was still had by all, and they resolved to do it again.

The contest was almost *too* successful. After an article on the challenge appeared in *Sports Illustrated,* a national chili cooking craze ensued, and the *Goat Gap Gazette* was born. There was enough Terlingua and chili to go around for everyone—until the early eighties, that is. The story goes that in 1982, Tolbert came to the cookoff with two European friends and insisted that they be allowed to cook. Many of the other cooks protested because they had had to earn enough points to compete in what was then called the World Championship by qualifying at other cookoffs, and the foreign invaders had not qualified. The protesting cooks' rationale was that everyone should observe the same rules and regulations.

Tolbert found the protestations ridiculous and set up a separate cookoff with his own loyal faction at Terlingua the following year. It was nicknamed the "Behind the Store" cookoff, because it was held behind Arturo White's store, where it still exists to this day, known more formally as the vocal chord–gagging "The Original Viva Terlingua International Frank X. Tolbert–Wick Fowler Memorial Championship Chili Cookoff."

Just as tempers on both sides were reaching a boiling point, the groups became completely divided after a run of deceptions, tricks, and other assorted nastiness. In 1983, the two warring cookoffs were held on the same day. Tolbert then began the first litigation with a petition for trademark status of the term *Chili Appreciation Society* for his cookoff. By the time the trademark was issued in 1984, Frank Tolbert had died.

Each year the flames of controversy between the cookoffs grew. In 1988, a lawsuit was filed on behalf of the protesting cooks' group, now known as

CASI, Inc., against the Fowler cookoff and the use of the tag line "Chili Appreciation Society International."

The U.S. federal judge who was assigned the case urged the two groups to work together to find an equitable solution, but there was no such luck. Judge Lucius Bunton of the Twelfth Western District ruled that the Tolbert faction had no claim to the trademark and gave it instead to CASI, Inc. However, the judge did refuse to rule whether either group had the right to call themselves the "original" Terlingua cookoff. With $40,000 in legal fees apiece, both groups simply went away aggravated, vowing to cook at their own "original" Terlingua cookoff.

Today, there are still two rival cookoffs in Terlingua. The CASI cookoff is called the "CASI Terlingua International Chili Championship," and the Behind the Store cookoff is dubbed "The Original Viva Terlingua International Frank X. Tolbert–Wick Fowler Memorial Championship Chili Cookoff."

In 1992, co-author Melissa Stock traveled to Terlingua to judge the Behind the Store cookoff to capture the "flavor" of a championship. Here is her report:

In the early fall of '92, *Chile Pepper* magazine publisher Robert Speigel received an invitation to be a chili judge at the Behind the Store cookoff in Terlingua. Robert couldn't make it, Dave DeWitt and Nancy Gerlach were busy galloping around the globe, so that left me. The most exciting thing I had planned for that weekend was doing laundry. I could definitely fit a little chili tasting into my schedule. My first official trip as an editor with *Chile Pepper*. How cool. Nothing could daunt my excitement. Never mind that when I asked about accommodations all I heard was laughter and the remark "gotta' tent?" I didn't even flinch when the same laughter accompanied my next question, "Just how far is it to Terlingua from Albuquerque?"

The Road to Terlingua

Among chili cookoff folks, and there's an estimated one hundred thousand or so of them that compete or attend, Terlingua is spoken about in almost mythical terms—the Super Bowl of chili, the Broadway of cookery. Lore surrounding the four-day event is just about as spicy as the chili served. Naked dancing, drunken debauchery, and, of course, the world's finest chili. It was my job to separate fact from fiction and not only judge the cookoff, but participate in the relatively new events, such as the Pea Off (relax, it's a black-eyed pea cooking contest), the Barbecue Brisket Contest, the Beans Only Cookoff, and the Peculiar Magarita Contest.

We packed up the car with what we thought was enough food and beer to last the weekend. And, of course, we also made sure to bring our accommodations—a tent and two sleeping bags. I figured that my husband, Dan, and I were either going to bond or contemplate murder during our thirteen-hour drive. Luckily, neither of us likes to sing show tunes while on the road, so the prospect of bonding was brighter.

How does one get to Terlingua from Albuquerque? According to Dan, you drive about ten hours to the middle of nowhere, and then go three hours more. Or as another person put it, drive until no matter where you go, you're on your way back. In truth, Terlingua is located in west Texas, very close to the Mexican border. Having never had the pleasure of visiting west Texas before, I was a bit shocked by the desolation. There were no trees except mesquite, and even the snakes were trying to get under the car to find some shade. (Notice how I've begun talkin' like a Texan?)

After thirteen hours we ran out of potato chips. We were down to Barry Manilow and the Bee Gees for tape selctions. Dan was suspiciously humming the tunes from *Oklahoma!* and *A Chorus Line*. We had to get there soon.

It was November 6, we had on shorts, had all of the windows down, and had just passed the "Terlingua Next Right" sign. We could smell the barbecue five miles out of town. It didn't matter that my back end had bonded with the car seat four hours earlier. Or that the windshield bug-splat count had passed 150. All was forgiven as that wonderfully delicious aroma of brisket tickled our tastebuds, leaving visions of dripping barbecue sauce dancing in our heads. Forget the shocks. We ripped down the dirt road to the check-in gate at warp speed.

And then we were there. Just rocks and a lone yucca or two. No trees, grass, or visible bathrooms. I had been to a place like this before, but just to drop off things I didn't need anymore. It occured to me that the brochure was right: Terlingua was located where the cookoff folks would have the place all to themselves. No other human being would go there on purpose. Dan started to laugh. I was still looking for the bathrooms. As we pulled up in our Honda to get our stickers and judging packet, I realized with horror that we were probably presumed to be two yuppie dorks lost in west Texas. I quicky flashed my best "I know what I am doing" smile and asked where we should put up our tent and where we could shower. Our greeter smirked and pointed out into the abyss, obviously confused by our lack of a motor home. As for showers, he informed us, we were only going to be there until Sunday, so what did we need one for?

Gary P. Nunn and Other Entertainment

I should tell you now that I am not a weenie. I have hiked rim to rim in the Grand Canyon twice. I bait my own hook and don't feel guilty. The idea of camping was no big deal. I just thought there would be fewer motor homes and more grass.

So there you go. It was Friday night and we were at the world famous Terlingua. We found a semiflat place and pitched our tent, finding the true meaning of the saying "between a rock and a hard place." But that barbecue smell was still thick, and our spirits soared. It was dusk and the band was scheduled to start soon. We grabbed a few beers and headed down to the gathering

1982 Terlingua champion Tom Skipper.

Jo Ann Horton

area, refusing to be intimdated by the fact that we had only two six-packs and most of our neighbors were sporting their own kegs. We made a note to make friends with them later.

The Terlingua headquarters included a bandstand, a chili judging area, a few food vendors, and the Lone Star Beer concession stand. We also located the facilities, which were as elegant as I had imagined. The decor of the Port-A-Potties didn't alarm me. However, with a single potty for each gender, I was a little alarmed, considering the amount of beer and chili being consumed by what looked like a couple thousand people. I made a note to carry TP with me at all times.

Our hunger was fierce, so we began to search for the brisket. Unfortunately, we could not find it. We then asked a knowledgable-looking person, who sadly informed us that the brisket cooking had been in the afternoon. It would be burgers for us that evening.

We grudgingly ate our burgers next to the "Please Don't Puke Here" sign and waited for the band to start. Country-western band Gary P. Nunn was the headliner, and a big name on the chili circuit. The weather was beautiful, a star-filled cool desert evening. The crowd was having a great time as people of all ages drank and danced the night away. We met chiliheads from all over the United States, many of whom travel a week or more to get to Terlingua each year. We even met a couple from Sweden, and another from Canada. I quickly dropped the "you won't believe how far we drove to get here" routine from my witty repartee.

Saturday started early. I had to check in at the judges' table by 10 A.M. to find out which round of the chili cookoff I would judge. So I trotted down to the bandstand, deciding to walk instead of hitching a ride on what I think was a Model-T pickup that drove the circuit picking up mostly highly spirited revelers and taking them down to the bandstand area.

Dan had a hangover and I was on my own. As I checked in, I noticed a strange thing. Everybody was drinking what appeared to be margaritas—I had just entered the Peculiar Margarita Contest zone. But since it was my job to have the full Terlingua experience, I quickly joined in. After all, they said it would clear my palate for the chili judging. After about three margaritas, my palate was positively transparent. It was 10:45 A.M.

I still had a little more than an hour until I was slated to judge, so I decided to go talk to the cooks. It was then that I noticed that no, Jose Cuervo was not playing tricks on me, but rather, dozens of different booths had sprung up, each sporting a different theme and show, and their own brand of chili.

Dan was back from the dead and was taking pictures of the crazy cooks and their teams. There were two different types of entertainment competitions: the Open Show, which consisted of five or more people, and the Limited Show, which was four or fewer team members. There were teams of nerds, chili Elvises, and one group who assembled an entire train. My personal favorites were the Skeeter Meat Chili Company, who dressed in black mosquito suits and handed out shots of skeeter juice (which I think was a very potent version of jungle juice), and Pharter Starters Chili, whose motto was "a warm breeze on the chili scene." Dozens of these groups danced and sang and had a great time, obviously having been stung by a bit of skeeter juice themselves.

It was finally my turn to help judge. I was assigned to table number two, where I would taste the semifinals with about twenty other bleary-eyed judges. Although everything at Terlingua is wacky and fun, these chiliheads are deadly serious about the judging. Each judge must follow the directions exactly. Each container of chili is numbered and counted. We tasted each one once, judging texture, taste, consistency, aroma, and appearance, then changed spoons and started over. Between chilis we cleared our palates with beer and fruit.

It was all excellent. Truly the best I have ever had. I could not find one that did not have a rich, reddish brown texture, succulent sirloin, or a flash of heat. For those not familiar with real Texas chili, ground beef and beans are heresy. Blends of secret spices, red chile powder, and long slow cooking make its magic. Each cook must qualify to cook at Terlingua, entering and winning competions during the year to accumulate enough points to cook.

After judging, the rest of the trip was what you might expect: napping, and lots of visiting and friendly discussions concerning whether this year's chili was as good as last year's, or the chili from ten years ago. A highlight was an extraordinary conversation with Hallie Stillwell, a judge of the very first Terlingua cookoff, who at ninety-two or so was there plugging her first book, *I'll Gather My Geese*, her life story about ranching in west Texas since 1918. Meanwhile, everybody waited patiently for the final competition results.

The chili cookoff winner was Dorene Ritchey—the third Terlingua championship under her belt. The Skeeter Meat people placed fourth in the Open Show category. Dan and I were ready for another fascinating, thirteen-hour drive home, having lived to tell about Terlingua. Maybe west Texas wasn't so bad after all. I had seen the drunken debauchery and tasted the world's finest chili. All I missed was the naked dancing. Maybe next year.

ICS — A History, Maybe

In 1988, International Chili Society director Jim West and historian Ormly Gumfudgin teamed to write a brief history of ICS that appeared in *Chile Pepper* magazine. What follows here is based on their work and our research.

The International Chili Society was booted out of Texas in 1974 and reborn in California. Here's how it happened. During the 1974 cookoff, C. V. Wood and Carroll Shelby flew a network TV crew into Terlingua to cover the festivities. Of course, it was only natural that the media people would interview the people they had traveled with, but Frank Tolbert didn't like it one bit. After standing around on the sidelines and not receiving any attention from the TV crew, he got mad. In a letter to Wood and Shelby, he invited ICS to take the World's Championship Chili Cookoff to California and "save the freight." So they did. It was as simple as that.

The most vital item on the agenda was to decide where it could be held so that there would be a sufficient space for the thousands of people expected. ICS needed hotels, an area for recreational vehicles, a location with the charm of a ghost town like Terlingua, plus many other details. After much searching, Tropico Gold Mine was selected. It's located three miles west of Rosamond in the Mohave Desert. One other little detail was that ICS trademarked the phrase *World Championship Chili Cookoff.*

The first Championship Chili Cookoff held in California was twice as big as expected—about twenty thousand people attended. Maybe some of them were star-struck by the celebrity judges: William Conrad, Robert Mitchum, Ernest Borgnine, Peter Marshall, Dale Robertson, and John Derek. The "Miss Chile Pepper" was Diana House, who went on to spice up *Playboy* magazine —but that's another story.

Meanwhile, back in Texas, Frank Tolbert was busy organizing the Chili Appreciation Society International and promoting the Terlingua cookoff. Although relations with the two societies seemed to be heated, they were in constant communication with Frank.

Early in 1976, ICS began to get really organized by finding corporate sponsors. Pepsi, Budweiser, Hunt–Wesson, Tabasco Brand, the American

Spice Trade Association, and Tequila Sauza came on board to help raise money for various charities. By 1977 the turnout at Tropico Gold Mine for the championship exceeded thirty-five thousand. That year Tommy Lasorda, Leslie Uggams, Andy Granatelli, and Bobby Unser were added to the celebrity judging staff, and by the end of the fourth championship, more than $50,000 had been raised for charity.

Cash prizes were growing as well. In 1978, the World's Champion Chili Cook, LaVerne "Nevada Annie" Harris, picked up $14,000—which wasn't shabby for three hours of cooking. That year ICS started its official publication, *Chili*.

In 1980 the Tropico Gold Mine was sold lock, stock, and barrel, as the saying goes. The old Paramount Ranch in Agoura was chosen as the new site, but the World Championship Cookoff was eventually moved back to Tropico.

The 1988 championship was held on October 30 in Tropico with more than $35,000 in cash prizes and awards. Since 1975 ICS has raised over $10 million for charities and nonprofit organizations. There are nearly 15,000 members worldwide and about 350 sanctioned cookoffs every year with nearly 10,000 contestants and 5,000 judges. Obviously, chili cookoffs today are no longer off-the-wall events, but rather viable fundraising efforts.

In addition to raising money, ICS also has a lot of fun, which is demonstrated by some of the events at the Tropico Gold Mine. In 1988, the Tulsa, Oklahoma, Jaycees built the World's Largest Pot of Competition-Style Chili.

Wick Fowler at the Ladies' Only Chili Cookoff in Luckenbach, Texas, when all the hurricanes were named for women.

The 750 gallons of chili were made with 75 pounds of bacon, 3,000 pounds of chili-grind meat, 1,500 pounds of onions, 1,200 cloves of garlic, nearly 30 pounds of spices—and, of course, more than 50 pounds of fresh chiles. The concoction, based on a recipe called Chili from Hell, was served to more than twenty thousand chiliheads at Tropico in a benefit for the St. Jude's Children's Hospital in Memphis.

In 1992, the twenty-sixth annual World's Championship Chili Cookoff was moved to Rawhide, an 1880s western town located in Scottsdale, Arizona. The following year, the championship moved to Reno, Nevada.

The Roving Chili Pot

In an effort to revive the Chili Bill that was introduced into Congress in 1984 to make chili America's official food, the ICS and Hyundai Motor America teamed up in 1993 to move a three-hundred–pound copper chili pot from Washington, D.C., to their World's Championship Chili Cookoff in Reno, Nevada. The pot was mounted on a motorized stagecoach—which was the first stagecoach to travel across the country since the late 1800s. Jim Lotito did the driving and Ormly Gumfudgin rode shotgun.

Chiliheads pledged $10 for every mile the stagecoach traveled, and for their pledge they had a chance to win a Hyundai automobile. The stage with the chili pot arrived in Reno on October 1—just in time for the championship cookoff.

ICS Procedures and Hints

In 1980, the legendary C. V. Wood (1920–1992) wrote an article on how to judge a chili cookoff. "There are no absolute guidelines on how each judge will or should make the winning selections," he wrote. But he did offer some major characteristics for winning chili:

- Good chile pepper taste ("not too hot, not too mild").
- Good texture of the meat ("not too tough, not too mushy").
- Good consistency ("not too thick, not too thin").
- Good blend of spices.
- Good aroma (a personal preference).

Interestingly enough, Wood wrote: "Color has little to do with a good bowl of chili." Later cooks disagreed with that comment. Wood's final estimation of the best way to choose a winning bowl was, "If I'm only going to have one type of chili for the rest of my life, which bowl on this table would I choose?"

Here's some advice from Tom Valentine, who wrote about how to get the most out of a chili cookoff in the early issues of the ICS publication, *Chili* magazine.

- A chili team can have no more than four members—"the head cook and three elves."
- Everything for chili must be prepared on-site. Prechopped ingredients such as onions are not permitted, but canned chiles and tomatoes are allowed.
- Each contestant must cook at least a gallon of chili.
- Don't try to be exotic. "Carrots and weiners and saffron and turnips do not impress chili-conditioned palates."
- Forget using sugar. "It's for sissies."
- "Cumin can make or break a superior bowl of chili."
- Judges usually rate 60 percent on flavor, 30 percent on texture, and 10 percent on consistency.

Additionally, Randy Robinson, the 1991 World's Champion, offered the following sage advice (no, don't put sage in your chili):

- Use a recipe and keep notes. Randy found it hard to believe that many cooks just "throw together" their chili. Without a recipe, there is no way to repeat success even if they happen to win. "Without a basic recipe and past notes to guide you," he wrote, "you can't hope to address the consistency question."
- Chili that looks good is bound to taste better. He recommended a "combination of finely cubed (¼ inch) and coarsely ground meat."
- Strive for "no flaws" chili. That means, according to Randy, "no unusual, overbearing, or distracting flavors." The blend of seasonings should be "balanced, harmonious, and complex."
- "Know thy Jury." Randy does his research and visits the favorite chili parlor in a town with a cookoff to determine "everyman's taste" that the judges will be looking for.

- To perfect your chili, "practice, judge, and kibbitz." Randy advised: "The fastest way to learn how to win is by judging chili and stealing secrets from good chili cooks."

Basic CASI Rules and Judging, Plus Hints

As might be imagined, there are extensive CASI rules and regulations for cookoffs, many too technical to get into here. The booklet *Official CASI Rules* contains forty pages of dense type and complicated regulations. But here are the basics:

- All chili must be cooked on-site and be prepared in the open.
- All chili must be cooked from scratch, which means starting with raw meat. Commercial chili powder is permitted, but commercial mixes are not. Marinating meat is not allowed. Health requirements forbid home-butchered meat.
- No fillers, such as beans, macaroni, rice, or hominy, are permitted.
- Each cook is responsible for cooking one pot of chili and turning in just one judging cup from that pot.
- Cooks must prepare and cook chili in a sanitary manner and cook it under the cover of a tent or umbrella. The cleanup procedure requires three containers: one with soap and water, one with clean rinse water, and one with a small amount of bleach.
- Any cook failing to comply with CASI rules is subject to disqualification from the cookoff.

An entire book or epic poem could be written on judging chili and probably will be someday. Until then, here are the basics on CASI judging:

- Aroma: Chili should smell good.
- Red Color: Chili should look good and the color should range from reddish to reddish brown. Shades of "gray, black, pink, or camouflage" are unappealing, as is excess grease.
- Consistency: Chili should be a good balance of meat and gravy. The meat should be tender but not mushy.
- Taste: Chili should taste good. Judges believe that an excellent-tasting chili will always stand out.

- Aftertaste: Residual taste should be pleasant. A chile pepper "afterbite" is also permitted, but the degree of heat is a matter of personal preference.

There are numerous hints on how to prepare championship chili scattered throughout this book, but here are some specific ones for CASI cookoffs, courtesy of the ChiliHeads of Arizona:

- Meat should be cubed; ground meat very seldom places.
- All fresh ingredients (onions, garlic) should be run through a blender to make them smooth, because chunks tend to get low scores.
- Some judges dislike beer or other alcohol in chili.
- Use two spoons to taste your chili to avoid putting the spoon that was in your mouth back into the chili.
- Ask other cooks to critique your chili.
- Try your recipe at home and have friends and relatives critique it.
- As other experts have advised, you are cooking chili to please the judges, not yourself. Remember that judging varies from cookoff to cookoff, so don't change your recipe too rapidly.

Cookoff Recipes

Originally, when we planned this book, we intended to include recipes from the cookoffs of both the major associations. So we retained some chiliheads to scour the cookoffs and collect recipes from winning cooks—and good recipes from cooks who weren't fortunate enough to win major prizes. We had great luck with the CASI-sanctioned cookoffs and the Behind the Store competitors. But we ran into a dead end with ICS.

We wrote to Jim West, ICS director, requesting permission to reprint some winning ICS recipes that had already been published in their own publications. At first we received no response. Finally, after a phone call to the ICS offices, we were faxed a letter from Edward A. Sokolski, the attorney who represents the ICS for patent, trademark, and copyright causes.

"The International Chili Society," he wrote, "has written agreements with all competitors in its chili cookoffs which provide for the assignment of exclusive rights to the publication of any recipe used in the competition. Rights to publish such recipes have already been committed by my client and therefore permission for you to publish them cannot be granted."

We warned you that the chili world could be downright contrary. In light of Mr. Sokolski's letter, we were afraid to publish *any* recipe associated with an ICS-sanctioned event, so we have not knowingly done so. Instead, we offer a single recipe, ICS-Style Chili, which was created by us. If readers wish to find ICS competition recipes, we suggest looking in *The International Chili Society Official Chili Cookbook,* by Martina and William Neely, which is listed in our bibliography.

Following our ICS-Style Chili recipe, however, are a bunch of great recipes from CASI cookoffs, Terlingua, and the Behind the Store cookoff.

You Forgot the Beer

❝During the early days of the last war, when a lot of people were buying up sheets, pillowcases, sugar, and razor blades, I invested my money in the 'necessities of life'—bourbon whiskey and Texas chili, and my safe return from the war was evidently influenced by the good physical condition which that diet produced.❞

—Gen. C. R. Smith, former president, American Airlines

ICS-Style Chili

Since this chili is our own creation and has never been entered in any ICS-sanctioned cookoff, we are permitted to publish it here. It utilizes many of the ingredients and techniques common to ICS-style chilis.

3   pounds sirloin steak, cut into ¼-inch cubes
¼   cup vegetable oil
1   cup chorizo sausage
1   large onion, minced
3   cloves garlic, minced
1   stalk celery, minced
2   cups beef broth
2   cups tomato sauce
1   12-ounce bottle Corona beer
¼   cup New Mexican red chile powder (your choice, hot or mild)
3   tablespoons chili powder (your choice)
½   cup diced New Mexican green chiles
1   tablespoon cumin
2   teaspoons Mexican oregano
Salt, white pepper, cayenne, cumin, and brown sugar, to taste

Sauté the steak in the oil in a skillet until lightly browned. With a slotted spoon, remove the steak and reserve. Add the sausage to the same skillet and fry for 5 minutes and remove with the slotted spoon and reserve. Add the onion, garlic, and celery to the oil and sauté until the onion is soft. Remove with the slotted spoon and reserve.

Transfer the steak, sausage, and onion-garlic-celery mixture to a chili pot or Dutch oven. Add the beef broth, tomato sauce, and beer and bring to a simmer. Cook for a half hour.

Add the New Mexican chile powder, your choice chili powder, green chiles, cumin, and oregano, and simmer uncovered for 1 hour, stirring occasionally.

The next step is the most difficult. Taste the chile and add salt, white pepper, cayenne, cumin, and brown sugar to make the chili perfect. Simmer an additional 15 minutes.

Serves: 6

Chili Cook's Hints   Experiment with other spices to make your chili unique. Some suggestions are: ¼ to ½ teaspoon of paprika, coriander, cilantro, sage, and basil. You might also want to draw attention to your chili by floating an habanero chile on top, but omit the cayenne and take care that the habanero does not burst!

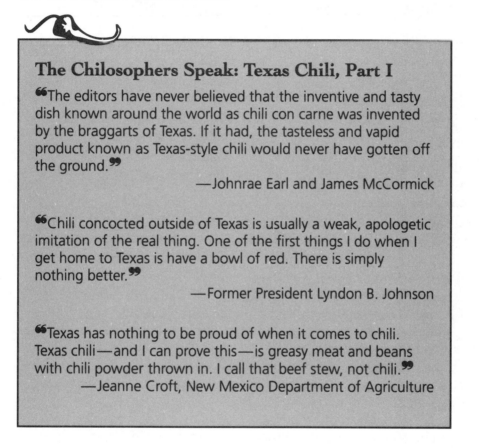

The Chilosophers Speak: Texas Chili, Part I

❝The editors have never believed that the inventive and tasty dish known around the world as chili con carne was invented by the braggarts of Texas. If it had, the tasteless and vapid product known as Texas-style chili would never have gotten off the ground.❞

—Johnrae Earl and James McCormick

❝Chili concocted outside of Texas is usually a weak, apologetic imitation of the real thing. One of the first things I do when I get home to Texas is have a bowl of red. There is simply nothing better.❞

—Former President Lyndon B. Johnson

❝Texas has nothing to be proud of when it comes to chili. Texas chili—and I can prove this—is greasy meat and beans with chili powder thrown in. I call that beef stew, not chili.❞

—Jeanne Croft, New Mexico Department of Agriculture

Dorene Ritchey's 5-R Chili

Dorene Ritchey says the most important ingredient in award-winning chili is luck. However, as a three-time Terlingua champion, we believe there's more than luck involved with her chili. Please note that a great bowl of red is not quickly made. Total cooking time of this recipe is 2½ to 3 hours.

1	tablespoon vegetable shortening
2	pounds beef, boneless, trimmed of fat, and cubed—shoulder arm, chuck, or chuck tender preferred
1½ teaspoons hot sauce	
1	cup tomato sauce
2	beef bouillon cubes
Water	
2	jalapeños, slit down the middle

Spice Mixture

6	tablespoons New Mexican red chile powder
4	teaspoons ground cumin
1	tablespoon granulated onion
1	teaspoon granulated garlic
1	teaspoon MSG (optional)
½	teaspoon salt
½	teaspoon white pepper
⅜	teaspoon ground cayenne
¼	teaspoon dried oregano
⅛	teaspoon crushed bay leaf

Melt the shortening and quickly sear the meat. Add the hot sauce, tomato sauce, bouillon cubes, water to cover, and 1 whole jalapeño. Simmer, covered, for 40 to 60 minutes, stirring occasionally. Add water as needed and remove the jalapeño when it becomes soft. Squeeze any juice from the jalapeño into the mixture and discard the pulp and seeds.

Mix together the ingredients for the spice mixture, then divide it into three equal portions. During the last hour of cooking time add one-third of spice mixture and the second jalapeño. Continue cooking, adding water as needed. During the last half hour of cooking, remove the second jalapeño and squeeze in the juice, discarding the pulp and seeds. Add the second third of the spice mixture. Continue cooking, adding water as needed.

During the last 15 minutes, add the remaining spice mixture. Taste for seasoning and adjust the chile powder, cumin, and salt if needed during the last 5 minutes.

Serves: 6

Hot Pants Chili

This recipe is from the legendary Allegani Jani Schofield, who won the CASI Terlingua Cookoff in 1974. She is from Fredericksburg, Texas.

4   pounds beef stew meat, ground once
3   onions, chopped
2   tablespoons vegetable oil
Salt and pepper to taste
2   heaping teaspoons *comino* (cumin) seeds
6   cloves garlic
Water
1   12-ounce can tomatoes
1   teaspoon sugar
½   can beer

2   packs Vanco chili seasoning (or chili powder of your choice)
1   small pack Vanco chili powder (or chile powder of your choice)
3   teaspoons *mole* paste
1   teaspoon Tabasco sauce
1   teaspoon salt
1   quart water
4   jalapeños, chopped
½   cup masa (corn flour)
Water

Brown the meat and onions in the oil. Season with salt and pepper to taste.

Using a *molcajete* (mortar and pestle), grind the comino seeds and the garlic with a little water and add to the meat.

In a blender, combine the tomatoes, sugar, beer, chili seasoning, and chile powder. Add the mixture to the meat.

Add the *mole* paste, Tabasco, salt, water, and jalapeños and cook for 2½ hours, stirring well from time to time.

At the end of the cooking time, make a runny paste of masa and water and add it to the chili. This will thicken the chili, but stir it fast or it will be lumpy. Cook a half hour more.

Serves: 6

Buzzard's Breath Chili

Tom Griffin, a Houston stockbroker, was the CASI Terlingua champion in 1977 with this interestingly named chili.

8 pounds boneless beef chuck, cut into ⅜-inch cubes and trimmed of gristle and fat
¼ cup vegetable oil
2 8-ounce cans tomato sauce
2 cups water
2 large onions, chopped
5 cloves garlic, chopped and crushed
2 jalapeños, wrapped in cheese cloth

¼ cup chili powder
2 teaspoons ground cumin
¼ to ½ teaspoon dried oregano
Cayenne powder to taste
Salt to taste
1 quart beef stock, homemade preferred
Masa harina
1 to 2 teaspoons paprika

Brown the meat in oil in an iron skillet, about 2 pounds at a time, until gray in color. Place in a large, cast-iron chili pot.

Add the tomato sauce and water. Add the onion, garlic, jalapeños and chili powder.

Simmer for 20 minutes and then add the cumin, oregano, cayenne, and salt to taste. Add the beef stock and simmer, covered, until the meat is tender, about 2 hours, stirring occasionally.

Add the masa to achieve the desired thickness, if needed.

Add the paprika for color and cook 10 additional minutes. Correct the seasoning to taste, discard the jalapeños, and serve.

A small amount of additional cumin enhances the aroma when added during the last 10 minutes.

Serves: 12

Judge Arly P. Haffazz Chili

This was the winning recipe at the CASI Terlingua International Chili Championship in 1980. It's from Bob Moore of Terlingua, Texas.

5   pounds boneless sirloin tip roast or a good shoulder cut, cubed

4   tablespoons kidney fat, minced

2   medium white onions, minced

1   12-ounce can beer

1   8-ounce can tomato sauce

1   cup hot water

1¼ cups beef stock

6   large cloves garlic, mashed with 1 tablespoon vegetable oil into a puree

5   tablespoons paprika

2   teaspoons salt

1   tablespoon flavor enhancer (Accent or MSG)

1½ teaspoons white pepper

11 tablespoons unblended chile powder (he grinds his own with various Mexican chiles—see hint)

5½ tablespoons finely ground cumin

1   teaspoon dried oregano

¼   teaspoon ground Japanese, de arbol, or cayenne chile (for additional heat)

In a skillet, brown the meat with 3 tablespoons rendered kidney fat until gray in color. Place the meat and natural juices in a cooking pot.

In the skillet, sauté the onions in 1 tablespoon rendered kidney fat until translucent. Add to the cooking pot.

Add the beer, tomato sauce, hot water, beef stock, half the mashed garlic mixture, 2 tablespoons paprika, 1 teaspoon salt, flavor enhancer, and 1 teaspoon pepper. Simmer over a low heat 2 hours until the meat is tender. Be sure the pot has a tight lid as this will help the tenderizing process. Stir occasionally.

When the meat is tender, add the remaining garlic mixture, unblended chili powder, cumin, 3 tablespoons paprika, oregano, 1 teaspoon salt, ½ teaspoon pepper, and the hot chile powder.

Continue cooking for 15 more minutes. Turn off the heat and let sit for 1 to 2 hours so the flavor of the spices is absorbed.

After resting for 1 to 2 hours, turn the heat back on and continue to simmer for 1 more hour. Total cooking time is 3 hours, 15 minutes.

Serves: 10 with hearty appetites

Chili Cook's Hint   If you don't want to make your own chili powder, Bob suggests you use 10 tablespoons of a good commercial chili powder, cut the cumin down to 2½ tablespoons, cut the paprika to 2 tablespoons, and omit the oregano.

John Billy's Chili

This recipe is from John Billy Murray, of Humble, Texas, who won the Behind the Store cookoff in 1984. He notes: "The chili should be of a thick consistency so that a ten-inch wooden spoon will stand upright in it, and then sink slowly to the bottom."

2   tablespoons rendered beef kidney suet, chopped, or the same amount of vegetable oil

2   pounds beef chuck, cut in sugar-cube–sized chunks

1   medium onion, finely chopped

4   large cloves garlic

1   tablespoon garlic powder

½   tablespoon MSG (optional)

½   tablespoon salt

¾   cup (or more) beef bouillon or broth

1   8-ounce can tomato sauce

4   heaping tablespoons chili powder

1   heaping tablespoon ground red New Mexican chile or 1 large ancho chile, softened and peeled (see hint)

2   tablespoons cumin

⅜   teaspoon paprika

White pepper to taste, about 1 to 1½ tablespoons

1   large or 2 small jalapeños, seeds and stems removed, cut in half

In a large stainless steel pot, render enough fat from the suet to make approximately 2 tablespoons of fat. Remove the suet and discard. Add the beef cubes and cook over high heat until the meat turns gray.

Add the onion, garlic cloves, garlic powder, ¼ tablespoon MSG, ¼ tablespoon salt, and the beef bouillon. Cover and cook over medium heat at a rapid boil until the meat is tender, about 45 minutes. (The meat should be tender enough to squeeze flat between your fingers without bouncing back.)

Reduce the heat, add the tomato sauce, and cover and simmer for 15 minutes. If desired, remove the garlic or mash the cloves and incorporate into the chili. Add the remaining MSG and salt, chili powder, ancho chile, cumin, paprika, white pepper, and jalapeño halves. Cover and simmer an additional 45 minutes, stirring frequently.

Add additional broth (or liquid from softened ancho) very sparingly as needed during remaining cooking time to prevent meat from becoming dry. At the end of the cooking time, remove the jalapeños and discard.

Serves: 10 to 12

Chili Cook's Hint   To soften the dried ancho chile, seed and stem the pod and place under a broiler to blacken the skin. Soak the blackened chile in warm water for 10 to 15 minutes. Scrape the pulp from the skin and discard the skin.

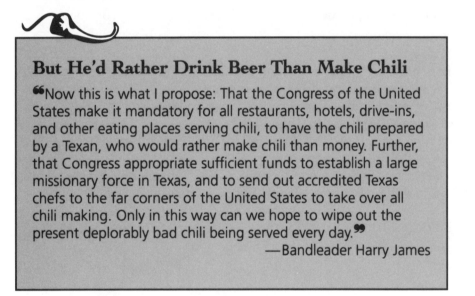

But He'd Rather Drink Beer Than Make Chili

❝Now this is what I propose: That the Congress of the United States make it mandatory for all restaurants, hotels, drive-ins, and other eating places serving chili, to have the chili prepared by a Texan, who would rather make chili than money. Further, that Congress appropriate sufficient funds to establish a large missionary force in Texas, and to send out accredited Texas chefs to the far corners of the United States to take over all chili making. Only in this way can we hope to wipe out the present deplorably bad chili being served every day.❞

—Bandleader Harry James

Community Chili

From Jim Ivy of Irving, Texas, the Behind the Store champ in 1985, comes this winning recipe.

3 pounds beef chuck, cubed	½ teaspoon cayenne pepper
1 medium onion, chopped	1 teaspoon paprika
1 8-ounce can tomato sauce	1 teaspoon garlic powder
3 jalapeños	½ teaspoon oregano
4 tablespoons chili powder	1 teaspoon MSG (optional)
3 tablespoons cumin	1 teaspoon black pepper

Put meat, onion, and tomato sauce in a large pot with water to cover. Wash and prick the jalapeños and drop them in whole. Add 1 tablespoon each of chili powder and cumin. Bring to a boil, cover and reduce heat. Cook until the meat is tender, about 2 to 2½ hours.

After 1 hour, remove the jalapeños and mash them through a strainer. Throw away the pulp and add the juice to the chili.

Place the remaining spices in a cup or bowl with a lid and shake to mix. Put about half the mixture in the pot about 30 minutes before the chili is done.

Add the remaining spices for the final 15 minutes of cooking time.

Serves: 6

1845 Brand Chili

This recipe is a living testament to the phrase "if it ain't broke, don't fix it." Richard S. Slocomb won the 1972 Texas Men's State Championship with this tried-and-true treat.

5   pounds ground chuck beef

5   tablespoons *comino* (cumin) seeds

5   large onions, chopped

10 cloves garlic, crushed

10 New Mexican red chile pods

6   cups water

Oregano to taste

Salt and pepper to taste

In a large skillet, brown the beef. Once the meat is done, place the beef and its juice in a medium-sized stew pot. Add the *comino* seeds, chopped onion, and garlic to the chili. In a medium pot, place the water to boil, adding the red chile pods once the water is bubbly. Boil for 10 minutes, or until the pods are very soft. Remove the soft pods and puree in a blender. Add the pureed pods, oregano, salt, and pepper to the stew pot, stirring the mixture well. Cook the chili from 3 to 4 hours over medium heat, adding water and stirring as necessary.

Serves: 6 to 10

Grand Prize Chili

Ray Calhoun was right to name his fare Grand Prize Chili; it captured the Texas Men's State Championship in 1980.

1 tablespoon olive oil	Water
3 pounds flank steak, cubed into ¼-inch pieces, or coarsely ground chuck	4 teaspoons cumin powder
	1 teaspoon garlic powder
1 8-ounce can tomato sauce	½ teaspoon MSG (optional)
1 tablespoon onion powder	½ teaspoon oregano
1 tablespoon paprika	½ teaspoon black or white pepper, ground
1 teaspoon cayenne powder	6 tablespoons New Mexican red chile powder
2 beef bouillon cubes	
1 chicken bouillon cube	Salt to taste

In a medium stew pot, heat the oil and briefly sear the meat. Add the tomato sauce, onion powder, paprika, and cayenne. Add the beef and chicken bouillon, along with enough water to cover the entire mixture. Stir the chili well and simmer for 1½ hours. Next add the cumin, garlic, MSG, oregano, pepper, and red chile powder. Stir well and cook the chili an additional 30 minutes, or until the meat is tender.

Serves: 4 to 6

Inspired Chili

Pat Moriarty's chili inspired enough judges at the 1989 Texas State finals to take home a championship.

3 pounds lean beef, chili grind
1 tablespoon New Mexican red chile powder
½ teaspoon cumin
1 medium onion, finely diced
1 clove garlic, squeezed through a press
1 cup water
1 can beef broth
1 teaspoon New Mexican red chile powder
¼ teaspoon celery salt
⅛ teaspoon basil

¼ teaspoon oregano
1 8-ounce can tomato sauce
3 fresh jalapeños, seeds and stems removed
3 tablespoons New Mexican red chile powder
1 tablespoon cumin
1 clove of garlic, squeezed through a press
½ teaspoon salt
¼ teaspoon cayenne powder
¼ teaspoon white pepper
2 teaspoons paprika

Brown the ground beef in a medium pot. Add the red chile powder, cumin, onion, and garlic and sauté. Add the water, beef broth, red chile powder, celery salt, basil, oregano, tomato sauce, and jalapeños. Stir the chili and simmer for 1 to 2 hours, or until the meat is almost tender.

Remove the jalapeños, squeezing their juices into the chili. Discard the jalapeños after the juice is removed.

Stir the chili well and add the red chile powder, cumin, garlic, salt, cayenne, white pepper, and paprika. Cook the chili 30 minutes more or until the meat is completely tender. Add salt and additional cayenne pepper to taste.

Serves: 4 to 6

Pedernales River Rat Chili

The recipe features the creations of Lynn Hejtmancik, the 1988 winner of the CASI Terlingua International Championship.

2   tablespoons Crisco
3   pounds beef chuck, chili grind
    or ¼-inch cubes
2   tablespoons paprika
1   tablespoon onion powder
¼   teaspoon oregano
1   can (14½ ounces) beef broth
2   beef bouillon cubes
½   chicken bouillon cube
1   tablespoon garlic powder
½   teaspoon black pepper
2   tablespoons jalapeño hot sauce
    (your choice of brand)
Water
4   tablespoons red chili powder
    (Dave Mark's Chili Powder
    from San Antonio preferred)
2   tablespoons Chimayo (New
    Mexican) red chile powder
1   teaspoon garlic powder

1   teaspoon onion powder
¼   teaspoon cayenne
2   tablespoons jalapeño hot sauce
    (your choice of brand)
8   ounces salt-free tomato sauce
¼   teaspoon brown sugar
1   teaspoon MSG (optional)
¼   teaspoon black pepper
2   tablespoons cumin powder
1   tablespoon mild New Mexican
    red chile powder
1   tablespoon garlic powder
1   teaspoon onion powder
Salt
Powdered beef base
Garlic powder
Cumin powder
Cayenne pepper
White pepper
Arrowroot or flour

Heat the Crisco in a medium cooking pot. When the Crisco has melted and is very hot, add the meat and stir until it is gray and starts to make its own juice. Add the paprika, onion powder, oregano, beef broth, the beef and chicken bouillon cubes, garlic powder, black pepper, and jalapeño hot sauce. Mix well and add enough water to cover the meat plus about 1 inch. Stir the chili every 10 minutes, and cook covered at a medium boil for 30 minutes.

Skim all of the unwanted grease off of the top of the chili, then add the chili powder, Chimayo red chile powder, garlic powder, onion powder, cayenne, and jalapeño hot sauce. Continue to stir and cook the chili until the meat is tender. Once the meat is done, lower the heat and add the tomato sauce, brown sugar, MSG (if desired), and black pepper. While the chili continues to cook, in a separate bowl combine the cumin powder, New Mexican mild red chile powder, garlic powder, and onion powder. Mix well, and add to the chili a teaspoon at a time, stirring and tasting between each addition, until you are pleased with the taste. You need not use the entire spice combination. Finally, adjust to taste with powdered beef base (if it needs more salt), garlic, cumin, cayenne, and white pepper. Thin the chili with beef broth or water if necessary. To thicken, add arrowroot or flour. Turn off the heat—the chili is now ready to eat, chill, or freeze.

Serves: 4 to 6

Hoot Owl Chili

Maxine Reed's chili was found to be the finest at the 1988 Original Viva Terlingua International Frank X. Tolbert–Wick Fowler Memorial Championship Chili Cookoff.

1	teaspoon paprika		2	tablespoons cooking oil
1	tablespoon onion powder		3	pounds chuck tender, cut in ¼-inch cubes
2	teaspoons garlic powder			
1	teaspoon MSG (optional)		2	cups water
1	teaspoon cayenne		1	cup tomato sauce
1	tablespoon cumin		1½	cups beef broth
1	teaspoon white pepper		1	medium onion, finely chopped
5	tablespoons New Mexican red chile powder		4	medium jalapeños
			½	teaspoon cumin

In a bowl, mix together the paprika, onion powder, garlic powder, MSG (if desired), cayenne, cumin, white pepper, and red chile powder. Mix the spices until well blended. Next coat a 4-quart pan with the cooking oil, and sear the meat. Add the water, tomato sauce, beef broth, and onion. Remove the stems from the jalapeños and slit each one with a knife. Add the jalapeños and half of the spice mixture. Cover the chili and simmer 1½ to 2 hours, stirring occasionally.

    Remove the jalapeños after 1 hour and set aside. Add the remaining spice mixture and ½ teaspoon of cumin. Add the juice from the jalapeños to the chili by pressing each jalapeño separately through a strainer into the mixture. Discard the pods. Cook for 30 more minutes, or until the meat is tender.

Serves: 4 to 6

Fat Dog Chili

This chili could have been called Double Luck Chili, having won both the Texas Men's State Championship in 1987, and the CASI Terlingua International Chili Championship the same year! This recipe by David Henson will definitely delight your guests.

4½ tablespoons minced onion

½ teaspoon garlic

1 teaspoon hot sauce (Trappey's Green Dragon preferred)

½ teaspoon salt

2 tablespoons Crisco

2½ pounds chuck tender, cut in ½-inch cubes

1 can beef broth

4 to 6 whole jalapeños

3 tablespoons commercial chili powder (an assortment of brands)

2 teaspoons cumin

¼ teaspoon cayenne

¼ teaspoon oregano

¼ teaspoon crushed bay leaf

½ teaspoon salt

½ cup tomato sauce

3 tablespoons New Mexican red chile powder (an assortment of types and brands)

2 teaspoons cumin

½ teaspoon garlic powder

½ cup tomato sauce

1 teaspoon Gebhardt's Chili Powder

½ teaspoon cumin

1/16 teaspoon sweet basil

1/16 teaspoon brown sugar

In a nonreactive bowl, soak the minced onion, garlic, hot sauce, and salt together for 20 to 30 minutes before starting the chili.

In a medium stew pot, melt the Crisco and brown the meat. Add the soaked onion and the beef broth, floating the jalapeños on top of the mixture. Cook the chili for 1 hour, then remove the jalapeños, squeezing the juice from them into the chili and discarding the pods. Next, add the chili powder, cumin, cayenne, oregano, bay leaf, salt, and tomato sauce. Cook for 1 hour, stirring frquently.

Add the red chile powder, cumin, garlic, and tomato sauce. Continue to cook the chili on medium heat. About 15 minutes before serving, add the Gebhardt's Chili Powder, cumin, basil, and brown sugar. Stir well and serve.

Serves: 4 to 6

Yahoo Chili

Barbara Britton from Mesquite, Texas, won the 1989 CASI Terlingua International Chili Championship with this recipe, and it's worth ya-hooting and hollering over!

1　teaspoon Crisco
2½ pounds beef chuck/mock tender or round steak cut in ½-inch cubes
1　8-ounce can of salt-free tomato sauce
1　14½-ounce can of beef broth
2½ cups water
2　tablespoons commercial chili powder
2　tablespoons onion powder
½　teaspoon ground cayenne
2　teaspoons beef-flavored base or 1 beef bouillon cube
1　teaspoon chicken-flavored base

or 1 chicken bouillon cube
½　teaspoon salt
1　tablespoon New Mexican red chile powder
1　tablespoon cumin
2　teaspoons garlic powder
3　tablespoons commercial chili powder
¼　teaspoon ground black pepper
½　teaspoon salt
⅛　teaspoon cayenne
1　tablespoon commercial chili powdcr
1　teaspoon ground cumin
½　teaspoon onion powder

In a 5-quart Dutch oven, melt the Crisco and brown the beef, retaining the juice from the meat in the oven. Add the tomato sauce, beef broth, and water.

Combine the chili powder, onion powder, cayenne, beef- and chicken-flavored base, salt, and red chile powder and add to the chili. Bring the chili to a boil, then reduce the heat and simmer for 1¾ hours. Add small amounts of water if the chili gets too thick.

In a separate nonreactive bowl, combine the ground cumin, garlic powder, commercial chili powder, and ground black pepper. Add this mixture to the chili and simmer for 30 more minutes.

Combine the last spices—the salt, cayenne, chili powder, cumin, and onion powder and add to the chili. Simmer 15 more minutes and serve.

Serves: 4 to 6

Bandit Chili II

This recipe is from our friends Phebe and Dywane Cude, who helped us collect a great many of the award-winning chili recipes in this book. They travel all over the West participating in chili cookoffs, and usually take home a prize or two, each cooking their own pot. Phebe says that although they share the same recipe, their chili always turns out differently. Even married chili cooks are sly that way, and most have a few secret ingredients up their sleeve!

2 pounds beef, in ½-inch cubes, or chili grind	1 package Goya Sazon (available in Latin markets)
1 15-ounce can beef broth	1 teaspoon brown sugar
1 8-ounce can salt-free tomato sauce	3 to 4 jalapeños, seeds and stems removed, cut in half lengthwise
½ tablespoon onion powder	2 teaspoons cumin
½ teaspoon cayenne	½ tablespoon garlic powder
1 teaspoon beef bouillon granules	⅛ to ¼ teaspoon black pepper
1 or ½ teaspoon chicken bouillon granules	4 tablespoons New Mexican red chile powder
¼ teaspoon salt	¼ teaspoon Texas Gunpowder (powdered jalapeño, optional)
½ teaspoon New Mexican red chile powder	Salt to taste

In a large pot, briefly sear the meat and then add the broth. Cover the pot and boil for 30 minutes. Add the tomato sauce and cover and simmer for 30 more minutes.

Add the onion powder, cayenne, beef and chicken bouillon granules, salt, chile powder, Goya Sazon, brown sugar, and jalapeños. Cook and stir for another 45 minutes, or until the meat is tender, then turn off the heat.

About 30 minutes before you are ready to serve or turn in the chili for judging, bring the chili to a boil and add the cumin, garlic powder, black pepper, red chile powder, and Texas Gunpowder (if desired). Remove the jalapeños, add water if the chili is too thick, and adjust the salt. Turn in and win!

Serves: 4 to 6

The Chilosophers Speak: Texas Chili, Part II

"Texas chili is a bowlful of attitude. It is ornery, rude, and starts fights and feuds. It inspires homesickness, chauvinism, braggadocio, tears (of agony as well as longing), dozens of tumultuous cookoffs each year, and more philosophizing than Marcel Proust's madeleines.**"**

—Jane and Michael Stern

"What really spoiled Texas chili was the same thing that used up Elvis Presley and John Belushi and made young martyrs of the likes of Joan of Arc and Jesus of Nazareth and the Kennedys and Dr. Martin Luther King: success.**"**

—Sam Pendergrast

"I like beans in my chili, but not enough to argue about it with Texans.**"**

—Calvin Trillin

Hike 'n Fire Chili

Chili master Les Doss was judged the best of the best at the 1988 Texas Men's State Championship with this sixteen-ingredient chili.

2½ to 3 pounds chuck roast or tender, cut into ½-inch cubes
1   large onion, diced
5 to 6 drops vegetable oil
1   tablespoon garlic powder
2   cups tomato sauce
2   teaspoons paprika
1   teaspoon salt
1   8-ounce can beef stock
2   teaspoons MSG (optional)
¼   tablespoon white pepper

1   tablespoon garlic powder
4   teaspoons cumin
¼   teaspoon oregano
¼   teaspoon white pepper
3   tablespoons dark chili powder
1   tablespoon light pure chili powder
4   teaspoons paprika
1   teaspoon salt
¼   teaspoon cayenne

Separate the meat and onion into 3 equal batches. In a large skillet, add the oil and heat. When the oil is warm, add the first batch of the meat and onion and sear. Do each batch separately, then place all the meat and onion in a large chili pot and simmer for 30 minutes. Add the garlic powder, tomato sauce, paprika, salt, beef stock, MSG (if desired), and white pepper. Cook the chili on medium heat, stirring frequently, until the meat is tender, at least 1 hour.

Add the garlic powder, cumin, oregano, white pepper, dark chili powder, light pure chili powder, paprika, salt, and cayenne pepper. Cook 15 minutes longer and serve.

Serves: 4 to 6

North Texas Red

The winning year for Tom Tyler was 1985, when he was named chili champ at the Texas Men's State Championship. This recipe leans toward the traditional, requiring about three hours of preparation.

1 tablespoon Crisco	¼ teaspoon oregano
2½ pounds beef, cubed in ½-inch pieces	⅛ teaspoon ground bay leaf
Water	1 8-ounce can tomato sauce
4¼ tablespoons minced onion	2 beef bouillon cubes
1 teaspoon granulated garlic	3 tablespoons commercial chili powder
1 teaspoon salt	2 teaspoons cumin
¼ teaspoon cayenne	¼ teaspoon cayenne
4 fresh jalapeños	1 teaspoon granulated garlic
3 tablespoons commercial chili powder	½ teaspoon MSG (optional)
2 teaspoons cumin	Salt and cayenne to taste

Heat the Crisco in a large pot. When the oil is hot, add the beef and cook until the meat is gray. Add enough water to cover the meat about 2 inches. Bring the mixture to a boil and add the onion, garlic, salt, and cayenne. Float the jalapeños on top of the chili and cook for 1 hour at a moderate boil.

Remove the jalapeños, squeeze the juice through a strainer into the chili, and discard the pods. Add the chili powder, cumin, oregano, bay leaf, tomato sauce, and bouillon cubes. Keep the level of the liquid at least ½ inch over the meat level, and simmer for 2 hours.

Add the chili powder, cumin, cayenne pepper, garlic, and MSG (if desired). About 10 minutes before serving, add salt and cayenne to taste.

Serves: 4 to 6

No Name Chili

Lynn Weber proves that chili doesn't have to have a clever name to be a winner.

3   pounds beef, cubed in ¼-inch pieces
1   medium onion, diced
Water
3   fresh jalapeños
1   cup tomato sauce
4   tablespoons commercial chili powder

3   tablespoons cumin
½   teaspoon oregano
1   teaspoon garlic powder
1   teaspoon MSG (optional)
1   teaspoon black pepper, ground
½   teaspoon cayenne

Place the meat and onion in a heavy covered pot. Add water to cover. Wash and pierce the jalapeños with a knife; add to the pot. Cook over medium heat until the meat is gray, about 30 to 40 minutes.

Add the tomato sauce, chili powder, cumin, oregano, garlic powder, MSG (if desired), black pepper, and cayenne. Cook over low heat until the meat is tender, about 1½ to 2 hours. Remove the jalapeños before they break apart. Adjust the seasonings and add more salt and cayenne if needed.

Serves: 4 to 6

Contrary to Ordinary Chili

Bob Ritchey, Jr., won the 1982 Texas Men's State Championship with this out-of-the-ordinary chili. And, great chili must run in the family—his wife, Dorene Ritchey, is a chili champ herself with a recipe in this book too!

2 tablespoons vegetable oil

1 medium yellow onion, diced

3 large cloves garlic, crushed

3 pounds lean beef, cubed in ¼-inch pieces

Water

2 teaspoons salt

1 tablespoon MSG (optional)

1½ teaspoons hot sauce (Trappey's Green Dragon preferred)

1 cup tomato sauce

7 heaping tablespoons chili powder

1 tablespoon ground cumin

¼ teaspoon ground oregano

¼ teaspoon garlic powder

Pinch sweet basil

In a large aluminum pot, add the cooking oil and sauté the onion and garlic until translucent. Add the meat to the pot and brown on high heat, stirring often. Add water to cover, and the salt, half of the MSG (if desired), and hot sauce. Cook at low boil, adding water as necessary to cover the meat. Add the tomato sauce to the mixture and continue to boil for 45 minutes. Add the remaining ingredients except the basil and reduce the heat to a low simmer for 45 minutes. About 10 minutes before serving, add the basil and stir.

Serves: 4 to 6

Tom Mix Chili

Lonnie Gibbs of Grand Prarie, Texas, borrowed this famous name for his 1981 Texas Men's State Championship chili.

3   pounds beef, chili grind
1   14½-ounce can beef broth
1   8-ounce can tomato sauce
Water
5   heaping tablespoons minced onion
2   tablespoons garlic powder
½   tablespoon salt
2   teaspoons paprika
2   teaspoons cumin

½   teaspoon cayenne
¼   teaspoon white pepper
3   fresh jalapeños
8   tablespoons commercial chili powder
2   teaspoons cumin
¼   teaspoon oregano
¼   teaspoon thyme
½   teaspoon MSG (optional)

In a large pot, brown the meat and pour off the juice. Add the beef broth, tomato sauce, and enough water to cover the meat. Add the minced onion, garlic powder, salt, paprika, cumin, cayenne, and white pepper. Float the jalapeños on top of the mixture and boil for 2 hours.

Add the chili powder, cumin, oregano, thyme, and MSG (if desired). Remove the jalapeños and squeeze the juice into the chili for an extra bite of heat. Discard the pods and simmer for 1 hour.

Serves: 4 to 6

Chill Lee's Two-Time Texas State Championship Recipe
(Soon to Be Three)

There's no lack of confidence in Ed Paetzel's chili. Ed does offer this one tip, however: "Stick with the recipe and add only one can of beer. Do not add more beer! I've lost more chili cookoffs that way!" And he should know; Ed won the Texas Men's State Championship in both 1974 and 1979.

5   pounds beef, chili grind
1   large onion, finely chopped
4   cloves garlic, finely chopped
2   jalapeños, stems removed, chopped with the seeds
1   package Chill Lee's Championship Texas Home Style Chili Makins'
1   15-ounce can tomato sauce

2   tablespoons ground New Mexican red chile
1   teaspoon paprika
1   teaspoon ground black pepper
1   teaspoon MSG (optional)
1   teaspoon salt
1   can beer
2   cups water

In a medium chili pot, brown the meat, remove, and set aside. In the same pot, brown the onion, garlic, and jalapeños. Return the meat, add the remaining ingredients except the beer and water, and stir well.

Add the beer and let the chili marinate with no heat for 1 hour. After marinating, add the water. Cook the chili for approximately 2 hours on medium heat, or until the meat is tender. Check the chili during cooking time to see if it is too thick. If it is, add water a tablespoon at a time to thin.

Serves: 4 to 6

Sam Le Gear's Red Leg Chili

Sam's recipe has been the one to beat in the nineties at the Texas Men's State Championship. He was the champ in both 1991 and 1993.

1   tablespoon vegetable oil
½   pound beef, cubed in ¼-inch pieces
¼   teaspoon jalapeño powder
1   teaspoon garlic
1   teaspoon salt
2   cups water
¾   teaspoon cayenne
½   tablespoon onion powder
1   tablespoon paprika
1   teaspoon beef bouillon granules
1   teaspoon chicken bouillon granules

1   8-ounce can tomato sauce
½   teaspoon seasoning salt
1   teaspoon garlic powder
½   teaspoon cumin
¼   teaspoon black pepper
2   tablespoons commercial chili powder
1   tablespoon Gebhardt's Chili Powder
1   teaspoon MSG (optional)

Coat a medium pot with the oil. Brown the meat and add the jalapeño powder, garlic, salt, water, cayenne, onion powder, paprika, beef and chicken bouillon granules, and tomato sauce. Cook, covered, on medium heat for 1 hour.

Add the seasoning salt, garlic, cumin, black pepper, chili powder, Gebhardt's Chili Powder, and MSG (if desired). Cook, covered, for 30 more minutes.

Serves: 3 to 4

Lone Star Red Chili

Frank Fox went for the nickname of Texas to describe his chili. Could it be because everything in Texas is bigger and better?

1　teaspoon Crisco

3　pounds beef chuck, cubed in ¼-inch pieces

½　cup salt-free tomato sauce (Hunt's preferred)

1　8-ounce can ⅓-less-salt chicken broth (Swanson's preferred)

1　8-ounce can beef broth (Swanson's preferred)

1　tablespoon onion powder

2　teaspoons beef bouillon granules (Wyler's preferred)

1　tablespoon chili powder (McCormick's preferred)

2　tablespoons Texas-style chili powder

½　teaspoon cayenne

1　teaspoon chicken bouillon granules (Wyler's preferred)

1　tablespoon cumin

3　tablespoons Texas-style chili powder (McCormick's preferred)

½　cup salt-free tomato sauce

2　teaspoons garlic powder

¼　teaspoon ground black pepper

½　teaspoon salt

1　teaspoon chili powder (McCormick's preferred)

½　teaspoon onion powder

⅛　teaspoon cayenne

1　teaspoon cumin

In a 5-quart pot, melt the Crisco and brown the meat. Retaining the juice from the meat in the pot, add the tomato sauce and the chicken and beef broth.

In a separate container, combine the onion powder, beef bouillon granules, chili powder, Texas-style chili powder, cayenne, and chicken bouillon granules. Mix well and add to the chili pot. Bring the chili to a boil, reduce the heat, and simmer for 90 minutes.

In a separate container, combine the cumin, Texas-style chili powder, tomato sauce, garlic powder, and black pepper. Add to the chili, stir well, and simmer for 30 minutes.

Last, mix the salt, chili powder, onion powder, cayenne, and cumin in a separate container and add to the chili and simmer for 15 to 20 minutes. Adjust the salt and heat level to taste.

Serves: 4 to 6

Competition and Eating Chili

Larry Burgess points out the similarities and differences between these two styles of chili: "Much ado has been made about the difference between eating chili and competition chili. In the early years of chili cookoffs, the eating chili and competition chili were one and the same. As a general rule, chili grind was the choice of the cooks, and no one would dream of cooking less than five pounds of meat. The following is a recipe that seems to bridge the gap between the two cooking techniques. It not only has a good flavor, but it's not too heavy and has done reasonably well in competition."

2½ pounds beef, cubed into ¼-inch pieces

½ cup ⅓-less-salt chicken broth

½ cup beef broth (Swanson's preferred)

1 8-ounce can salt-free tomato sauce

2 tablespoons your favorite chili powder blend

1 tablespoon onion powder

1 tablespoon garlic powder

1 tablespoon paprika

2 teaspoons chicken bouillon granules

1 teaspoon beef bouillon granules

½ teaspoon jalapeño powder

½ teaspoon white pepper

1 large fresh jalapeño, stem removed

3 tablespoons your favorite chile powder blend

1½ tablespoons cumin

1 teaspoon onion powder

1 teaspoon garlic powder

⅛ teaspoon oregano

Chile powder blend and cumin to taste

In a large pot, brown the meat and add the chicken broth, beef broth, and tomato sauce. Bring the mixture to a hard boil, and add the chili powder blend, onion powder, garlic powder, paprika, chicken bouillon granules, beef bouillon granules, jalapeño powder, and white pepper. Float the jalapeño on top of the chili, cover, and boil until the meat is tender. Check frequently to make sure liquid is covering the meat at all times. If more liquid is needed, add small amounts of water and beef broth.

After the meat is tender, turn off the heat and let the chili rest. About 45 minutes before you are ready to serve or turn in the chili for judging, reheat the chili and bring to a slow boil. In a separate container, combine the chile blend, cumin, onion powder, garlic powder, and oregano. Mix the spices well and add to the chili before serving guests. For cookoffs with only two rounds of judging, add the spices 20 minutes before turn-in. For cookoffs with more than two rounds of judging, add the spices 10 minutes before turn-in. Fine-tune the taste with additional chile blend or cumin.

Serves: 4 to 6

Chili Cook's Hints   "An inexpensive way to test your chili powder blend is to add a small amount to boiling water. Check for color, aroma, and flavor. Keep adding and mixing the different chili powder blends until you achieve your desired taste. Also, 8 or 9 drops of fresh lime juice will smooth out a bitter taste."

Out of Site Chili

Doris Coats and the Bottom of the Barrel Gang are the keepers of this great recipe. Doris won the 1991 CASI Terlingua International Chili Championship with this American original.

1 teaspoon shortening	½ teaspoon salt
2½ pounds chili-grind ground beef	½ teaspoon McCormick Season-All Seasoned Salt
1 14½-ounce can beef broth	½ teaspoon onion powder
1 8-ounce can tomato sauce	2 tablespoons McCormick Mexican Hot Chili Powder
2 teaspoons onion powder	
2 teaspoons garlic powder	2 tablespoons McCormick Texas-Style Chili Powder
1 teaspoon beef-flavored base or instant bouillon	¼ teaspoon cayenne
1 teaspoon chicken-flavored base or instant bouillon	¼ teaspoon salt
1 cup water	2 teaspoons paprika
2 teaspoons ground cumin	1 teaspoon ground cumin
¼ teaspoon white pepper	1 tablespoon chili powder
½ teaspoon cayenne	

In a Dutch oven, melt the shortening and brown the beef, retaining the juices in the oven. Add the beef broth and tomato sauce.

Combine the onion powder, garlic powder, beef and chicken base, and water. Add to the beef mixture and bring to a boil. Reduce the heat and simmer for 30 minutes.

In a separate container, combine the cumin, white pepper, cayenne, salt, seasoned salt, onion powder, and chili powders. Mix well and add to the chili. Stir the chili and cover and simmer for 45 minutes. Add small amounts of additional water if the chili gets too thick.

Combine the cayenne, salt, paprika, cumin, and chili powder in a separate container. Stir it into the chili, cover, and simmer for 30 minutes. Top with pinto beans, chopped onions, or grated cheese.

Serves: 6

High-Octane Chili

Jerry Hunt of Shreveport, Louisiana, won the granddaddy of all cookoffs— the CASI Terlingua International Chili Championship—in 1990 with this top recipe.

3 pounds chili-grind beef	½ teaspoon black pepper
1 10½-ounce can beef broth	½ teaspoon onion powder
1 8-ounce can tomato sauce	½ teaspoon garlic powder
4 tablespoons onion flakes	½ teaspoon white pepper
2 teaspoons beef-flavored base or instant bouillon	1 tablespoon cumin
1 teaspoon chicken-flavored base or instant bouillon	1 tablespoon paprika
1 teaspoon garlic powder	4 tablespoons chili powder
2 tablespoons chili powder	½ teaspoon cayenne
2 teaspoons hot pepper sauce	3 tablespoons chili powder
	1 teaspoon ground cumin
	½ teaspoon cayenne

In a Dutch oven, brown the beef, retaining the juices in the oven. Add the beef broth and tomato sauce to the beef. Combine the onion flakes, beef and chicken base, garlic powder, chili powder, and hot pepper sauce in a separate container. Add the spice mixture to the beef and bring to a boil. Reduce the heat, cover, and simmer for 1 hour.

Combine the black pepper, onion powder, garlic powder, white pepper, cumin, paprika, chili powder, and cayenne in a separate container. Add the spices to the chili and simmer for 45 minutes to 1 hour.

Last, combine the chili powder, cumin, and cayenne. Add to the chili, stir, cook for 30 minutes, then serve.

Serves: 4 to 6

Cindy Reed's 1993 Championship Chili

Cindy Reed comes from a long line of chili champions. Here's her winning recipe from the 1993 CASI Terlingua International Chili Championship.

1	teaspoon vegetable oil		1	tablespoon New Mexican red chile powder
2	pounds of beef chuck tender, cut into ⅜-inch cubes		½	teaspoon salt
1	tablespoon dark red chili powder		2	serrano chiles
2	teaspoons garlic granules		1	tablespoon paprika
1	8-ounce can tomato sauce		1	package of Goya Sazon (available in Latin markets)
1	14½-ounce can beef broth		1	teaspoon MSG (optional)
1	teaspoon chicken bouillon granules		1	teaspoon onion powder
1	teaspoon jalapeño powder		½	teaspoon garlic powder
1	tablespoon onion powder		½	teaspoon white pepper
2	teaspoons garlic powder		5	tablespoons medium and dark chili powders
½	teaspoon cayenne		2	teaspoons cumin
1	teaspoon white pepper		⅛	teaspoon salt
2	cups spring water			

Coat a 3-quart heavy saucepan with cooking oil, add the beef, the dark chili powder, and garlic, and brown the beef.

    In a separate container, combine the tomato sauce, beef broth, chicken bouillon granules, jalapeño powder, onion powder, garlic powder, cayenne, white pepper, spring water, red chile powder, salt, and whole serrano chiles. Add this mixture to the chili, bring to a boil, then reduce the heat and simmer for 1½ hours. Next, in a separate container combine the paprika, Goya Sazon, MSG (if desired), onion powder, garlic powder, white pepper, and chili powders. Add to the chili, bring to a boil, then reduce the heat and simmer for 20 minutes. Add small amounts of water if the chili is too thick. Remove the serranos when they become soft. Last, add the cumin and salt and simmer for another 10 minutes, then serve.

Serves: 6 to 8

Snake Rattle & Roll No-Beans Chili

Darrell Bahner of Sacramento, California, has been competing with the Snake Rattle & Roll Chili team for more than ten years. They have won many cookoffs, including the Northern California Regional and the High Sierra Regional. And Darrell and his gang always make sure there is lots of fun as well as cooking going on. "My brother Delbert, at one cookoff, was having a jolly good time when during the cooking he and his partner got a little happy from the aroma of their chili. They got so tangled up in their chili table that they pulled the whole damn thing onto the asphalt. Since then we call them the Asphalt Chili Company!"

2   tablespoons mild New Mexican red chile powder

1   tablespoon hot New Mexican red chile powder

2   tablespoons Gebhardt's Chili Powder

1   tablespoon chili powder (California Fancy preferred)

3   tablespoons cumin

1   tablespoon paprika

1   teaspoon black pepper

1   teaspoon MSG (optional)

1   14-ounce can chicken broth

1   14-ounce can beef broth

1   14-ounce can tomato sauce

1   7-ounce can whole mild green chiles, chopped

3   pounds tri-tip or London broil, cubed in ¼-inch pieces

1   pound snake meat, if available (rattlesnake preferred)

1   cup minced onion

7   cloves garlic, minced

Combine all the ingredients in a large chili pot except the beef, snake meat, onion, and garlic. Simmer the mixture for 1 hour.

During that hour, brown the beef, snake meat, onion, and garlic. After the cooking time is up, add the meat mixture to the chili pot. Simmer for 1 more hour and serve.

Serves: 8 to 10

Heavy Weight Chili

Carl Blattenberg of Sacramento, California, says the secret ingredient in his chili is sugar. The Heavy Weight team, which Carl says could have been contenders, is made up of a retired food inspector, a mechanic, and an electrician. Their chili is great, *and* they know what to do if the stove goes out—who could ask for more?

3	pounds beef chuck, cubed in ½-inch pieces	1	6-ounce can tomato paste
Vegetable oil		½	teaspoon cayenne
4	cups water	2	tablespoons cumin
2	tablespoons vegetable oil	2	teaspoons salt
1	large onion, diced	3	teaspoons oregano
5	cloves garlic, minced	2	tablespoons paprika
		¼	teaspoon sugar

In a large pot, brown the meat in the oil. When the beef is cooked, add the water and simmer for 30 minutes.

Add the remaining ingredients and simmer for 2 hours. Serve and enjoy!

Serves: 4 to 6

Cock-Eyed Black Bull Chili

Eddie La Cross and his team have been cooking and performing together for seven years. He says the funniest thing that ever happened at a cookoff was when he accidentally left half of his chili spices at home, and he *still* won the competition!

2½ cups beef broth

¼ cup tomato sauce

2 ounces canned jalapeños, pureed

2 medium onions, pureed

5 cloves garlic, pureed

7 tablespoons New Mexican mild red chile powder

2 tablespoons Californian mild chile powder

1 tablespoon New Mexican hot chile powder

3 tablespoons cumin

½ teaspoon oregano

1 teaspoon paprika

1 tablespoon brown sugar

1½ pounds London broil, cut into ½-inch cubes

1 pound beef chuck, cut into ½-inch cubes

½ pound lean pork, cut into ½-inch cubes

2 teaspoons salt

In a large stockpot, combine the beef broth, tomato sauce, jalapeños, onion, garlic, chile powders, cumin, oregano, paprika, and brown sugar. Stir well and heat to almost boiling.

Brown the meats in a large skillet. Drain the meat through a colander, and add it to the stock pot. Cook the chili for 1 hour, then add the salt. Stir well and then cook for 1 more hour or until the meat is tender.

Serves: 8 to 10

Doggone Good Chili

This recipe was contributed by Terlingua resident A. Vann York. A prerequisite to living in that Texas town is probably a recipe for lip-slurping chili. Here's a great one!

2½ pounds beef, cubed in ½-inch pieces
2 tablespoons Crisco
1 8-ounce can beef broth
1 8-ounce can tomato sauce
Water
2 teaspoons paprika
2 teaspoons onion powder
1 teaspoon cayenne
2 teaspoons beef bouillon granules
1 teaspoon chicken bouillon granules
1 teaspoon salt
1 tablespoon mild New Mexican chile powder
1 tablespoon hot New Mexican chile powder

1 tablespoon cumin
1½ teaspoons garlic powder
½ teaspoon very fine black pepper
1 package Goya Sazon (available in Latin markets)
3 tablespoons New Mexican Light Chili Powder mix
1 tablespoon Gebhardt's Chili Powder mix
¼ teaspoon salt
½ teaspoon cayenne
1 tablespoon Gebhardt's Chili Powder mix
1 teaspoon cumin
¼ teaspoon onion powder
¼ teaspoon garlic powder
¼ teaspoon salt

In a large stockpot cook the cubed meat in the Crisco until gray. Add the beef broth, tomato sauce, and enough water to cover the meat by at least 1 inch. Slowly boil the mixture for 30 minutes.

Add the paprika, onion powder, cayenne, beef bouillon granules, chicken bouillon granules, salt, and chile powders. Slow boil the chili for another hour and then add the cumin, garlic powder, black pepper, Goya Sazon, chili powders, and salt. Add more water if needed, and slow boil for an additional 30 minutes.

Finally, add the cayenne, chili powder mix, cumin, onion powder, garlic powder, and salt. Add additional Gebhardt's and salt if necessary. Mix well and serve.

Serves: 8 to 10

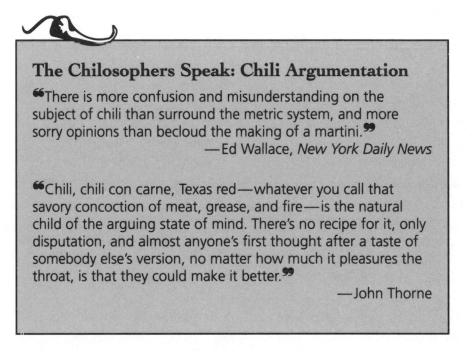

The Chilosophers Speak: Chili Argumentation

"There is more confusion and misunderstanding on the subject of chili than surround the metric system, and more sorry opinions than becloud the making of a martini."
—Ed Wallace, *New York Daily News*

"Chili, chili con carne, Texas red—whatever you call that savory concoction of meat, grease, and fire—is the natural child of the arguing state of mind. There's no recipe for it, only disputation, and almost anyone's first thought after a taste of somebody else's version, no matter how much it pleasures the throat, is that they could make it better."
—John Thorne

4

Southwestern Chilis

Texans may rightfully claim that chili originated in their state, but the fact remains that the folks in the rest of the Southwest have been cooking up similar stews for centuries. "The extravagant use of red pepper among the [New] Mexicans has become truly proverbial," wrote Josiah Gregg in 1844 in *The Commerce of the Prairies*. "It enters into nearly every dish at every meal, and often so predominates as entirely to conceal the character of the viands."

As is so often true in chili lore, the rivalries among the states involve nomenclature as well as recipes. As we discovered in Chapter 1, New Mexicans and others in the Southwest use the word *chile* to describe the plant, the pod, and various dishes made with chile peppers, whereas to Texans, "chili" is a very specific dish. In New Mexico, to further complicate matters, chile cookoffs usually have three distinct categories: Red, Green, and Texas-Style.

But even such generosity has not prevented a series of chili—and chile —wars.

The Congressional Controversy

According to chili legend, in 1974 Senator Barry Goldwater of Arizona noticed that the National Press Club Restaurant in Washington, D.C., served a Texas-style chili. It is reported that the senator exclaimed, "Texans don't know chili from shit."

Senator John Tower replied on the Senate floor that comparing Texas chili to Arizona chili was like comparing Sophia Loren to Phyllis Diller and

---

An udderly ridiculous team at Flatonia, Texas.

Jo Ann Horton

challenged Goldwater to a cookoff. Senator Henry Bellman of Oklahoma supported Goldwater regarding Texas chili, but indicated that to trade the "ketchup and sand" Arizona chili for the "crude-oil flavored" Texas chili would only aggravate the situation.

Senator Robert Taft of Ohio decided that the issue was important enough to take to the *Congressional Record*. Speaking of Tower and Goldwater, he stated, "Each likened the other chili to barnyard apples, and possibly each spoke truly." Taft went on to lambast the origin of Texas chili as "Texans mowing down helpless Mexicans and then ransacking their mess kits." He was, of course, touting Cincinnati chili, which he said "draws on the subtleties of the Balkans for its spicing."

Senator Joseph Montoya of New Mexico added fuel to the fire by stating that anyone born north of the border could not know anything at all about chili, so he entered his wife's Mexican chili! The cookoff was judged to be a tie between Goldwater and Tower, but a subsequent cookoff sponsored by *McCall's* magazine was won by Tower.

The congressional controversy continued in 1983 when Senator Pete Domenici of New Mexico stated in the *Congressional Record* that despite the fact that the dictionary preferred the spelling *chili*, the correct spelling was *chile* for the dish of meat and chile pods. "Knowing that criticizing the dictionary is akin to criticizing the Bible, I nevertheless stand here before the full Senate and with the backing of my New Mexican constituents state unequivocally, that the dictionary is wrong."

Domenici went on to ask, "Would Florida be any less offended if oranges were suddenly spelled *orangis*? Would there be no outcry from the state of Washington if their apples were suddenly spelled *applis*?" As a result of Domenici's impassioned plea, on November 14, 1983, the *Albuquerque Journal* caved in and announced, "The I's of Texas are no longer upon us. 'Chili' is dead. The only time we will use 'i' will be when we quote the written word of some Texan."

Interestingly enough, it was Congressman Manuel Lujan of New Mexico who sponsored the Chili Bill in 1984, which called for making chili the official national food. House Joint Resolution 465 (some sources say 255 and some say 337!) of February 2 spelled the dish *chili*, which touched off even more controversy. "Where I come from, we spell it 'c-h-i-l-e,'" Lujan said.

The Chile Challenge

Regional politics continued to provoke frequent debates and contests. An offshoot of the chile-chili wars was sparked by a "Mexican" terminology. One might think that Mexico City, or perhaps Puebla, Oaxaca, or Cuernavaca, would be the culinary capital of that diverse cuisine called "Mexican." Think again, because in 1987, Tucson Mayor Lew Murphy proclaimed his city "The Mexican Food Capital of the World and Elsewhere." In a blistering letter to the mayors of San Antonio, El Paso, Los Angeles, San Diego, Santa Fe, and Albuquerque, Murphy challenged the cities to a chile cooking contest in Tucson. "It's time to put your Mexican menu where your mouth is," Murphy wrote.

Such a cavalier attitude produced fumes from Santa Fe Mayor Sam Pick, who retorted: "We've been eating chile here in Santa Fe before Tucson was even thought of." Pick was alluding to the fact that Santa Fe was founded 165 years before Tucson, and he called for a citywide contest to pick a chile cook to represent the City Different at the Tucson chile challenge.

Murphy's proclamation of Tucson as the Mexican food capital included a statement which seems to indicate that he was suffering from irreversible chile addiction: "Tucson's growth has been due not as much to climate as chimichangas, not as much to colossal scenery as carne seca, not as much to great contemplation as to green corn tamales."

Eventually, the cities of Phoenix, El Paso, Albuquerque, and Santa Fe collided with Tucson in early December 1987 to give a heated response to the chile challenge. The event was called, incredibly, "The Great American Mexican Food Cook-Off." The judges of the contest were all Mexicans—not Hispanics, mind you, but real Mexican chile aficionados imported from Tijuana. One of them was president of the Tijuana Restaurant Owners' Association.

The results of the contest proved that Tucson's claim to be the capital of Mexican food was invalid. Overall winners were, in order: Santa Fe, Phoenix, and Albuquerque. Santa Fe councilman John Egan announced tersely, in a good imitation of a heavyweight boxer's manager: "As far as we're concerned, the trophy lives in Santa Fe. You want it, you come and get it."

The stunning Santa Fe victory led to a number of developments. In January 1988 a bill was introduced in the New Mexico State Legislature calling for the memorialization of Santa Fe's culinary reputation. Representatives Max Coll (D–Santa Fe) and Gary Robbins (R–Roosevelt-Curry) praised the Santa Fe chefs in their memorial, which threatens that any New Mexican who misspells *chile* as *chili* will "automatically be deported to Texas." The memorial concluded by acclaiming Santa Fe as "The Mexican Food Capital of the Universe."

Such political attention resulted in Mayor Sam Pick's announcement of his city's defense of the chile crown. On November 18 and 19, 1988, Santa Fe chefs successfully defended their city's modified title of "Mexican Food Capital of the World and Elsewhere" at the Mayor's Chile Challenge held at Sweeney Center.

The winning Santa Fe cooking team consisted of chefs Bill Weiland, Alex Valdivia, Todd Sanson, and Robert Valencia, plus two nonprofessional cooks, Betsy Honce and Barbara Timber. The judging panel consisted of one representative from each city, and the official order of finish was Santa Fe, Española, and El Paso. Santa Fe Mayor Sam Pick announced that Santa Fe would again host the competition in 1989. But it was never held, and the competition faded away because of a failure of the political leadership.

The Chile-Chili War

The interstate conflict was revived again in 1992, when Texas declared war on New Mexico. The initial volley in the campaign was fired off by Hill Rylander of the Travis County Farmer's Market in Austin and Nacho Padilla of El Paso, who proclaimed Texas to be the "Chili Capital of the World." Rylander even went so far as to erect a beautiful engraved glass plaque at the Farmer's Market that announced the site to be the "Capsicum Capital of the World."

New Mexicans were furious and pointed out that not only did their state grow more jalapeños than Texas, the Lone Star State did not even keep records of their chile acreage! Ignoring such facts, Texas accelerated the attack with a proclamation from the El Paso County Commission, which stated on September 9, 1992: "Whereas, chili first made its way into El Paso County in 1598; and whereas New Mexico fraudulently claims that they are the chile capital of the Southwest; and whereas New Mexico has misrepresented and misspelled chili since the State of Texas gave them the first chili pepper seeds; now, therefore, be it resolved that El Paso County joins the State of Texas in declaring war on the State of New Mexico by sanctioning the First Annual Placita de Ysleta Texas/New Mexico Chili War Festival at the Placita de Ysleta in El Paso County on the Mission Trail on August 20–22, 1992."

The Texas governor, Ann Richards, kept up the pressure with her Official Memorandum of November 13—but she spelled the word both ways!

Chili bard Kent Findlay sings "If You Know Beans About Chili, You Know Chili Has No Beans," with plastic friend.

Jo Ann Horton

"Texas *is* the chili capital of the Southwest," she bragged. "The State of Texas grows more than 100 varieties of chiles in its various climates and soil conditions throughout the entire year." She then stated, "The duty now falls on Texas chili chefs to uphold our state's reputation as Chili Capital of the Southwest. The only thing that stands between us and our rightful title is the willingness of New Mexico chili chefs to actually show up and fight." In light of what transpired, that comment would undoubtedly come back to haunt her.

New Mexico fought back. Governor Bruce King's spokesman, John McKean, went on the record: "Even some Texas canneries that produce that awful brown stuff they call chili say they get their chiles from New Mexico, although I don't know if that's the best use for our product."

The New Mexico State Legislature and Governor King quickly passed Senate Joint Memorial 5, which stated, in part and with considerable exaggeration: "Whereas, despite New Mexico's long and rich chile history and prehistory, with solid archaeological evidence indicating the continuous use of both red and green chile since the time of Folsom Man some twelve thousand years ago [this is not true], we now find 'Texas Man' claiming the noble chile as his; and whereas despite the facts, we hear boasting from east of the Pecos that 'The Lone Star State' is the chili capital of the Southwest . . . and Texas chefs malign the noble 'red and green' by blending it into a slurry of kidney beans and onions called chili; now, therefore, be it resolved by the Legislature of the State of New Mexico that the Land of Enchantment bets the 'whole enchilada' and its reputation as the Chile Capital of the World against the Lone Star State in the Mother of All Chile Wars Festival to be held May 29–31, 1993, at the Doña Ana County Fairgrounds."

New Mexico's ploy was clever. By holding the Chile War Festival prior to the contest in El Paso in August, the New Mexicans hoped to deflate the Texans' claims. Led by expert festival organizer Bill Gomez, the Chile War Festival was an enormous success, with more than fifteen thousand people attending. About a hundred chile cooks showed up, with the Texans outnumbered four to one. There were five different categories for the competition: Red Chile, Green Chile, Salsa, Unique, and Texas-Style. There was even a sanctioned CASI cookoff.

The New Mexicans won the Chile War Festival. As the *Las Cruces Sun News* reported, "Temperatures flared, the food was hot, and New Mexico prevailed over Texas." In the professional chefs' portion of the competition,

Jo Ann Horton

Frank Fox and Duke Walton in their "four-fours" (too large for tutus) at the Mexican International Cookoff in Nuevo Laredo.

chef Bill Keller of Albuquerque won both the Green Chile and the Texas-Style divisions! Later, Nacho Padilla of El Paso presented the Chile War bronze chile statue to Governor Bruce King, and admitted the Texas defeat.

But did the Texans have their revenge in August? No. Dispirited and disillusioned, the Texans failed to hold their contest and, as Bill Gomez noted, "They declared war but never followed through." Their failure proved what the New Mexico Legislature had claimed in its memorial: "It's painfully clear that the noises from Austin and El Paso are nothing more than Texas-style boasting."

Given the history of such interstate rivalry, there is no doubt that the chile-chili wars will continue. Meanwhile, readers can decide for themselves about the quality of Southwestern chile-chili dishes with the recipes that follow.

Pueblo Red Chile

Here is a very ancient recipe from New Mexico's Pueblo Indians, although it's not nearly twelve thousand years old.

5 dried red New Mexican chiles, seeds and stems removed	1 teaspoon pork fat
1 cup water	½ teaspoon oregano
2 pounds pork, cut into ¼-inch dice	1 clove garlic, minced
	Cornstarch to thicken, if necessary

Combine the chiles and water in a blender and puree into a paste.

Fry the pork in a skillet with the fat until browned. Drain off the fat. Add the pureed chiles and the remaining ingredients and cook, covered, for about 1 hour or until the pork is tender. Add water if the chile is too thick, and cornstarch if it is too thin.

Serves: 4 to 6

By the Great God Chiligula

The Houston Pod of CASI swears an oath by Chiligula, the God of Chili, as follows: "I pledge allegiance to the Houston Pod of the Chili Appreciation Society—International, camaraderie for which it stands; one comestible indigestible, with heartburn and gas pains for all; so help me Chiligula."

Mission Chili

This slightly modified recipe, originally published in the *Mission Cookbook* of the St. Ann's Society of Tucson in 1909, was a chili con carne that was also called *picadillo*. It is a rather primitive chili recipe that sometimes was "fancied up" with raisins, wine, and olives.

1 pound beefsteak, coarsely ground	Salt and pepper to taste
1 onion, diced	1 to 2 tablespoons chili powder
2 tablespoons lard or shortening	2 cups boiling water
1 tablespoon flour	1 tomato, diced

Combine the beefsteak and onion and mix well. Heat the lard in a pan and add the beefsteak-and-onion mix. While it browns, sprinkle it with the flour, and salt and pepper to taste.

Add the chili powder to the boiling water and boil for 5 minutes. Add the chili water to the browned meat, reduce heat, and simmer for 30 minutes. Add the tomato and simmer for 20 minutes or until thickened to desired consistency.

Serves: 4

Alice Stevens Tipton's Chile con Carne

According to Alice, writing in *The Original New Mexico Cookery* in 1916, "So many spurious receipts for this delicious dish of New Mexico have been given publicity, that it is appalling to even contemplate the disastrous results of preparing a dish according to some of the rules laid down by those utterly ignorant of the first principles to be followed in making chile con carne. The average American cook seems to think that if the food is hot with any kind of pepper, it is all that is necessary . . . the result is a sloppy concoction unfit for the human stomach. . . ." So Alice, let's have a bottle of home-brew while we have a little talk on what's happened since 1916. But, let's start with the black olives. Alice, these come from California! So, admit it, Alice, you have been influenced. Even back in 1916, California did have some products used in New Mexican cuisine.

2 tablespoons lard or drippings

3 onions, chopped

4 cloves garlic, chopped

2 pounds New Mexico boiling mutton, cut into 1-inch cubes

1 pound New Mexico pork, cut into 1-inch cubes (or substitute 2 pounds New Mexico round steak)

1 quart can tomatoes, put through a coarse colander or use an equal amount of fresh tomatoes, put through a coarse colander

1 quart chile pulp (see method, page 37)

Salt to taste

2 tablespoons dried oregano

3 bay leaves

1 pint of black olives

Heat the lard or drippings in a large kettle. Add the onions and garlic and brown. Then add the cubed meat, stirring to mix. Turn down the heat to a simmer, cover, and let the meat steam for 2 to 3 minutes.

Add the tomatoes and stir them in; cover and let the mixture simmer for 30 minutes.

Add the chile pulp and simmer 15 to 20 minutes, covered. Add salt to taste.

Add the oregano and the bay leaves. Cover and cook slowly for 3 hours.

Add the olives and cook at least 1 hour, covered.

Serves: 6

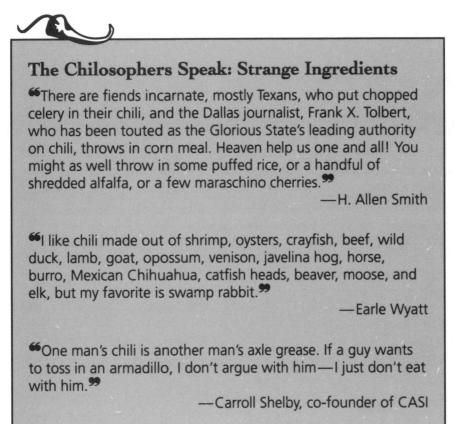

The Chilosophers Speak: Strange Ingredients

"There are fiends incarnate, mostly Texans, who put chopped celery in their chili, and the Dallas journalist, Frank X. Tolbert, who has been touted as the Glorious State's leading authority on chili, throws in corn meal. Heaven help us one and all! You might as well throw in some puffed rice, or a handful of shredded alfalfa, or a few maraschino cherries."

—H. Allen Smith

"I like chili made out of shrimp, oysters, crayfish, beef, wild duck, lamb, goat, opossum, venison, javelina hog, horse, burro, Mexican Chihuahua, catfish heads, beaver, moose, and elk, but my favorite is swamp rabbit."

—Earle Wyatt

"One man's chili is another man's axle grease. If a guy wants to toss in an armadillo, I don't argue with him—I just don't eat with him."

—Carroll Shelby, co-founder of CASI

Pete's Red Chile

Pete Benavidez was the owner of the long-gone Videz Café in Albuquerque. This recipe is for his classic red chile, as collected by Dick Beeson in *Chile Pepper* magazine.

6 dried New Mexican red chiles, seeds and stems removed

1 clove garlic

1 teaspoon ground Mexican oregano

Salt to taste

½ pound pork, either cubed from a roast, or chops, or even bones with meat

1 to 1½ pounds very lean ground beef

Cover the chiles with very hot water and soak for 20 to 30 minutes or until limp and partially rehydrated. Place the chiles in a blender (they should loosely fill three-quarters of the container; if more, make two small batches). Fill the container near the top with water. Drop in the clove of garlic and sprinkle the top with the oregano. Add a little salt at this stage if you wish. Blend for 2 to 3 minutes on high or until a homogeneous or orangish-red mixture is obtained.

Pour the mixture into a saucepan and add the pork. Cook, covered over very low heat or uncovered at a slight bubble, for 2 to 3 hours. If cooked uncovered, periodically add water back to original level to maintain proper consistency—medium soupy.

Remove the pork pieces and save for another meal such as carne adovada. Place the chile sauce in the refrigerator and cool. Remove any fat that congeals on the top.

Season the beef with a little salt and pepper and sauté until the meat is no longer pink.

Combine the reserved sauce and beef and simmer, covered, for an additional 30 to 45 minutes.

It is better if the sauce is on the thin side; it can always be thickened with a flour-and-water paste and cooked for an additional 10 minutes.

Serves: 4 to 6

New Mexican Red Chile

Here is a classic recipe from Nancy Gerlach, food editor of *Chile Pepper* magazine. She wrote: "When you order 'chili' in New Mexico, this is what you will be served. It is a basic recipe that has its roots in very old Pueblo Indian cooking. Beef can also be substituted in this recipe."

6 to 8 dried red chiles, stems removed

2 pounds pork, cut into 1½-inch cubes

2 tablespoons vegetable oil

3 cloves garlic, minced

3 cups water or beef broth

Salt to taste

Place the chiles on a sheet pan in a 250°F oven and toast for 15 minutes, being careful not to let them burn. Place the chiles in a saucepan, cover with water, and simmer for 15 minutes until soft. Place them in a blender, with the water, and puree until smooth.

Brown the pork in the oil. Add the garlic and sauté. Pour off any excess fat.

Combine the chile mixture, pork, and remaining water, bring to a boil, then reduce the heat and simmer until the pork is very tender and starts to fall apart—at least 2 hours.

Serves: 6

Doña Josefita's Ranch-Style Green Chile

This recipe is a classic version of New Mexican green chile. It first appeared in *New Mexico Magazine* in 1947 and was later reprinted in *Chile Pepper* magazine.

12 large green New Mexican chiles, roasted and peeled, seeds and stems removed

1 clove garlic, minced

1 large tomato, sliced

Salt and pepper to taste

¾ pound round steak, chopped into ¼-inch cubes

2½ cups water

Chop the chiles into small pieces, the smaller the better. Place the chiles and garlic in a skillet. Add the tomato; season with salt and pepper. Add chopped round and fry.

Add 2½ cups of water to the fried meat. Boil for 10 minutes.

Serves: 4

New Mexican Green Chile Stew

This is a staple dish with as many variations as there are cooks. It is a basic in New Mexican cookery and is often cooked in its own category in Southwestern chili cookoffs.

2 pounds lean pork, cubed
2 tablespoons vegetable oil
1 large onion, chopped
2 cloves garlic, minced
6 to 8 New Mexican green chiles, roasted and peeled, seeds and stems removed, chopped

1 large potato, peeled and diced (optional)
2 tomatoes, peeled and chopped
3 cups water

Brown the pork in the oil. Add the onion and garlic, and sauté for a couple of minutes.

Put the pork, onion, garlic, and the remaining ingredients in a kettle or crockpot and simmer for 1½ to 2 hours or until the meat is very tender.

Serves: 6

Keller Green Chile Stew

Albuquerque chef and caterer Bill Keller won second place at Tucson's Great American Mexican Food Cook-Off in 1987 with this simple but delicious green chile.

2 tablespoons lard

1½ pounds pork butt, diced

2 tablespoons white pepper

2 tablespoons granulated garlic

4 tablespoons cumin

½ onion, diced

2 tablespoons chicken bouillon granules

8 ounces chopped hot New Mexican green chiles

2 cups hot water

1 large potato, peeled and diced

Heat the lard in a skillet and add the pork. Cook but don't brown the pork. Add the remaining ingredients except the potato and cook for 30 minutes. Add the potato and cook until the potato is done, about 20 minutes.

Serves: 4 to 6

Chavez Green Chile Stew

Ben Chavez, former chef at the Hilton de Santa Fe, used this innovative recipe to win first place in the "Use of Green Chile" category at the Tucson Great American Mexican Food Cook-Off in 1987.

Step 1

7 or 8 New Mexican green chiles, roasted and peeled, seeds and stems removed

5 dried green chiles (*chile pasado*)

1½ pounds pork bones, lightly browned in the oven

1 quart double-strength homemade chicken stock

¼ white onion, chopped fine

Combine all ingredients and braise in a 350°F oven for 2 hours.

Step 2

¼ pound pork loin, cut into julienne strips

¼ pound beef sirloin, finely julienned

1 tablespoon vegetable oil

2 fresh New Mexican green chiles, roasted and peeled, seeds and stems removed, chopped fine

¼ tablespoon cayenne

¼ medium white onion, chopped fine

½ medium tomato, chopped fine

½ garlic clove, minced

½ tablespoon minced fresh cilantro

2 cups chicken stock

Sauté the pork and beef in the oil until browned. Add the rest of the ingredients in step 2 and cook over medium heat for 10 minutes. Add all of the ingredients in step 1 except the pork bones and cook 15 minutes.

Serves: 8 to 10

Santa Fe Trail Chile

Scott Almy of Santa Fe placed third in Tucson's Great American Mexican Food Cook-Off in 1987 with this amalgam of Texas and Southwestern styles.

omit

¼ cup vegetable oil

omit 1 pound pork butt, cut into ¼-inch dice

1 pound beef chuck, cut into ¼-inch dice

1 pound ground pork

1 pound premium ground beef

red

1 ~~2~~ ~~green~~ bell peppers, seeds and stems removed, diced

2 stalks celery, diced

1 ~~2~~ medium yellow onions, chopped

½ pound frozen or canned chopped Hatch New Mexican green chiles

~~1 beer (12 ounces)~~

Water as needed

1 can 2 cups cooked pinto beans

1 can 2 cups cooked kidney beans, including the liquid

~~1 cup diced canned tomatoes~~

1 cup tomato sauce

2 tablespoons oregano

1 tablespoon cumin

3 tablespoons minced fresh garlic

¼ to 1 cup Chimayo red chile powder (cook's choice)

SALT & PEPPER TO TASTE.

Heat the oil over medium heat, add the cubed pork and beef, and sear until a rich, dark color develops. Add the ground pork and beef and cook until browned. Drain off all fat.

Add the bell peppers, celery, onion, and green chiles. Pour in the beer. Simmer, covered, for 20 minutes over very low heat.

Add the remaining ingredients and simmer 1 hour, adding water if necessary. Cool and refrigerate overnight, and reheat and serve the next day.

Serves: 12

1993 New Mexico Chili Champ Chili

Sue Seehusen won the New Mexico championship title in Alamogordo, New Mexico. The cookoff was held to raise money for the community's zoo. This makes sense as chili cookoffs are pretty wild! This is a CASI-style chili, which proves that even in the Southwest, it's possible to cook like they do in Texas!

3   pounds beef rump roast, diced into ¼-inch cubes
1   teaspoon Crisco
1   can beef broth
1   8-ounce can tomato sauce
1½ cups water
1   tablespoon New Mexico mild red chile powder
2   tablespoons New Mexico hot red chile powder
1   tablespoon onion powder
1½ teaspoons cayenne
2   teaspoons beef bouillon granules
1   teaspoon chicken bouillon granules
½   teaspoon salt

1   tablespoon ground cumin
2   teaspoons garlic powder
2   tablespoons Texas-style chili powder
½   tablespoon New Mexican hot red chile powder
½   tablespoon New Mexican mild red chile powder
¼   teaspoon ground black pepper
1   tablespoon brown sugar
½   teaspoon seasoning salt
2   tablespoons Gebhardt's Chili Powder
1   teaspoon onion powder
1   teaspoon cumin
Jalapeño powder to taste

In a large pot, brown the beef in the Crisco. Add the beef broth, tomato sauce, and water. Simmer the mixture for 15 minutes, then bring to a boil and add the mild red chile powder, hot red chile powder, onion powder, cayenne pepper, beef and chicken bouillon granules, and salt. Cover the pot, reduce the heat, and simmer for 1 hour.

When the hour is up, let the chili set for 15 minutes without any heat. Bring the chili back to a boil and add the ground cumin, garlic powder, Texas-style chili powder, mild red chile powder, hot red chile powder, black pepper, and brown sugar. Continue to cook until the meat is tender.

Finally, 15 minutes before you are ready to serve, add the seasoning salt, Gebhardt's Chili Powder, cumin, and onion powder. Add the jalapeño powder to taste.

Serves: 4 to 6

Chili Dogs

From chili cook John "Professor Fosdick" Foster comes this true story: "From the start we have had a tradition of making up humorous labels for our team and putting them on soup cans for display purposes, or selling them for $1 each to raise money for the charity at hand. We would always tell the people that it was only soup that was in the can itself. We found that on more than one occasion, people would steal our cans, probably assuming our chili was inside. So, we started putting our labels on cans of dog food. Hopefully, those that tried to circumvent the charity donation got an unpleasant surprise."

Short Rib Chili

This chili recipe, one of Mary Jane's favorites, is easy to make, cooks in 2½ hours, and combines the best of both red and green chiles. Serve it with fresh bread or cornbread and a big green salad. It is a nutritious meal in a bowl.

4   pounds beef short ribs
2   tablespoons corn oil
1   onion, chopped
1   green bell pepper, chopped
2   cloves garlic, chopped
1   beef bouillon cube
2   cups water, or substitute 2 cups of beef stock and omit the bouillon cube

2   tablespoons New Mexican red chile powder
1   can stewed tomatoes, crushed
1   cup New Mexican green chiles, chopped
2   cans kidney beans, pinto beans, or black beans, drained
1   can whole kernel corn or 2 cups fresh corn off the cob

Trim the excess fat from the short ribs. Heat the oil in a large Dutch oven and brown the ribs. Add the onion, bell pepper, and garlic and sauté for 1 minute.

Dissolve the bouillon cube in the water and add to the sautéed mixture (or add the 2 cups of beef stock).

Add the remaining ingredients—except the beans and corn—and bring to a boil. Reduce the heat to a simmer. Cover and cook for 2½ hours, stirring occasionally.

Just before serving, add the drained corn and the drained beans and heat through. For convenience, you may want to cut the meat off the bones while it is in the pot.

Serves: 8

Carne Adovada Black Bean Chili

Even though this recipe requires prior preparation, it is well worth the effort; you also get enough carne adovada left over for another meal!

2 tablespoons corn oil

1 onion, chopped

1 pound cooked carne adovada, slightly shredded (see recipe, page 139)

1 8-ounce can tomato sauce

¼ cup water

2 tablespoons chili powder (Chugwater preferred)

2 fresh tomatoes, coarsely chopped

½ teaspoon oregano

¼ teaspoon ground cumin

1½ cups cooked black beans

SALT & PEPPER TO TASTE

Garnishes: fresh chopped onion, sour cream, slices of avocado

In a large, heavy casserole, heat the oil and sauté the onion for a minute. Add the shredded carne adovada and stir until it is coated with the onion.

Add the remaining ingredients except the cooked beans and bring the mixture to a boil. Reduce the heat, cover, and simmer for 45 to 60 minutes or until the mixture is well blended and slightly thickened. If it isn't thick enough, continue cooking with the cover off, stirring occasionally. Add the beans and heat through.

Ladle into warm bowls and garnish.

Serves: 5 to 6

SUBSTITUTED SMOKED ELK FOR CARNE

SMOKED ELK

- SALT & PEPPER & WORCESTERSHIRE BOTH SIDES OF ELK STEAK
- SMOKE ON TRAEGER FOR 2 HRS (~180°F)
- INCREASE TEMP TO 325°F - 350°F COOK UNTIL MED TEMP, ~145°F

New Mexican Carne Adovada

This is a classic meat recipe that has some basic relation to chili con carne.

1½ cups crushed dried red New
    Mexican chiles, seeds included
4   cloves garlic, minced
3   teaspoons dried oregano

3   cups water
2   pounds pork, cut into 1-inch
    cubes

Combine the chiles, garlic, oregano, and water and mix well to make a caribe sauce.

Place the pork in a glass pan and cover with the chile caribe sauce. Marinate the pork overnight in the refrigerator.

Bake the mixture in a 300°F oven for 2 hours, or until the pork is very tender.

Serves: 4 to 6

Turkey Chili

This chili is a taste treat because of the combination of red chili powder and green chiles. It's a meal in a bowl when it is served with warm bread or cornbread and a tossed green salad.

1	tablespoon vegetable oil		1	tablespoon chili powder
1	pound ground turkey		½	teaspoon ground cumin
1	large onion, chopped		½	teaspoon dried oregano
2	cloves garlic, minced			Salt and pepper to taste
½	cup chopped bell pepper		1	bay leaf
1	16-ounce can tomatoes, drained and coarsely chopped		2 to 3	cups cooked and drained pinto beans or kidney beans
1	cup tomato sauce			
½	cup chopped New Mexican green chiles			

In a large, heavy casserole, heat the oil and brown the turkey. Add the onion, garlic, and bell pepper and sauté until the onion is translucent.

Add the remaining ingredients, except the beans, and stir to mix. Cover and cook over low heat for 1 hour, stirring occasionally and adding a little water or broth if the mixture gets too thick.

Add the drained beans and continue cooking until the beans are heated through.

Serves: 4 to 5

Hardfat Bentley's Lone Star Chile or Chili

Our friend Jon Bentley, who grew up in Texas but lives in New Mexico, has divided loyalties. This recipe was originally published in *Chile Pepper* magazine in 1989 and reveals influences from both states. He noted: "For the roadkill version, substitute armadillo, 'coon, 'possum, or other tooth-some, recently procurred meat. As with all game, double the amount of chile and beer. Oil guests appropriately with beers, tequila, or mezcal."

6	tablespoons sunflower oil	1 or 2	Lone Star longneck beers
1	teaspoon olive oil	10 to 15	New Mexican red chile pods, seeds and stems removed
1	teaspoon crushed New Mexican red chiles	8	cups water (or more if needed)
2	medium onions, chopped	1¼	cups tomato paste
5	cloves garlic, minced	2	dashes cumin
6	pounds coarsely ground chuck		Salt and pepper to taste
8	cups water		

Heat the two oils in a large pot and add the crushed red chile and stir well. Add the onion and garlic and cook until the onion is soft. Add the chuck, water, and beer and simmer until the meat turns gray, stirring often.

Meanwhile in a separate pot, combine the chile pods and water and boil rapidly for 10 minutes. Puree the mixture in a blender and add to the simmering meat.

Add the rest of the ingredients and simmer for 2 to 3 hours until the mixture has thickened. You may need to add more water if it is too thick.

Serve with Lone Star or Mexican beer and beans on the side, but don't put any beans in the damn chile!

Serves: 10 to 12

Beef and Black Bean Chili

The addition of corn gives this chili a little crunch, and the cilantro adds another dimension of flavor. Black beans are our favorite beans to use in chili.

1   pound lean ground beef
1   large onion, chopped
2   cloves garlic, minced
1   to 2 tablespoons chili powder
Salt and pepper to taste
1   teaspoon cumin
2   tablespoons chopped fresh cilantro

2   16-ounce cans stewed tomatoes, chopped and not drained
2   16-ounce cans black beans or 3 cups cooked black beans
1   cup corn, frozen, canned, or fresh off the cob

Garnishes: shredded Monterey Jack or Asiago cheese and chopped cilantro

Brown the beef and add the onion and garlic; sauté for a minute. Drain off any excess fat.

Stir in the chili powder, salt and pepper, cumin, cilantro, and tomatoes. Cover and simmer for 30 minutes, stirring once.

Add the beans and corn; cover and simmer for 20 minutes.

Serve in warm bowls and garnish with grated cheese and chopped cilantro.

Serves: 6

Garlic Festival Chili

Caryl Simpson and Tom Reed of Gilroy, California, wrote to *Chile Pepper* magazine: "Down there in chileland you think chiles make the world go 'round, but out here in the Garlic Capital of the World, we know better. After all, what would chili be without garlic? So, for all you chile wimps laboring under the delusion that the chiles make the chili, we've got one to share with you in honor of Garlic Festivals everywhere and people who think anything worth doing is worth doing to excess."

50 (yes, fifty) medium garlic cloves, peeled

4 to 5 pounds pork loin, 2 inches thick, trimmed of fat

2 tablespoons Garli Garni seasoning

3 onions, peeled and sliced 1 inch thick

⅓ cup vegetable oil

¼ cup flour

¼ cup paprika

3 tablespoons chili powder

1 jalapeño chile, seeds and stem removed, chopped

1½ tablespoons filé powder

5 cups chicken or pork stock

2 cups pureed fresh tomatoes

2 poblano chiles, seeds and stems removed, chopped

Blanch the garlic cloves in boiling water until tender, 7 to 10 minutes, then drain.

Prepare a bed of hot coals for grilling. Season the pork with the Garli Garni seasoning and brush the pork and onion slices with some of the vegetable oil. Grill the pork until it is brown on the outside and rare on the inside, and grill the onions until they are charred. Allow both to cool. Dice the pork and onions to ½-inch pieces and set aside.

Heat the remaining vegetable oil in a deep skillet over medium heat until very hot. Reduce the heat and whisk in the flour until the roux is deep brown. Allow to cool. Combine the paprika, chili powder, jalapeño, and filé powder in a bowl.

Bring the stock, tomatoes, and poblanos to a simmer in a saucepan. Over low heat, whisk the paprika mixture into the roux and cook 5 minutes, stirring constantly. Whisk in the hot stock, one cup at a time. Add the grilled onions and bring to a boil. Add 1 to 2 tablespoons of Garli Garni, reduce heat, and simmer for 1 hour, stirring occasionally.

Add the blanched garlic and simmer until thickened, about 30 to 40 minutes, stirring occasionally. Add the pork and simmer until cooked through, about 15 to 20 minutes. The chili tastes best when refrigerated overnight and served the next day. It goes great with garlic bread!

Serves: 4 to 6

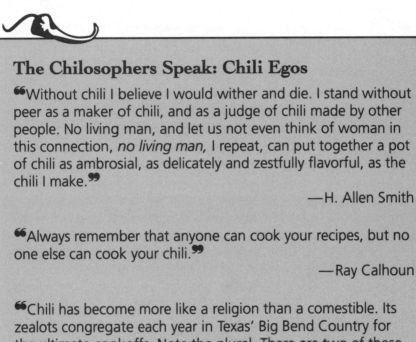

The Chilosophers Speak: Chili Egos

66Without chili I believe I would wither and die. I stand without peer as a maker of chili, and as a judge of chili made by other people. No living man, and let us not even think of woman in this connection, *no living man,* I repeat, can put together a pot of chili as ambrosial, as delicately and zestfully flavorful, as the chili I make.99

—H. Allen Smith

66Always remember that anyone can cook your recipes, but no one else can cook your chili.99

—Ray Calhoun

66Chili has become more like a religion than a comestible. Its zealots congregate each year in Texas' Big Bend Country for the ultimate cookoffs. Note the plural. There are two of these giant contests and they don't speak to each other. Chilidom split into two factions several years ago. Some compare chili to the Baptists because of that.99

—Thom Marshall, former *Houston Chronicle* columnist

La Fonda Frijoles

Here is a side dish for chili from the famed La Fonda Hotel in Santa Fe, which shows how beans are prepared in New Mexico. With the addition of the chile, it becomes almost a vegetarian chili! Pinto beans are an important crop in New Mexico.

2   cups dried pinto beans

4   slices raw bacon, diced

2   cloves garlic, minced

1   teaspoon onion, finely chopped

2   New Mexican green chiles, roasted and peeled, seeds and stems removed, finely chopped

1   teaspoon salt

Vegetable oil for frying

Freshly grated Parmesan cheese

Wash the beans and soak overnight in cold water to cover. Drain and add fresh water when you are ready to cook the beans. Add the bacon, cover, and bring to a boil. Add the garlic, onion, chile, and salt. Reduce heat and simmer for 4 hours or until the beans are done. Remove the bacon and drain and cool the beans.

At this point, the beans may be added to chili or refried as a side dish. To refry, mash the mixture slightly with a fork. Refry the beans in 1 to 2 tablespoons of vegetable oil, stirring well. Serve with grated Parmesan sprinkled over the top.

Serves: 6

5

Chilis of Celebrities, Chefs, and Friends

By far, the most unusual chili recipes we collected appear in this chapter. Freed from any necessity to be either authentic or sanctioned, a wide range of styles and ingredients are represented here. But before we get to them, let's hear from a very vocal minority about what's wrong with chili cookoffs.

The following diatribe is an excerpt of an article that originally appeared in *Chile Pepper* magazine. It is by Sam Pendergrast of Abilene, Texas, whom we introduced then as "inconoclasic, bombastic, and pyroclastic."

"Requiem for Texas Chili"

When a dozen chili nuts got together in 1967 at an abandoned opry house in the manforsaken desert at Terlingua to compare their chili and hooraw one another, and a few thousand all-purpose renegades heard about it and decided to kibbitz the authorities on chili while falling over the prickly pears and digging life on the frontier, it was all fun nonsense.

But the chili was real chili.

Within a surprisingly few years, the original thesis was gone, lost in the sweet yesteryears of memory with the charming and mostly tongue-in-cheek founders. Wick Fowler, Texas columnist and one of the first two contestants in a chili cookoff, was the first to go. Then, in 1976, the delicious Americonoclast H. Allen Smith, who had been the other contestant for the first chili bash in '67, passed away. When Frank X. Tolbert went to the great cookoff in the sky in '84, the Founding Stirrers of record were gone, and maybe that's what happened to Texas chili.

In the early days, the contestants were for the most part people who cooked chili and wanted to see how their recipe would stand up against those of other people who made chili. A couple of years later, the field of contestants broadened and the operational individual goal shifted to one of producing a winning recipe rather than evaluating existing recipes.

But probably it was something more functional and less portentous than the passing of the Chili Titans that tainted first the cookoffs and eventually the manna of middle Texas. Where there had been in the formative days one citadel of chili (at Terlingua) and one arbiter of excellence for the record (Tolbert), the proliferation of cookoffs soon required a vastly expanded clergy to administer to the far-flung kingdom. Anointments became, of practical necessity, casual, multifarious, and largely self-administered. Anybody who had ever heard of chili could start a cookoff, name himself administrator, and pursue whatever procedures he deemed appropriate.

And that, I'm sorry to say, is where we began to screw up contest chili— and, by slipshod supervision and casual expedience, eventually dealt a mortal

Jo Ann Horton

Cowchip Chili wins yet another showmanship trophy at Flatonia, Texas.

(if unintentional) blow to what had by then become the State Dish of Texas. Lesser cookoffs tended to attract fewer dispassionate judges, or judging administrators simply took the easy way out. They started using chili cooks to do at least the preliminary judging—and often the final judging as well. This procedure worked so well that now it is difficult to find a cookoff in which there are not members of cooking teams serving as judges at some level.

When I judged at Terlingua in 1984, there was mercifully no sign of a preponderance of cubed-steak chili, and the farther you get from Houston the less likely you are to be assaulted by it. So what's the problem if cookoff contestants want to make steak with brown gravy and call it chili, and contest administrators are dumb enough to let them do it?

Aside from compromising the integrity of the greatest grassroots culinary movement in modern times, the long-term effect will be to confuse people about what is *real* chili. In literally thousands of portions of chili I have tasted from Terlingua, I can't recall a single bowl of real old-time diner chili. You're more likely to find more or less traditional chili in the lower-level cookoffs and more probably on the preliminary tables rather than among the finalists.

At every high-powered cookoff that comes to mind, there is just a world of slop no more akin to real chili than was Michener's *Texas* to the real thing.

And how do we get back to the real chili if we want to?

The first step is to institute an absolute ban on allowing any member of any cooking team to have anything to do with judging. The VIP system, where the local sheriff, the school dietitian, or the campaigning politician do the judging, really works—so long as they have no connection with the cooks. Or just get a dozen people off the street to judge. Despite the mythology of the Big Chili Cadre that judging is some sort of God-given talent, the general public is still likely to be the best judge of basic chili. Also, cookoff administrators should not be allowed to tell judges what they think is good chili.

After Sam's article ran in *Chile Pepper,* he wrote to tell us that he had received three bomb threats on his life. "Not to worry," he advised, "they were all from close friends."

Bill Renfro's Triple

Just so people will not accuse us of being anti-cookoff, we present the story of a man who is the first person in the country to do an extraordinary thing: judge three world championship chili cookoffs in one year! During 1993 Bill Renfro

Two of the winningest chili cooks ever, Dorene Ritchey and Bob "Hizzoner" Moore, on stage at Terlingua.

Jo Ann Horton

was a judge at the ICS World's Championship Chili Cookoff in Reno, Nevada, the first week in October, as well as at both the CASI Terlingua International Chili Championship and the Behind the Store/Original Viva Terlingua International Frank X. Tolbert–Wick Fowler Memorial Championship Chili Cookoff on the first Saturday in November.

And why would any human being with a working stomach attempt such a feat? Renfro says it was a matter of doing something that had never been done before. "I just enjoy chili and chili people. I would do it again anytime!"

The chili at both of the Terlingua cookoffs was all Texas-style, whereas the ICS Reno competition, according to Renfro, had a bit more of a California flair. "The Terlingua chili had more meat and spices; the ICS chili used a bigger variety of chile peppers and even used some bell pepper." Renfro, who owns Renfro Foods of Forth Worth, Texas, admitted that he enjoyed the CASI Terlingua competition of 263 cooks the most, simply because he had a lot of friends there. Great friends and chili also helped him to forget the cold front that hit Terlingua that weekend.

As for judging tips, Renfro says he got to the point where he could tell exactly what the chili was going to taste like just by the way it looked and

Goat Gap Gazette editor Jo Ann Horton dressed as Luckenbach Mayor Hondo Crouch at the first Ladies' Only Chili Cookoff in Luckenbach, Texas.

Richard Horton

smelled. As for his favorite chili, Renfro says he's a medium-hot, beef, onion, and tomato man. Although he wouldn't tell us his secret chili recipe, he did say that he simply cooks what he likes, and nothing else.

Eclectic Chilis

Chili cooks, being independent and ornery, sometimes include such ingredients as shark meat or eggplant or a half cup of cumin in their creations. In the remainder of this chapter, we present a wide range of chilis from friends, chefs, and celebrities. In some of the other chili books, the celebrities represented include Dwight Eisenhower, Dr. Joyce Brothers, Richard Nixon, Perry Como, James Garner, and Betty Ford (Addictive Chili?). We have examined their recipes and have found them to be, well, average. So we have rounded up our own celebrities and have extracted recipes from them. They include Bill Mauldin, Ian Tyson, Lady Bird Johnson, and an infamous resident of Texas named Bubba.

We have also collected recipes from our friends across the country who make their living cooking for others. One would imagine that if anyone knows how to make a great chili, it's a great chef. We'll see about that shortly.

By the way, we should warn chili purists that all bets are off concerning the ingredients used in this chapter, and that our strictures put forth in Chapter 2 are hereby suspended for the duration of this chapter.

Sam Pendergrast's Original Zen Chili

Here is Sam's recipe for good ol' cafe chili. Note the extreme amount of cumin. Interestingly enough, in the version of this recipe that appeared in *Texas Home Cooking,* the amount of cumin was mysteriously *doubled.* Could Sam be addicted to cumin? Sam is also the author of *Avenida Juarez,* a novel that has to be read to be believed.

1 pound fatty bacon	Water
2 pounds coarse beef, extra-large grind	1 teaspoon cayenne
½ cup whole *cominos* (cumin seed —yes, one-half cup!)	Salt, pepper, and garlic powder to taste
½ cup pure ground New Mexican red chiles	

Render grease from the bacon; eat a bacon sandwich while the chili cooks. (Good chili takes time.)

Sauté the ground beef in bacon grease over medium heat. Add the *cominos* and then begin adding the red chile until what you are cooking smells like chili. (This is the critical point; if you add all the spices at once, there is no leeway for personal tastes.) Let the mixture cook a bit between additions, and don't feel compelled to use all of the red chile.

Add water in small batches to avoid sticking, and more later for a soupier chili. Slowly add the cayenne until smoke curls your eyelashes. Palefaces may find that the red chile alone has enough heat.

Simmer the mixture until the cook can't resist ladling a bowlful for sampling. Skim the excess fat for dietetic chili, or mix the grease with a small amount of cornmeal for a thicker chili.

Finish with salt, pepper, and garlic powder to individual taste, paprika to darken. Continue simmering until served; continue reheating until gone. (As with wine, time enobles good chili and exposes bad.)

The result should be something like old-time Texas cafe chili: a rich, red, heavily cominesque concoction with enough liquid to welcome crackers, some chewy chunks of meat thoroughly permeated by the distinctive spices, and an aroma calculated to lure strangers to the kitchen door.

Serves: 4

Variation: For cookoff contest chili, drink bad tequila two days before starting the chili; burn mixture frequently; sprinkle occasionally with sand and blood; serve cold to a dozen other drunks and call them "judges"; and keep telling yourself you're having a great time.

Mauldin Chili

"My wife's a great chili maker," brags Bill Mauldin, the famous political cartoonist. "Of course, she makes enough for a battalion in the infantry." His soldiering background and pride in his mate's culinary skills combine as Mauldin reviews the family's favorite recipe.

2 to 3 pounds ground beef
1   tablespoon New Mexican red chile powder
2   tablespoons olive oil
2   large onions, chopped
4   cloves garlic, minced
3   bell peppers, coarsely chopped (preferably 1 red, 1 green, and 1 yellow)
2   8-ounce cans whole tomatoes, chopped
1   8-ounce can tomato paste

4   cups water
1   cup black coffee
1   tablespoon sugar
2   tablespoons vinegar
1   teaspoon oregano
1   teaspoon cumin
2   tablespoons salsa
2   tablespoons chile powder (1 tablespoon each of cook's choice)
2   8-ounce cans kidney beans

Brown the beef, sprinkling in the red chile powder while it cooks. Drain the fat off the browned beef and set aside. In a large soup pot, add the olive oil and sauté the onions, garlic, and bell peppers until they are soft.

Add the chopped tomatoes and tomato paste to the sautéed vegetables along with the 4 cups of water. Stir in the coffee, sugar, vinegar, oregano, cumin, salsa, chile powder, and browned-beef mixture. Bring the chili to a boil, reduce the heat, and simmer for 1 hour. Add the beans and cook for another 15 minutes.

Serves: 8 to 10

Lady Bird Johnson's Pedernales River Chili

This recipe originally contained beef suet, but that ingredient was omitted after LBJ's severe heart attack when he was Senate Majority Leader. Remember to skim the fat off the chili. Lady Bird wrote: "So many requests came in for the recipe that it was easier to give the recipe a name, have it printed on a card, and make it available. It has been almost as popular as the government pamphlet on the care and feeding of children."

4   pounds coarsely ground beef
1   large onion, chopped
2   cloves garlic, chopped
1   teaspoon oregano
1   teaspoon ground cumin

6   teaspoons New Mexican red chile powder (or more for heat)
2   16-ounce cans tomatoes
2   cups hot water
Salt to taste

Combine the beef, onion, and garlic in a skillet and sear until the meat is lightly browned.

Transfer this mixture to a large pot, add the remaining ingredients, and bring to a boil. Reduce the heat and simmer for 1 hour.

When done, transfer the chili to a bowl and place it in the refrigerator. When the fat has congealed on top, remove it with a spoon.

Reheat the chili and serve it as LBJ liked it—without beans and accompanied by a glass of milk and saltine crackers.

Serves: 12

Tyson Ranch Chili

Between albums, Canadian cowboy musician Ian Tyson always makes time to enjoy his wife's chili. Chock-full of venison, this chili is truly unique.

1   12-ounce can beef consommé
1½ cups red wine
4 to 6 ounces tomato sauce
2   bay leaves
4   cinnamon sticks
Pinch ground coriander
1   tablespoon dried oregano
2 to 3 tablespoons vegetable oil
4   cloves garlic, chopped
4 to 5 venison steaks cut into
    bite-sized cubes

1   large onion, chopped
1   green bell pepper, seeds and
    stem removed, chopped
1   red bell pepper, seeds and stem
    removed, chopped
1   4-ounce can New Mexican
    green chiles, chopped
2 to 3 jalapeños, seeds and stems
    removed, chopped
6 to 8 large dried apricots, chopped
Cooked fettucine noodles

Garnishes: feta cheese, sour cream, and hot sauce

Combine the consommé, wine, tomato sauce, bay leaves, cinnamon, coriander, and oregano in a large pot.

Heat the oil in a pan until hot. Add the garlic and meat and brown. Remove the garlic and meat and add to the cooking pot. Add the onion, green and red bell peppers, and New Mexican green chile to the oil and sauté for 1 to 2 minutes. Add to the pot. Add the jalapeños and apricots to the mixture and simmer for 2 hours. Turn off the heat and let stand for 1 hour. Reheat before serving.

Serve the chili on top of the fettucine noodles, topped with the feta cheese, sour cream, and hot sauce.

Serves: 6

Bubba's Chili

No book on chili con carne would be complete without a recipe from a person from Texas named Bubba. This wonderful recipe requires three hours cooking time and a bit of Texas magic!

2	pounds very lean, coarse chili-grind beef, or beef cubed in ½-inch pieces
1	8-ounce can beef broth
4	ounces tomato sauce
2	tablespoons hot chile powder (California Fancy preferred)
¼	teaspoon oregano
½	teaspoon cayenne
2	teaspoons onion powder
1	teaspoon white pepper
½	cup tomato sauce
1	tablespoon New Mexico Light chili powder
½	teaspoon MSG (optional)
1	teaspoon paprika
1	teaspoon garlic powder
2	teaspoons cumin
1	teaspoon onion powder
1	teaspoon beef bouillon granules
1	package Goya Sazon (available in Latin markets)
2	tablespoons commercial chili powder of your choice
½	teaspoon black pepper
1	teaspoon garlic powder
⅛	teaspoon jalapeño powder
1	teaspoon chicken bouillon granules
½	cup tomato sauce
1	teaspoon cumin
½	teaspoon garlic powder
1	tablespoon commercial chili powder of your choice
½	teaspoon onion powder
⅛	teaspoon cayenne

Salt and cayenne to taste

Brown the meat in a large pan on medium heat. Add the beef broth and tomato sauce, stir lightly, and cover. When the mixture has started to reach a light boil, add the California Fancy or other hot chile powder, oregano, cayenne, onion powder, white pepper, tomato sauce, New Mexico Light, MSG (if desired), paprika, and garlic powder and cook for 2 hours, or until the meat is tender. If the meat is tender before 2 hours, turn off the burner and let the pot rest.

One hour before serving time, reheat the chili on low heat, and add the cumin, onion powder, beef bouillon granules, Goya Sazon, chili powder of your choice, black pepper, garlic powder, jalapeño powder, chicken bouillon granules, and tomato sauce. Stir the chili well and add water if the mixture is too thick.

About 15 minutes before serving, add the cumin, garlic powder, chili powder of your choice, onion powder, and cayenne. Just before serving, add salt and cayenne to taste.

Serves: 4 to 6

Pecos River Red XX Chili

Jeff Johnson, manager of The Loon Café, says that because of the extremely cold winters in Minneapolis, chili and other hot and spicy foods have developed "quite a religious following." The restaurant has been open for more than ten years and specializes in five different kinds of chili, which year after year win readers' polls in various magazines and newspapers. The recipe for the number one–selling chili at The Loon is given below, in a quantity large enough to serve at a party. The cayenne makes this chili extremely hot, so watch out!

5	pounds trimmed beef (no fat), cut into small cubes
1	large onion, chopped fine
1	cup chopped New Mexican green chiles
⅓	cup cayenne
½	cup New Mexican red chile powder
1	cup paprika
2	tablespoons minced jalapeños
2	tablespoons crushed red chiles

2	tablespoons cumin
1	tablespoon oregano
2	quarts tomato sauce
2	cups water
1	dash Tabasco sauce
3	tablespoons chicken base (bouillon granules)
1	cup masa harina
2	cups water
Salt to taste	

Garnishes: Cheddar cheese, minced green onions, and sour cream

In a large pot, brown together the beef, onion, and green chile. Add the cayenne, chile powder, paprika, jalapeños, crushed red chile, cumin, and oregano. Simmer for 15 minutes.

Add the tomato sauce, water, Tabasco, chicken base, and simmer for 20 minutes.

Mix the masa harina with the water and make an extremely smooth paste. Add this to the chili, stirring constantly. Simmer for 15 minutes. Add salt to taste if necessary.

Serve the chili topped with shredded Cheddar cheese, minced green onions, and a dollop of sour cream.

Serves: 10 or more very hungry people

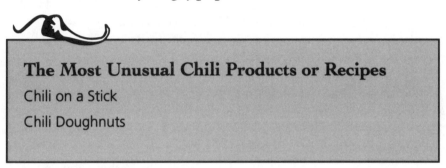

The Most Unusual Chili Products or Recipes

Chili on a Stick

Chili Doughnuts

Chili Darter's Chili

Jack Curry, along with his Chili Darter's team, has won or placed in thirty cookoffs during fifteen years of competition. He says they make a people-pleasing chili—one that is very well liked by the cookoff attendees. Jack and his wife Debi also own the Prince of Wales Pub in San Mateo, California. Every Thursday at lunch they feature their competition all meat chili. They also sponsor a chili party for the Stanford University baseball fans and umpires. They have competed in more than 135 cookoffs in California, Oregon, Arizona, Hawaii, Texas, and Nevada.

7 pounds tri-tip beef, cubed	5 tablespoons pasilla chile powder
2 tablespoons vegetable oil	2 tablespoons cumin seeds, toasted and ground
¼ teaspoon garlic salt	
½ cup Worcestershire sauce	1 tablespoon freshly ground oregano
2 cups medium green chile salsa (Ortega's preferred)	
	½ tablespoon cilantro
2 cups vegetable broth (Swanson's preferred)	1 tablespoon chipotle (smoke-dried jalapeño) chile powder
8 ounces diced New Mexican green chiles	1 tablespoon fresh garlic
	½ tablespoon cayenne
8 tablespoons New Mexican red chile powder	4 tablespoons Goya Sazon
	MSG to taste (optional)

Brown the beef in the oil and garlic salt in a large stockpot. Add the Worcestershire sauce, green salsa, and vegetable broth. Bring the mixture to a boil, then add the diced green chiles, and cook for 45 minutes on medium heat.

In a separate container, combine the New Mexican red chile powder, pasilla powder, cumin, oregano, and cilantro. Mix well, and add one-fourth of this spice mix to the chili. Stir the chili well and cook for 1¾ hours.

Add the chipotle powder and 2 tablespoons of the spice mix. Cook for 15 more minutes and add the rest of the spice mix, the garlic, cayenne, and the Goya Sazon. Stir well and add the MSG if you wish. Simmer 10 more minutes and serve.

Serves: 15 to 20

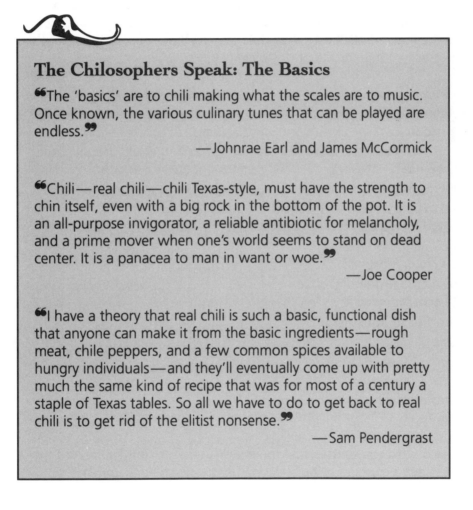

The Chilosophers Speak: The Basics

❝The 'basics' are to chili making what the scales are to music. Once known, the various culinary tunes that can be played are endless.❞

—Johnrae Earl and James McCormick

❝Chili—real chili—chili Texas-style, must have the strength to chin itself, even with a big rock in the bottom of the pot. It is an all-purpose invigorator, a reliable antibiotic for melancholy, and a prime mover when one's world seems to stand on dead center. It is a panacea to man in want or woe.❞

—Joe Cooper

❝I have a theory that real chili is such a basic, functional dish that anyone can make it from the basic ingredients—rough meat, chile peppers, and a few common spices available to hungry individuals—and they'll eventually come up with pretty much the same kind of recipe that was for most of a century a staple of Texas tables. So all we have to do to get back to real chili is to get rid of the elitist nonsense.❞

—Sam Pendergrast

Ed's Buffalo Snort Red Chili

Ed Dorfman, winner of many awards and trophies for his barbecue and chili, says that the ambience of his restaurant (the Texas Chili and Rib Company in Phoenix, Arizona) is that of a small Texas bar. Basically a carry-out, his "small joint" seats about thirty people who dig in to his brisket, ribs, chicken wings, and several different kinds of chili. About his love for chiles, he calls himself a "capsaicin-holic" who uses chile in everything he cooks—note the eight chile-related ingredients of this recipe.

½   pound bacon with fat

2   pounds Spanish onions, chopped fine

5   tablespoons New Mexican red chile powder

2   tablespoons cayenne powder

4   jalapeño chiles, seeds and stems removed, chopped

½   cup canned New Mexican green chiles, chopped

1   dried New Mexican red chile pod, stem removed

1   pound Italian hot sausage

Dash Tabasco sauce

1   teaspoon Hungarian hot paprika

3   pounds crushed Italian tomatoes

1   tablespoon Mexican oregano

10   ounces T-bone steak, chopped fine

5   pounds coarsely ground chuck

1½ cups water

1   bottle Lone Star beer

2   teaspoons salt

1½ cups chopped bell pepper

1   tablespoon garlic in oil, chopped

2   tablespoons Worcestershire sauce

1   tablespoon raw sugar

5   tablespoons cumin

1   pound fresh armadillo meat (optional)

Fry the bacon in a soup kettle, add the onion, and sauté until soft. Add the remaining ingredients and bring to a boil. Reduce heat and simmer for about 2 hours, stirring frequently.

Serves: More than 10

Ed's Buffalo Snort Green Chili

Ed Dorfman has been called a "chili doctor," a "barbecue baron," a "chili guru," and a "spiceologist," but he says that he's just a chef who, through trial and error, has invented recipes that people other than himself enjoy. Despite all his awards, he believes that the best chili judges are his customers.

1   cup chopped scallions
2   teaspoons crushed garlic
3   tablespoons bacon fat
3   pounds pork loin, cut into ¼-inch cubes
2   cups canned New Mexican green chiles, chopped
6   NuMex Big Jim green chiles, roasted and peeled, seeds and stems removed, chopped
4   jalapeños, seeds and stems removed, chopped

2   teaspoons Tabasco sauce
12 small tomatillos, quartered
2   tablespoons Mexican oregano
3   tablespoons cumin
2   teaspoons salt
1½ tablespoons dried cilantro
1   tablespoon brown sugar
4   chicken bouillon cubes
1   bottle beer
1   tablespoon filé powder

Sauté the scallions and garlic in the bacon fat until soft. Add the pork loin and sear until crisp. Add the rest of the ingredients and simmer until done, approximately 2 hours.

Serves: 6 to 8

Maria's Chili Verde

"I am probably the world's finest cooker of chili," states Bud Spillar, owner and chef of Maria's of Keno in Klamath Falls, Oregon, a claim that will undoubtedly be disputed by all the other chefs represented in this book. In support of his declaration, Bud has won chili cookoffs in El Paso and Austin, placed fourth in the Great Northwest Chili Cookoff, and is frequently a judge at the famous CASI Terlingua International Chili Championship in Texas. Home cooks can judge for themselves by fixing this hot and colorful concoction.

2	pounds skirt or flank steak	1	teaspoon salt
3	quarts beef bouillon	4	tablespoons Mexican oregano
12	fresh jalapeños, stems removed, diced with seeds	1	large onion, diced
3½	cups canned chopped New Mexican chiles	1	tablespoon granulated garlic
1	habanero chile, stem removed, seeded and diced (optional)	12	strips Monterey Jack cheese cut ½ inch by 2 inches

Cook the steak in a pressure cooker with 2 cups of water at 10 pounds pressure for 1 hour. Remove the steak, shred, and keep warm.

Place the bouillon in a stock pot, add the remaining ingredients except the cheese, and bring to a boil. Reduce heat and simmer for 30 minutes.

Place the broth mixture in bowls, add the shredded steak, and add 2 pieces of cheese to form a cross in the bowl. Serve with corn or flour tortillas brushed with butter.

Serves: 6 to 8

Black Bean Chili

The Galley del Mar in Ridgeland, Mississippi, is an "upscale resort-area restaurant for fine, casual dining," according to owners Wayne Craft and Larry McCandless. Its specialty is spicy seafood dishes prepared by a collaboration of their cooking staff supervised by Lloyd Kent, but occasionally they drift off into the area of chili con carne.

1 pound black beans, cleaned	2 jalapeños, seeds and stems removed, chopped (or more for heat)
1 tablespoon red chile powder	
½ teaspoon cayenne	1 dried New Mexican red chile pod, seeds and stem removed
1 tablespoon cumin	
2 teaspoons paprika	1 tablespoon chopped fresh cilantro
1 tablespoon oregano	
1 bay leaf	1 pound tenderloin tips, cubed
1 tablespoon olive oil	2 teaspoons salt
1 onion, chopped	1½ teaspoons black pepper
4 cloves garlic, minced	1 ham hock
1 bell pepper, seeded and chopped	3 cups canned peeled tomatoes with liquid
2 cups canned chopped Rotel tomatoes with liquid	½ cup Burgundy wine
	Cilantro sprigs for garnish

Soak the beans overnight in water. Drain and refill the pot until the water just covers the beans, and bring to a boil. Reduce heat and simmer 1 hour.

Combine the red chile powder, cayenne, cumin, paprika, oregano, and bay leaf in a heavy skillet and toast until the spices are brittle, but do not burn. Remove and set aside.

Heat the olive oil and sauté the onion, garlic, and bell pepper until soft. Add the spices and tomatoes and sauté 15 minutes. Add the remaining ingredients and enough water to make a loose consistency and simmer, covered, for 2 hours. Adjust the water if necessary. Uncover and simmer, stirring occasionally, until thickened. Remove the ham hock and chile pod, add the cooked black beans, and serve in bowls garnished with sprigs of cilantro.

Serves: 8 to 10

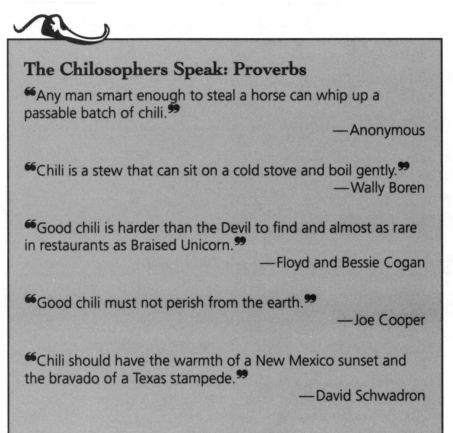

The Chilosophers Speak: Proverbs

"Any man smart enough to steal a horse can whip up a passable batch of chili."

—Anonymous

"Chili is a stew that can sit on a cold stove and boil gently."

—Wally Boren

"Good chili is harder than the Devil to find and almost as rare in restaurants as Braised Unicorn."

—Floyd and Bessie Cogan

"Good chili must not perish from the earth."

—Joe Cooper

"Chili should have the warmth of a New Mexico sunset and the bravado of a Texas stampede."

—David Schwadron

Chef Heywood's Chili

This chili is from the C.I.A.—the Culinary Institute of America. Chef Jim Heywood competed in fifteen chili cookoffs in 1992. "I've won a few along the way," he notes, "including the Connecticut State Championship in 1988 and the New Hampshire State Championship in 1991."

5   pounds lean beef (chuck or round), diced in ½-inch pieces

½   cup vegetable oil

1½ pound onions, diced

6   cloves garlic, minced

2   cups dark beer

2   cups beef broth

1   6-ounce can tomato paste

1½ cups diced New Mexican green chiles

2 to 3 jalapeños, seeds and stems removed, minced very fine

¾   cup chili powder

3   tablespoons freshly ground cumin seed

1½ tablespoons dried oregano

Salt and pepper to taste

Brown the beef in the oil. Remove and reserve the beef, leaving the oil in the pan.

Sauté the onions and the garlic in the remaining oil until soft. Add the beer, reserved beef, and tomato paste and bring to a boil. Reduce the heat and simmer for 1 hour, stirring frequently.

Add the remaining ingredients and simmer for another hour, stirring frequently.

Serves: 12 to 14 hungry chili addicts

Chef Rosa's Black Bean Sirloin Chile

Here is a delicious chile from chef Rosa Rajkovic of the Monte Vista Fire Station in Albuquerque. Dave has eaten this chile twenty times or more.

1   pound black turtle beans

1   tablespoon cumin

¼   teaspoon cayenne

2   teaspoons paprika

2   ancho chiles, seeds and stems removed

4   tablespoons olive oil

1   large red onion, chopped medium fine

2   teaspoons garlic, minced fine

2   cups plum tomatoes, peeled and seeded, diced and drained

2   fresh jalapeños, seeds and stems removed, chopped fine

2½ pounds sirloin, cut in 1-inch cubes

¼   cup cilantro, chopped fine

2   tablespoons fresh oregano, chopped fine

2   tablespoons fresh marjoram

Rinse the black beans in cold running water and place them in a heavy, 5-quart casserole or Dutch oven in enough water to cover by 2 inches. Bring the water to a boil over high heat and boil the beans for 2 minutes. Turn off the heat and let the beans soak for 2 hours at room temperature.

Meanwhile, heat a dry, heavy skillet over medium heat and cook the cumin, cayenne, and paprika until lightly toasted and fragrant, taking care not to let the mixture burn. Remove the spices from the heat and set aside in a small bowl. In the same skillet, toast the anchos. Grind the anchos in a grinder to a smooth powder. Add the ancho powder to the reserved spices and set aside.

In a large skillet, heat 2 tablespoons olive oil and sauté the onion until transparent and soft, about 20 minutes. Add the garlic and sauté an additional 3 minutes. Add the reserved spice mixture, tomatoes, and jalapeños and sauté over medium-low heat for about 20 minutes. Add this mixture to the casserole containing the black beans, along with water to cover by 4 inches. Bring to a simmer and cook, partially covered, for 2½ hours, or until the beans are tender.

While the bean mixture is simmering, heat the remaining olive oil in a skillet and sauté the sirloin cubes until lightly browned. Add the browned meat to the beans during the last hour of cooking. Add the cilantro, oregano, and marjoram to the chile 20 minutes before the end of the simmering time.

Serves: 6

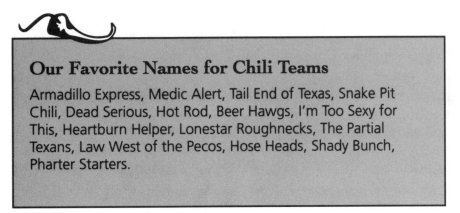

Our Favorite Names for Chili Teams

Armadillo Express, Medic Alert, Tail End of Texas, Snake Pit Chili, Dead Serious, Hot Rod, Beer Hawgs, I'm Too Sexy for This, Heartburn Helper, Lonestar Roughnecks, The Partial Texans, Law West of the Pecos, Hose Heads, Shady Bunch, Pharter Starters.

Judy's East of the Border Chili

Judy Howle contributed this interesting chili con carne recipe. She suggests topping the chili with grated Monterey Jack cheese and a slice of Jalapeño Cornbread from Chapter 6.

1½ pounds coarsely ground lean beef chuck or round

2 medium onions, chopped

2 cloves garlic, minced

4 ounces breakfast sausage, cooked and crumbled

1 15- to 16-ounce can tomatoes, pureed with juice

1 8-ounce can tomato sauce

1 can beef bouillon

4 ounces Absolut vodka

2 jalapeños, seeds and stems removed, chopped

2 tablespoons New Mexican red chile powder or ground ancho chiles

2 teaspoons oregano

1 tablespoon whole cumin seeds, toasted

1 teaspoon ground coriander

Salt to taste

Masa harina or cornmeal

Water

Sauté half of the beef with the onions and garlic until the meat turns gray. Add the rest of the beef and sauté. Pour the mixture in a large pot, add the rest of the ingredients, and simmer for 2 hours. If the chili needs thickening, make a thin paste of water and about 2 tablespoons masa harina or cornmeal. Add to the chili a little bit at a time, until it thickens to your desired consistency.

Serves: 4 to 6

Missile-Launcher Chili

Here's another contribution from Judy Howle—this chili is sure to send you flying!

¼ to ½ cup vegetable oil

4　pounds beef chuck, cut into ½-inch cubes

1　large onion, chopped

3　cloves garlic, finely chopped

5　fresh New Mexican green chiles, roasted and peeled, seeds and stems removed, chopped

8　fresh or canned jalapeños, seeds and stems removed, chopped

2　10-ounce cans tomatillos, drained, or 3 cups fresh

1　6-ounce can tomato paste

2　cups beef stock or beef broth

1½ teaspoons ground coriander

4　teaspoons ground cumin

1½ teaspoons salt

½　teaspoon ground black pepper

2　tablespoons masa harina or cornmeal

Water

Heat the oil in a skillet. Brown the beef one pound at a time, setting the browned beef aside each time. After all of the beef is browned, put the onion and garlic in the pan and cook until soft. Place the beef and the garlic and onion mixture in a large pot. Add the chiles, jalapeños, tomatillos, tomato paste, beef stock, coriander, cumin, salt, and pepper.

Cover the pot and simmer about 2½ hours, or until the meat is tender and well flavored. If the chili needs thickening, make a thin paste of water and masa harina or cornmeal and quickly stir into the chili. Cook and stir until thickened.

Serves: 6 to 8

Chef Todd's Man-Eating Chili

This fabulous dish improves with reheating, so try to make it a day ahead of time; the flavors become more mellow and more balanced, according to 1993 Santa Fe American Culinary Federation Chef of the Year Todd Sanson. Don't let the long list of ingredients scare you; most of them are probably in your cupboard at this very moment! It is a surprisingly easy recipe to prepare. We've divided the recipe into two parts—the marinade and then the cooking process.

Marinade

4   ounces gold tequila

1   tablespoon fresh lemon juice

1   teaspoon Worcestershire sauce

1   teaspoon ground New Mexican red chiles

¼   cup olive oil

½   cup tomato juice

2   garlic cloves, crushed

¼   cup chopped cilantro

2   pounds shark (or other really firm fish) cut into 1-inch cubes

2   pounds giant squid, ground in a food processor (pulsed) or in a meat grinder

4   tablespoons vegetable oil

In a large glass bowl, mix all of the marinade ingredients together with the shark and toss until the shark cubes are well coated. Marinate for 2 hours in the refrigerator. Remove the shark cubes and drain in a colander. Reserve in the refrigerator. Add the ground squid; toss that in the marinade and marinate in the refrigerator for 1 hour more.

Heat 2 tablespoons of the oil in a large skillet, add the shark cubes, and sear in the oil for 3 minutes. Place the seared cubes in a bowl and set aside.

Drain the ground squid in a colander. Heat the 2 remaining tablespoons of oil in the same skillet. Add the ground squid and sear for 2 minutes, treating the squid much like ground beef. Add the seared squid to the shark and set aside.

Chili

2 tablespoons vegetable oil

2 medium onions, diced

2 green bell peppers, seeds removed, diced

2 red bell peppers, seeds removed, diced

2 yellow bell peppers, seeds removed, diced

1 teaspoon salt

1 teaspoon ground cumin

1 teaspoon cayenne

1 teaspoon crushed chile caribe

½ teaspoon dried basil

1 teaspoon dried oregano

1 teaspoon dried thyme

3 bay leaves

4 jalapeños, seeds and stems removed, minced

½ cup New Mexican red chile powder, hot or mild

½ cup tomato paste

5 large tomatoes, peeled and diced

5 cups fish stock, or substitute 2 cups bottled clam juice and 3 cups water

1 16-ounce can pinto beans, drained

1 16-ounce can black beans, drained

2 16-ounce cans kidney beans, drained

½ cup cornmeal or falafel mix, mixed with 1½ cups water

Heat the oil in a large casserole, add the onions, and sauté for 10 minutes over moderate heat, stirring occasionally. Add the bell peppers and toss with the onions for 1 minute.

Add the salt, cumin, cayenne, chile caribe, basil, oregano, and thyme to the sautéed onion mixture and cook for 5 minutes, stirring repeatedly.

Add the bay leaves, jalapeños, shark-squid sauté, and the red chile powder and stir until the fish is just tender, about 5 minutes. Add the tomato paste, tomatoes, and fish stock and stir gently. Then bring the mixture to a boil.

Add all the beans, bring to a boil again, and then simmer for 15 minutes.

To thicken the chili, stir in a ½ cup of the cornmeal/falafel mixture and stir through the chili. Cook for a minute or two. If the chili isn't thick enough to your liking, add ¼ cup more, stir in, and cook for another minute. Repeat as needed.

To serve, remove the bay leaves and serve the man-eating chili in big, warm bowls.

Serves: 8 to 10

Seafood Chili

Connecticut resident Mark Pepin conjured up this nautical chili from the depths of the sea.

¼ pound bacon

2 large onions, thinly sliced

2 cloves garlic, minced

2 jalapeños, seeds and stems removed, minced

3 tablespoons chile paste (Lee Kum Kee preferred)

6 cups canned Italian plum tomatoes, coursely chopped, with the liquid

1 teaspoon oregano

1 teaspoon ground cumin

1 tablespoon white wine vinegar

Salt to taste

1 4-ounce can whole green chiles, cut into strips

1 pound boneless firm-flesh fish (cod or flounder preferred)

½ pound medium shrimp, peeled and deveined, tails removed

½ pound sea scallops, halved if real large

Cook the bacon in a large stock pot on medium heat until crisp, and then remove it with a slotted spoon. Add the onions to the bacon fat, lower the heat, and cook for 30 minutes. Add the garlic, jalapeños, and chile paste and cook for 5 minutes more.

Stir in the tomatoes with liquid, oregano, cumin, vinegar, and salt and simmer for 30 minutes. Crumble the reserved bacon and add to the pot along with the green chiles, fish, shrimp, and scallops. Simmer the chili until the seafood is cooked. Serve hot with crusty sourdough bread.

Serves: 6 to 8

Pork and Tomatillo Chili

We're getting fancy with our chili now! Another gourmet chili cook is Gary Tacket, who lives in Santa Ana, California.

1 cup orange juice	2 jalapeños, seeds and stems removed, diced
2 12-ounce bottles of dark beer or malt liquor	2 serranos, seeds and stems removed, diced
1 pound tomatillos, husks removed, quartered	2 habaneros, seeds and stems removed, diced
¼ cup peanut oil	3 tablespoons Tabasco sauce
10 cloves garlic, peeled	1 bunch cilantro leaves, chopped
2 pounds boneless pork, cut into ½-inch cubes	1 16-ounce can black beans with the liquid
Salt and pepper to taste	Cooked white rice
2 large yellow onions, quartered	
2 pounds Roma tomatoes, chopped	

In a large saucepan, combine the orange juice, beer, and tomatillos. Cook the mixture over medium heat for 15 to 20 minutes, then set aside.

Heat the peanut oil in a large skillet. Add the garlic and cook for 2 minutes. Stir in half the cubed pork and season with salt and pepper to taste. Brown on all sides, then remove the pork and add to the tomatillo mixture. Cook the remaining pork the same way, and add to the tomatillos. Brown the onions in the skillet, and add to the pork and tomatillo mixture.

Add the tomatoes, chiles, Tabasco, and cilantro to the chili mixture. Cover the chili and cook over low heat for 2 hours. Add the beans and cook, uncovered, for 30 minutes more. Adjust the seasonings to taste. Serve over the cooked rice.

Serves: 4 to 6

Crazy Cancun Chili

Plan a party and serve this fun chili contributed by Lynn Moretti. But make sure you reserve enough time. Lynn says this chili is at its best if made the day before and left to stand in the refrigerator overnight.

2   pounds ground chuck

1   pound chorizo sausage

1   large onion, diced

2   fresh jalapeños, seeds and stems removed, diced

1   stalk celery, diced

¼   cup fresh cilantro, chopped

¾   cup cooked black beans, drained

½   cup medium salsa (Gringo preferred)

1   28-ounce can crushed tomatoes

1   14½-ounce can salsa tomatoes with green chiles and onions (Rotell may be substituted)

2   15-ounce cans dark red kidney beans, drained

1   16-ounce can whole tomatoes, drained and chopped (reserve the juice in a microwave-safe dish)

2   corn tortillas

1   tablespoon beef bouillon base (granules)

⅓   cup New Mexican red chile powder

6   saffron stamens, crushed

Salt and pepper to taste

6½ tablespoons hot salsa of choice

1   tablespoon Tabasco sauce

1   dried habanero chile, crushed (¼ teaspoon habanero powder may be substituted)

In a large stockpot, brown the ground chuck, chorizo, onion, jalapeños, and celery. Add the cilantro, black beans, salsa, crushed tomatoes, salsa tomatoes, kidney beans, and whole tomatoes.

Break up the corn tortillas in small pieces and place in the juice. Microwave the juice and tortilla mixture for 2 minutes or until hot, then set aside. Add the remaining ingredients to the pot. Next, mash the tortilla pieces with a fork, and add the mixture to the chili. Simmer the chili for 1 hour, stirring frequently. Refrigerate overnight. Reheat and serve the next day.

Serves: 14 to 16

Jennifer's Absolut Chili

Absolut's Peppar vodka is a swell way to introduce a subtle heat to a variety of entrées, including chili con carne. This recipe was contributed by Mike and Penny Shtull.

3	tablespoons vegetable oil	1	cup Absolut Peppar vodka
1	large onion, diced	2	tablespoons cumin
3	medium garlic cloves, minced	1	teaspoon powdered black pepper
3	pounds lean beef, cut into ½-inch cubes	1	tablespoon dried oregano
5	tablespoons sweet Hungarian paprika	5	cups beef or chicken broth
		2	small tomatoes, diced
1	teaspoon cayenne	¼	cup corn flour

In a deep stockpot, heat the oil on high. When the oil is very hot, reduce the heat to medium-high and add the onion and 1 clove of the minced garlic. Add the meat to the mixture, a little bit at a time, stirring constantly until the meat is evenly browned. Stir in all of the remaining ingredients, except the corn flour. Bring the chili to a boil for 3 to 5 minutes, then reduce the heat to simmer. Cook the chili for a half hour.

When the cooking time is up, add the corn flour, stirring slowly to avoid lumps. Simmer for 30 minutes then stir the chili. Simmer for 10 minutes more, or until the beef is tender.

Serves: 6 to 8

Mike's Ridley Park Chili

This chili, contributed by Michael Perrupato of Ridley Park, Pennsylvania, is the perfect addition to any football tailgate party or game-day function.

⅓   pound lean bacon, diced

2   onions, minced

3   cloves garlic, minced

3   pounds lean ground beef

1   6-ounce can tomato paste

1   8-ounce can tomatoes, chopped

1   10-ounce can tomato sauce

1   4-ounce can jalapeños, drained, seeds and stems removed, diced

3   tablespoons red chile powder (Santa Cruz preferred)

1   teaspoon salt

2   16-ounce cans red kidney beans with liquid

Garnishes: Cheddar cheese and chopped raw onions

In a skillet, brown the bacon, onions, garlic, and beef. In a large pot, add the beef mixture along with the tomato paste, chopped tomatoes, tomato sauce, jalapeños, chile powder, and salt. Stir well and simmer for about 2 hours. Add the red kidney beans and simmer for another hour. Serve with shredded Cheddar cheese and chopped raw onions on top.

Serves: 6 to 8

Laszlo Eggplant-Soy Chili

This is perhaps the most unusual chili recipe in this book. Don Laszlo of Chicago promises with this recipe: "This is spicy chili that tastes like it's chock-full of meat and fat—yet the only fat in it is olive oil. Don't tell your guests it's a meatless chili; they simply won't believe you!" This recipe requires some prior preparation the day before you serve it, so plan ahead.

12	ounces red beans	2	cups vegetable stock
3	bay leaves	2	cups tomato paste
8	large cloves garlic, peeled and smashed with a knife blade	¼	cup extra-virgin olive oil
		¼	cup ground cumin
3	large onions, diced	¼	cup hickory-smoke sauce
3	tomatoes, chopped	¼	cup soy sauce
3	medium to large eggplants, unpeeled and diced into 1-inch cubes	¼	cup hot sauce of choice
		2	heaping cups of texturized vegetable protein (soy flake, available in health food stores)
2	cups red wine		

Combine the red beans and bay leaves in enough water to completely cover the beans. Soak overnight in the refrigerator, then drain the water and add fresh water. Cook the beans for 45 minutes, and set aside.

In a large nonstick skillet, sauté a third of the garlic, a third of the onion, and a third of the diced tomato over high heat. As the tomatoes break down, add a third of the eggplant. Stir gently, then cover and let cook on medium heat for 5 minutes. Next add a third of the wine and a third of the vegetable stock. Let the mixture simmer until the eggplant is soft, then transfer to a large stockpot. On medium heat, repeat the previous steps until all of the garlic, onion, tomatoes, eggplant, wine, and vegetable stock are added to the stockpot. Remove the bay leaves and add the beans to the stockpot. Add any remaining liquid and the tomato paste. Stir well and continue to cook the chili on medium heat.

Pour the olive oil into a small pot, and heat on medium-high. Mix in the cumin and quickly fry into a paste, then add to the chili, stirring well.

Add the rest of the ingredients, stir well, cover, and simmer for 30 minutes. Continue to stir frequently to keep the chili from collecting at the bottom of the pot. Add water in small amounts to attain a consistency of your choice. Turn off the heat and serve throughout the day.

Serves: 12 to 14

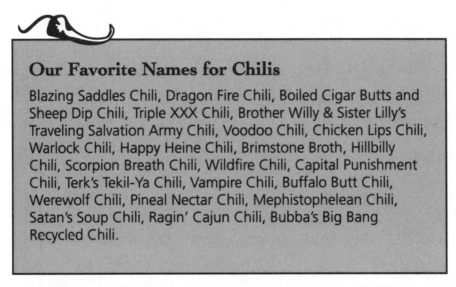

Our Favorite Names for Chilis

Blazing Saddles Chili, Dragon Fire Chili, Boiled Cigar Butts and Sheep Dip Chili, Triple XXX Chili, Brother Willy & Sister Lilly's Traveling Salvation Army Chili, Voodoo Chili, Chicken Lips Chili, Warlock Chili, Happy Heine Chili, Brimstone Broth, Hillbilly Chili, Scorpion Breath Chili, Wildfire Chili, Capital Punishment Chili, Terk's Tekil-Ya Chili, Vampire Chili, Buffalo Butt Chili, Werewolf Chili, Pineal Nectar Chili, Mephistophelean Chili, Satan's Soup Chili, Ragin' Cajun Chili, Bubba's Big Bang Recycled Chili.

Big Sky Chili

Patty Spiro says of her recipe, "The whole idea is to not rush this recipe. You may eat it right away, but it's better if it is left until the next day to allow flavors to combine and the chili to thicken."

1   pound red kidney beans
Water
1   teaspoon crushed hot dried chiles, such as Thai or piquin
1   tablespoon dried New Mexican red chiles, crushed
2   tablespoons Texas-style chili powder
1   clove garlic, minced
1   teaspoon freshly ground black pepper
¼   teaspoon salt
1   tablespoon olive oil

8   jalapeños, seeds and stems removed, chopped
13   dashes of Tabasco sauce
2   cloves garlic, minced
1   large onion, chopped
½   tablespoon dried New Mexican red chiles, crushed
1   pound lean beef, cut into ½-inch cubes
¼   cup Texas-style chili powder
1½   cups tomato paste
Salt to taste

Cover the kidney beans with water in a large pot. Add the crushed hot chiles, chili powder, garlic, black pepper, and salt. Cover and simmer until the liquid is absorbed. When the liquid is gone, add water to cover the beans again, then simmer, covered, until all but a little bit of liquid is absorbed. Stir occasionally to keep the beans from sticking.

In a separate skillet, sauté in 1 tablespoon of olive oil the jalapeños, Tabasco sauce, garlic, onion, chiles, beef, and chili powder until the mixture is brown, or the chili vapors get ya! Add the skillet contents to the large pot along with the tomato paste and salt to taste. Stir the chili well and simmer, covered, for 2 hours. Eat the chili immediately or refrigerate overnight and reheat.

Serves: 8 to 10

Black Bart's Chili

This chili utilizes black beans and chipotle chiles to conjure up a rich, smoky taste.

2   cups black turtle beans, soaked overnight
1   bay leaf
4   teaspoons cumin seeds
5   teaspoons paprika
½   teaspoon cayenne
4   teaspoons dried oregano
3   tablespoons corn oil
3   medium yellow onions, diced
3   tablespoons New Mexican red chile powder

4   cloves garlic, coarsely chopped
½   teaspoon salt
2   cups canned tomatoes, peeled, seeded, and chopped, with juice
2   teaspoons chopped chipotle chiles (smoked jalapeños)
1   tablespoon rice wine vinegar
4   tablespoons cilantro, chopped

Drain the beans, place them in a large pot, then cover with water by 2 inches. Bring the beans to a boil and add the bay leaf. Lower the heat and let the beans simmer while you prepare the rest of the ingredients.

Heat a small skillet over medium heat. Add the cumin seeds, paprika, cayenne, and oregano. Give a quick stir and remove from heat. Grind the spices in a mortar or spice mill to make a coarse powder.

Heat the oil in a large pan and sauté the onions over medium heat until they soften. Add the chile powder, garlic, salt, and spice mixture and cook for another 4 to 5 minutes. Next add the tomatoes, their juice, and 1 teaspoon of the chipotle chiles. Let simmer for about 15 minutes, then add to the beans, adding enough water to cover the beans by at least 1 inch. Continue cooking the beans slowly until they are soft, for about 1½ hours. Stir frequently and add more chipotles, the vinegar, and cilantro to taste.

Serves: 8

The Great Earth Veggie Chili

Not everyone in the world enjoys chili with meat, so we've come up with an alternative for those who love their veggies!

⅓ cup clarified butter

1 tablespoon salt

¾ teaspoon black pepper

1 tablespoon New Mexican red chile powder

2 teaspoons paprika

1 teaspoon dry mustard

¼ to ½ teaspoon cayenne

1 tablespoon cumin

1 tablespoon anise seeds

1 large onion, sliced

5 medium cloves garlic, chopped

2 stalks celery, chopped

1 large eggplant, peeled and cut into 1-inch pieces

2 small zucchini, peeled and cubed

1 red bell pepper, julienned

1 green bell pepper, julienned

½ cup olive oil

1 14-ounce can plum tomatoes, crushed into small pieces

2 teaspoons thyme

1 teaspoon dried rosemary

2 teaspoons dried basil

1 bay leaf

1 teaspoon Worcestershire sauce

1 tablespoon lemon peel

2 tablespoons honey

1 tablespoon ketchup

3 yellow squashes, peeled and cut into ½-inch circles

12 ounces red kidney beans, drained

13 ounces black-eyed peas, drained

¼ bunch fresh parsley, chopped

2 cups cooked brown rice

Garnishes: grated cheese, sour cream, and red onion

In a large deep skillet, fry in butter the salt, pepper, chile powder, paprika, mustard, cayenne, cumin, and anise seeds for 5 to 6 minutes. Add the onion, garlic, and celery and cook over medium heat for 5 to 10 minutes until the vegetables are soft. Add all of the remaining ingredients except the yellow squash, kidney beans, black-eyed peas, parsley, and rice. Simmer, stirring often, for 25 minutes. Add the squash, beans, and peas; cook 10 minutes longer, then stir in the parsley. Serve the chili in bowls over brown rice. Top with grated cheese, sour cream, and chopped red onion if desired.

Serves: 4 to 6

Pretty Damn Good Chili

This unusual recipe was given to us by Donald Downes, the Eatbeat editor of *Phoenix Magazine* and a graduate chef of the Scottsdale Culinary Institute. Donald says about his chili, from his Wyoming days, "I'd stir up a batch for a few buddies on many a wintry Wyoming night. The chili, like me, has gone through some changes, with the present version reflecting influences from Arizona."

1 pound beef sirloin, fat trimmed and coarsely ground (lean ground beef can be substituted)

1 pound pork sirloin, fat trimmed and coarsely ground (ground pork can be substituted)

2 teaspoons canola oil

2 medium onions, diced

2 carrots, finely diced

⅓ cup dry white wine

1 6-ounce can tomato paste

1½ cups chicken stock or low-sodium broth

1 28-ounce can whole peeled tomatoes, liquid drained and reserved, tomatoes cut into bite-sized pieces

2 cloves garlic, minced

1 7-ounce can diced New Mexican green chiles

½ 4-ounce can of diced, roasted jalapeños (a moderately spicy kick; for more fire, add the rest of the can)

½ teaspoon freshly ground black pepper

1½ tablespoons dried oregano

2 teaspoons powdered cumin

⅛ teaspoon cinnamon

½ teaspoon cocoa powder

Grated Asiago cheese for garnish

In a large sauté pan or skillet, brown the beef and the pork; drain and set aside.

In a 4½ quart heavy soup pot, heat the oil and then add the onions and carrots; cook until browned, stirring as needed—do not burn. Pour in the white wine to deglaze; stir in any browned bits. (If cooking on a gas stove, remove from the flame before adding the wine to reduce the chance of a flare-up.) Stir in the tomato paste and cook for 2 to 3 minutes.

Add the chicken stock, the liquid from the tomatoes, and the tomato pieces; stir to combine. Add the reserved browned beef and pork. Stir in the garlic, green chiles, jalapeños, black pepper, oregano, cumin, cinnamon, and cocoa powder. Reduce the heat to a simmer and cook for 1 hour, stirring occasionally. (Sampling is allowed.) Ladle into bowls and top with a handful of grated Asiago cheese. And, you have to have cold beer . . . that's a given.

This chili is thick and meaty. For a thinner batch, add more stock to the desired consistency.

Serves: 8 hungry people (10, if they're not too hungry or if you've got lots of side goodies from Chapter 6!)

Doctors' Road Chili aka Todd's Chili

You guessed it! It's Todd Sanson (*sans* shark) again, invading our chili buds. If you ever get to New Mexico, you have got to meet this guy. He is a chef extraordinaire, a great drink master, and a fine host.

2   tablespoons olive oil

3   onions, chopped

3   cloves garlic, minced

2   pounds lean beef, cut into 1-inch cubes

2   pounds very lean ground beef

2   teaspoons each: paprika, dried oregano, ground cumin, cinnamon, granulated sugar, veggie salt

¼   cup ground New Mexican red chiles

¼   cup chile caribe

4   jalapeños, seeds and stems removed, minced

2   chipotle chiles (smoked jalapeños), dried or canned, or substitute 2 yellow wax peppers

1½ cups water

1   cup dry red wine

2   cups chicken or beef broth, low sodium or homemade

2   16-ounce cans pinto beans, drained

1   16-ounce can kidney beans, drained

1   16-ounce can black beans, drained

2   20-ounce cans tomato sauce

1   6-ounce can tomato paste

1   16-ounce can stewed tomatoes

¼   cup masa, yellow or blue

¼   cup falafel mix (chick pea) blended in 1 cup water

Garnishes: grated cheese, chopped onion, chopped jalapeños

Heat the oil in a large heavy casserole, add the onion and garlic, and sauté for 1 minute. Then add the beef, herbs, ground red chile, and chile caribe and sauté for a minute or two more, until the cubed beef is browned.

Then add the jalapeños and chipotles and stir. Add the water, wine, broth, beans, tomato sauce, tomato paste, and stewed tomatoes. Cook for 1 hour on low heat, stirring frequently.

Add the masa and the falafel mixture and stir. Cook for 45 minutes. If the mixture becomes too thick, thin it with water.

Serve in big chili bowls with the garnishes.

Serves: 8 to 10

Jim Nelson's Chili

According to recipe author Jim Nelson, "This is excellent chili!" It certainly is interesting as it calls for both bitter chocolate and brewed coffee. Jim is from Milwaukee, and it's good to see that the Midwest is starting to heat up!

2 tablespoons vegetable oil	1 tablespoon paprika
2 pounds lean beef, cubed in ¼-inch pieces	1 14-ounce can kidney beans
	1 28-ounce can whole tomatoes, with juice, sliced
1 cup onion, diced	
1 clove garlic, diced	½ square bitter chocolate
2 teaspoons Tabasco sauce	2 cups brewed coffee
1 tablespoon salt	Water
1 cup celery tops, chopped	Crushed New Mexican red chiles to taste
3 tablespoons chili powder	
¼ cup white vinegar	

In a large stockpot, brown the beef and then add all of the other ingredients. Stir frequently while the chili simmers for the next 2½ hours. Add the water in small amounts if the chili is too thick. Add the crushed red peppers to taste.

Serves: 8 to 10

High Country Chili

Charles W. Rigby of Arlington, Texas, contributed this excellent, hardy recipe.

1 8-ounce can beef broth
1 8-ounce can tomato sauce
1 tablespoon California mild chili powder
1 tablespoon onion powder
1 tablespoon salt
½ teaspoon cayenne
1 teaspoon garlic powder
1 tablespoon paprika
2½ pounds chuck tender, cubed in ¼-inch pieces
3 tablespoons Gebhardt's Chili Powder

¼ teaspoon white pepper
⅛ teaspoon jalapeño powder
¼ teaspoon black pepper
½ teaspoon oregano
1 package Goya Sazon
Beef broth
3 tablespoons chili blend (Fort Worth Lite preferred)
½ teaspoon salt
⅛ teaspoon cayenne
½ teaspoon garlic powder
1 package Goya Sazon

In a chili pot, bring the beef broth and the tomato sauce to a slow boil.

In a separate container, combine the mild chili powder, onion powder, salt, cayenne, garlic powder, and paprika. Mix well and add to the chili pot. Bring the mixture back to a boil. Brown the meat in a skillet, and then add to the chili pot. Reduce to medium heat and cook for 1 hour.

In a separate container, combine the Gebhardt's, white pepper, jalapeño powder, black pepper, oregano, and Goya Sazon and add to the chili. Stir well and bring the mixture back to a slow boil for 30 minutes, adding beef broth as needed to keep the meat covered with liquid.

Combine the chili blend, salt, cayenne, garlic powder, and Goya Sazon and add to the chili; simmer for an additional 30 mintes, then serve.

Serves: 4 to 6

Duffy's Irish Chili

Contributor David A. Lorenz has made chili cooking a family affair. His wife competes against him, and both his mom and dad compete on the East Coast. His mom is the 1993 Massachusetts State Champ. David says the recipe below was developed over ten years of competing in chili cookoffs throughout Canada, twenty different states, and Mexico.

3	pounds sirloin, cut into ¼-inch cubes	3	tablespoons ground cumin
	Pam cooking spray	½	teaspoon ground oregano
5	tablespoons ground chili powder (California Fancy preferred)	½	cup chicken broth
		½	cup beef broth
3	tablespoons ground New Mexican red chile powder	¼	teaspoon MSG (optional)
		2	teaspoons salt

Sauté the meat in a skillet using the Pam to prevent sticking. Add to a 4-quart Dutch oven. Add the California chili powder, 2 tablespoons of the New Mexican red chile powder, cumin, oregano, chicken and beef broth, and MSG (if desired). Simmer the chili for 1½ hours. Add the salt and the rest of the New Mexican chile powder, and cook on medium heat for 1 hour more. Salt to taste, and serve.

Serves: 6 to 8

After-Burner Chili

Rolf and Jeanine Wiik of Escondido, California, contributed this recipe. They say their test tasters always want them to make the chili hotter. This is not a difficult job, given that their secret ingredients are fresh cayenne and serrano chile peppers!

1½ pounds chuck, cut into ¼-inch pieces
½ pound hot Italian sausage
2 large onions, chopped
1 16-ounce can kidney beans
1 16-ounce can pinto beans
6 fresh whole jalapeños
20 whole dried cayenne pods
1 8-ounce can tomato sauce

1 8-ounce can stewed tomatoes
2 tablespoons garlic powder
2 tablespoons salt
2 tablespoons pepper
2 tablespoons Lawry's Chili Seasoning
3 tablespoons New Mexican red chile powder
1 tablespoon paprika

In a large skillet, brown the chuck, sausage, and onions. Sauté until the chuck and sausage are completely cooked, and the onions are transparent. Transfer the meat-and-onion mixture to a large stockpot and add the rest of the ingredients and enough water to make a stew. Stir well and simmer for 4 hours. Remove the jalapeños and cayennes before serving.

Serves: 4 to 6

Professor Fosdick's Nasty Batch

John D. Foster, Jr., alias Professor Fosdick, has been competing with his team for thirteen years. Get ready to enjoy a unique bowl of Colorado's Arkansas River Valley's best. It's wonderful when served with warmed tortillas.

2 tablespoons extra-virgin olive oil

2 tablespoons vegetable oil

7 cloves fresh garlic, finely minced

3 pounds pork shoulder or butt, trimmed of excess fat and cubed into ½-inch pieces

¼ cup onion, chopped

¼ cup shallots, chopped

4 teaspoons lite salt

2 teaspoons white pepper

3 teaspoons white sugar

2 teaspoons seasoning salt (Lawry's preferred)

3 teaspoons cumin

1 teaspoon cilantro

¼ cup flour

1½ cups chicken broth

1 28-ounce can stewed tomatoes, crushed in a bowl

15 fresh New Mexican green chiles, roasted and peeled, seeds and stems removed, chopped (canned whole chiles may be substituted)

1 fresh jalapeño, seeds and stem removed, chopped

12 tablespoons green hot sauce of choice

Heat the oils in a 5-quart pot over medium heat and sauté the garlic for several minutes. Add the pork and sauté as well, covering the pot between stirrings. Stir the meat occasionally until it is gray and some liquid has formed—about 10 minutes.

Add the onion, shallots, salt, pepper, sugar, seasoning salt, cumin, and cilantro. Mix well and stir for 5 more minutes. Slowly mix in the flour until it forms a thick paste. Add the broth immediately. Stir well until the mixture is smooth, and simmer. To the bowl of crushed tomatoes, add the green chiles, jalapeño, and hot sauce and blend well. Add to the chili pot, stir, and simmer for 30 minutes more.

Serves: 8 to 10

Desert Storm Chili

David Finkelstein entered this recipe in the 1991 National Beef Cookoff in Colorado Springs. He didn't win a prize, but as far as the contestants and journalists at the cookoff were concerned, he was a real winner. A Navy medical petty officer, he conceived this recipe while serving in Saudi Arabia during Operation Desert Storm.

1½ quarts water

8 ounces dried red kidney beans

4 ounces dried Great Northern beans

1 pound coarsely ground beef (85 percent lean)

2 pounds boneless top sirloin steak, cut into ½-inch pieces

1 tablespoon vegetable oil

1 large onion, chopped

2 to 3 cloves garlic, minced

1 cup leeks, chopped

1 yellow or green bell pepper, chopped

1 tablespoon paprika

1 tablespoon crushed New Mexican red chiles

2 teaspoons cayenne

1½ teaspoons ground cumin

1 teaspoon dried oregano

Salt and pepper to taste

4 large tomatoes, peeled, seeded, and chopped

2 to 4 cups beef broth

Shredded Cheddar cheese for garnish

Crusty French bread

Combine the water and beans in a large Dutch oven. Bring to a boil and cook for 5 to 10 minutes. Remove from heat and let stand for 1 to 1½ hours.

Meanwhile, cook the ground beef in a large frying pan over medium-high heat, breaking the beef up into small pieces, until the beef is no longer pink. Remove the beef from the pan with a slotted spoon and reserve. Brown the sirloin pieces (in 2 batches) in the same frying pan over medium-high heat. Remove the sirloin from the pan with a slotted spoon after each batch is browned. Pour off the drippings.

Heat the vegetable oil in the same frying pan until hot. Add the onion and garlic; cook for 3 to 5 minutes or until the onion is translucent, stirring occasionally. Add the leeks and yellow pepper; continue to cook for 2 to 3 minutes, or until the vegetables are tender. Stir in the paprika, crushed red chiles, cayenne, cumin, oregano, and salt and pepper to taste. Cook for 2 to 3 minutes, stirring occasionally. Add the tomatoes, reduce the heat to medium or medium-low. Cook for 20 minutes, or until the tomatoes begin to break down. If necessary, add some beef broth to the tomato mixture to keep from scorching.

Drain and rinse the beans. Combine the beans, ground beef, sirloin pieces, tomato mixture, and enough remaining beef broth to cover in the same Dutch oven. Bring to a boil. Reduce heat; cover and simmer for 1¼ to 1½ hours or until the beans are tender, stirring frequently. Garnish with cheese and serve with crusty bread.

Serves: 12

Variation: Two to four cups of beer or water may be substituted for the beef broth.

The One and Only Recipe for Chili con Carne

Our friend Harold Timber authored this excellent chili recipe. As a world-champion Tex-Mex cook, Harold would tell you that as far as chili con carne goes, this recipe is all you'll ever need. We say tasting it is believing—give it a try and decide for yourself! Harold won the ICS World's Championship Chili Cookoff in 1983—but with a different recipe!

1 cup double-strength beef bouillon	1 teaspoon sugar
1 cup water	1 teaspoon celery salt
6 tablespoons medium-hot New Mexican red chile powder (Gebhardt's Eagle Brand Chili Powder may be substituted)	1 teaspoon salt
	½ teaspoon ground oregano
	½ teaspoon ground dry mustard
	2 teaspoons vegetable oil
1 tablespoon hot New Mexican red chile powder (cayenne pepper may be substituted)	1 cup onion, finely minced
	½ cup chopped canned mild New Mexican green chiles
1 tablespoon domestic paprika	1 tablespoon garlic, minced
1 scant tablespoon ground cumin	1 cup water
1 tablespoon masa harina corn flour (you may substitute flour in water to desired thickness)	1 cup tomato sauce
	1 bottle beer
2 teaspoons MSG (optional)	3 pounds sirloin, cubed in ¼-inch pieces

In a small saucepan, pour in the beef bouillon and water and bring to a boil. Then add the medium-hot chile powder, hot chile powder, paprika, cumin, masa harina, MSG (if desired), sugar, celery salt, salt, oregano, and mustard. Stir the mixture well, cover, and set aside.

In a 5-quart cast-iron cooking pot, add the vegetable oil and sauté the onion, green chiles, and garlic. When the onion is soft, add the water, tomato sauce, and beer. Bring the mixture to a boil, then reduce the heat and simmer.

In a separate frying pan, sauté half of the sirloin cubes at a time. When all of the beef is sautéed, add it to the cast-iron pot. Stir the chili well, and continue to simmer for 30 minutes. When the cooking time is up, add the saucepan of seasonings and simmer for 1 hour more, stirring occasionally. Turn off the heat and let the chili stand for 1 hour before serving. Correct the seasoning with hot sauce and salt.

Serves: 6 to 8

Chili Cook's Hints   If you want to add acidity, add 2 or 3 teaspoons of cider vinegar. If you like chili with beans, cook the beans separately and add to the chili as you serve each bowl.

6

Starters, Chili Accompaniments, and Fine Finishes

Mankind does not live by chili alone. Despite all of the recipes in this book for the bowl o' red, we realize that even the most dedicated chilihead must, occasionally, consume other foods. Even chili media guru Jo Ann Horton of the *Goat Gap Gazette* observes: "Don't go to the home of a dedicated competition chili cook and expect to get a pot of chili. Nope. Uh-uh. If there is one thing these folks don't cook for fun and for eating . . . it's chili! You might get a gourmet meal, a pot of beans, a can of squeeze cheese and a sleeve of Ritz crackers, but nix on a vat of chili. Why? Because competition chili cooks spend so many weekends tasting and mixing and stirring their pots of (hopefully) prizewinning chili, they simply don't want to eat it any other time."

In this chapter we have included starters and accompaniments for chili, beginning with cocktails. "As most of you must have heard," notes Jo Ann, "chili cooks are notorious for their love of alcoholic beverages—that's why they're called a 'stagger of chiliheads'—sorta like a gaggle of geese, you understand." Although many chiliheads would consider drinks and chili to be a complete meal, we've decided to include some salsas and sauces, snacks and appetizers, salads, breads, and desserts. Lots of desserts, in fact, because chiliheads are also notorious for their sweet tooth.

So, while you are creating the perfect chili, whip up some of our favorite accompaniments and make a complete meal!

Three Cheers from Todd

The following three drink recipes come from our friend Todd Sanson of Santa Fe Exotix condiments, who hit his bar at 6 A.M. to try some different combinations so he would have the recipes ready for us when we arrived for lunch. Todd was happy; we were happy.

The Tesuque Toad

1¼ ounce Absolut Citron vodka
1¼ ounce Herradura Silver tequila
½ ounce Grand Marnier

½ ounce Rose's lime juice
2½ ounces sweet and sour mix

Combine all the ingredients in a shaker with a few cubes of ice and shake for 10 seconds.

Pour the mixture into two Old-fashioned glasses with some ice cubes, or serve "up" in two elegant chilled cocktail glasses, with salted or unsalted rims.

Serves: 2

Pecos Blue Cocktail

1¼ ounce Absolut Kurant vodka
1¼ ounce Herradura Silver tequila
½ ounce Blue Curaçao

½ ounce Triple Sec
½ ounce Rose's lime juice
2   ounces sweet and sour mix

Mix and blend as the above drink.

Serves: 2

Ojo Caliente

1¼ ounce Absolut Peppar vodka   ½   ounce Rose's lime juice

1¼ ounce Herradura Gold tequila   2½ ounces Tavern sweet and sour

½   ounce Cointreau

Mix and blend as the above drink.

Serves: 2

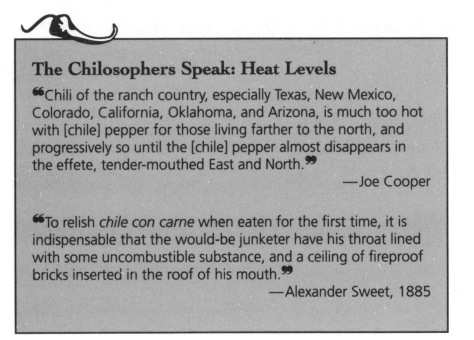

The Chilosophers Speak: Heat Levels

"Chili of the ranch country, especially Texas, New Mexico, Colorado, California, Oklahoma, and Arizona, is much too hot with [chile] pepper for those living farther to the north, and progressively so until the [chile] pepper almost disappears in the effete, tender-mouthed East and North."

—Joe Cooper

"To relish *chile con carne* when eaten for the first time, it is indispensable that the would-be junketer have his throat lined with some uncombustible substance, and a ceiling of fireproof bricks inserted in the roof of his mouth."

—Alexander Sweet, 1885

Shandygaff

This drink is a British concoction. Rumor has it that it made its way from England to India, where it was consumed by the Brits who drank it in great quantities as they devoured the addictive hot curries. We think it is a strange blending, but one that goes well with addictive hot chili.

2	large, chilled glasses	1	bottle chilled ginger beer
1	bottle chilled ale or beer		

Fill each of the glasses half full with the ale or beer. Then very, very gently stir in an equal amount of the ginger beer.

Serves: 2

Cadillac Bar Poppers

Larry Burruss, art director for the *Chilympiad Cookbook,* learned to make these "Poppers" at a bar in Piedras Negras, Mexico, in 1976. According to Jo Ann Horton, "Larry introduced Poppers to the chili world at The Way It Was Cookoff in Driftwood, Texas, several years ago. He mixed Poppers for everyone who wanted one (or many), and drank 'a few' himself. Much later in the evening, he decided he could fly. Firmly placing his feet on the top step of the motor home, flapping his arms wildly, and staring into the darkness, he gave it one big push, and off he went. Of course the flight lasted only a split second, and the bartender unceremoniously made landfall nose-first, two feet short of a giant cedar tree. So much for being invincible. That's what Poppers can do. Try them, but watch it!"

1½ ounces tequila   Splash of Kahlua
Splash of ginger ale

Pour the tequila in a shot glass with a heavy bottom. Then gently splash in a little ginger ale. Add a splash of Kahlua. Place clean towel over glass with palm of hand over top of glass. Grip the glass firmly and pound it on the table three times. Then *shoot!*

Serves: 1

Dangerous Slush

We all know that driving in slush can be dangerous, and drinking this slush with unbridled abandon can be dangerous too! It can be served before the meal or even as a highly potent frozen dessert to cool down those taste buds after some spicy chili.

1   large can frozen orange juice
    concentrate

1   large can frozen lemonade
    concentrate

1   large can frozen limeade
    concentrate

1   large bag frozen strawberries

1   fifth decent quality tequila

Pour all of the ingredients into a plastic 1-gallon container and shake to mix. Then add enough water to come up to within 2 inches of the top. Shake the container again.

Seal the container tightly and freeze overnight.

Cut a 3- to 4-inch hole at the top of the container and scoop the slush into dessert glasses. Serve with a spoon, followed by a straw for when the mixture starts to melt.

Serves: 10 to 15, depending on their imbibing habits and whether or not it is used as a dessert

Lemonade Bubbler

This recipe comes to us from Niki LaMont, who submitted it to *Chile Pepper* magazine for a recipe contest. We think this would be a fine drink to serve before, during, and after the great chili meal.

2   cups crushed ice

¾   cup Absolut Citron vodka, well chilled

1   small can frozen lemonade (6 ounces)

1   bottle dry champagne (Brut, not sweet), well chilled

Lemon slices or lemon twists to garnish

Into a blender, pour the ice, vodka, and lemonade and blend until slushy. Divide the mixture between six 8-ounce stemmed glasses. Top off each glass with the champagne, and garnish with a slice of lemon or a lemon twist.

Serves: 6

Tequila Sunrise

This version of the tequila classic is from Janie Burruss, wife of the inventor of Cadillac Bar Poppers. She lives in San Marcos, Texas.

1	ounce tequila	3	ounces orange juice
½	ounce apricot brandy	¼	ounce grenadine

Combine the ingredients over crushed ice and stir.

Serves: 1 drinker or 2 sippers

Montezuma's Cookoff

In a full-page ad for Montezuma Tequila in the first issue of the ICS publication, *Chili*, Barton Distillers ran some copy about how Montezuma, king of the Aztecs, invented the first Quetzalcoatl Chili Cookoff. The Aztecs starved themselves for six weeks just to "sharpen their taste buds." Then at the cookoff there was a maize-throwing contest, a throw-the-maiden-in-the-volcano contest, a wet loincloth contest, and a Chiligula (god of chili) look-alike contest that was won by Montezuma, Jr. "Then came the chili judging," the ad continued. "Montezuma himself deigned to taste the chili and awarded the winner with a lifetime supply of leg irons."

Land of Enchantment Salsa

Serve this salsa with blue corn chips—this recommendation comes from the recipe creator, Joan Bulkley, who submitted the recipe to *Chile Pepper* magazine. The roasted garlic mellows out the salsa and adds a rich flavor.

1 whole garlic bulb	½ bunch cilantro, leaves only
2 pounds ripe tomatoes, cored and quartered	3 whole oregano leaves, minced (about 1 teaspoon), or ½ teaspoon dried
1 pound tomatillos, husks removed, cored and halved	½ teaspoon ground cumin
¼ pound green jalapeños, seeds and stems removed	¼ cup habanero-style hot sauce
6 scallions, white part only	Freshly ground black pepper

In a small baking dish, roast the whole garlic bulb for 1 hour at 350°F. When cooled, squeeze the garlic puree out of each clove and set aside.

In a blender or food processor, chunk the tomatoes and tomatillos. Pour the mixture into a large mixing bowl. Then, in the blender or processor, add the jalapeños, scallions, and cilantro and blend for a few seconds; add to the mixing bowl.

Add the remaining ingredients to the bowl and stir until the mixture is well blended. Cover and chill for at least 1 hour.

Serves: 8 to 10

Guacamole with Chips

This classic Mexican dip goes well with chili. There are many variations of this recipe—from mild to wild. We add serranos to keep it hot.

4   serrano chiles, seeds and stems removed, chopped fine

3   ripe avocados, peeled, pitted, and mashed

1   small onion, minced

¼   teaspoon garlic powder

Salt to taste

Tortilla chips

Combine all the ingredients (except the chips) and allow to sit for a couple hours to blend the flavors.

Yield: 1 to 1½ cups

Trinidad Pepper Sauce Dip or Marinade

We thank our friends (and bottlers of this fine hot sauce) Mary Jane and Robert Barnes of Jacksonville Beach, Florida, for this recipe. It is an ideal dip for chips, toasted pita bread quarters, fresh crisp vegetables, or small cubes of grilled chicken breast.

1 cup Trinidad Habanero Pepper Sauce (see note)	1 cup honey (or more or less to taste)
1½ cups mayonnaise	½ cup Dijon-style mustard
½ cup fresh lime juice	2 teaspoons dry mustard

Mix all of the ingredients and refrigerate for several hours to blend the flavors.

To serve, let the dip sit at room temperature for 20 to 30 minutes to remove the chill. Stir before serving. Refrigerate any leftovers.

Yield: About 4 cups of dip

Note: Trinidad Hot Pepper Sauce is available at gourmet shops and by mail order.

Texas Salsa Verde

"This salsa is extremely versatile and can be served with all kinds of foods,"
says Pat Irvine, co-editor of the *Chilympiad Cookbook*. "It's a fun food and
gets a lot of interesting comments, especially from people who do not know
what a tomatillo is."

1   pound tomatillos

¼   cup minced cilantro

½   cup diced white onion

2 or 3 serranos or jalapeños, seeds
    and stems removed, minced

2   green onions, minced

Lemon juice to taste

Salt to taste

Drain the tomatillos if canned. If fresh, husk them and blanch them in
boiling water, covered until tender (about 12 minutes), then drain. Core the
tomatillos and mince them. Combine the tomatillos, cilantro, onion,
jalapeños, green onions, and lemon juice to taste. Add salt to taste just
before serving.

To make in a food processor, put the tomatillos, cilantro, onion, and
chiles in work bowl fitted with a steel blade, then process briefly. The
mixture should be slightly chunky. Stir in the green onions by hand and add
lemon juice and salt to taste just before serving. Serve with tortilla chips.

Serves: 6 to 8

Hot and Cold Dill Pickle Slices

This recipe comes from some people we met in the Paul Masson Wine Room in Monterey, California. We were swapping appetizer recipes, and they said this pickle recipe was a real crowd pleaser.

1   26- to 32-ounce jar of crinkle-cut dill pickle slices, most of the brine drained off

Sugar to almost fill the jar

¼   cup (or more) of hot sauce of choice

Add the sugar and hot sauce to the pickle jar and refrigerate for one week, turning the jar and shaking it slightly each day.

Serves: 6 hot-and-spicy-pickle lovers or 12 to 14 normal people

Killer Queso

This dip will whet your taste buds for more beer or margaritas and will really prime you for the meal to come. Some people have even poured a small amount of this dip over their chili con carne—is that permissible? Oh well, you can't exactly handcuff your guests, or can you?

8   ounces sharp Cheddar cheese, cut into ½-inch cubes

5   ounces Monterey Jack cheese, cut into ½-inch cubes

½ to ¾ cup milk

1   fresh habanero chile, minced, or substitute 1 teaspoon

    habanero powder or 1 teaspoon chiltepin powder

½   cup chopped green onion

¼   cup fresh tomato, finely diced

3   tablespoons chopped black olives

Place the cheeses in a double boiler, add the milk, and stir until the cheeses are melted. Add the rest of the ingredients and continue stirring until the mixture is heated through and all of the ingredients are well blended.

Serve hot with corn tortilla chips, deep-fried flour tortilla strips, or olives, pickles, and about anything else you can dip, including your finger when no one else is looking.

Serves: 4 to 6

Spicy Cashews

This nutty snack is quick to make and is positively addictive. It is something spicy to munch on while the other starters are being prepared. It can be served hot or cold, and any leftovers can be kept in an airtight container.

2 cups cashew nuts	½ teaspoon cayenne
1½ tablespoons butter or margarine	½ teaspoon ground cumin
1 teaspoon salt	

In a large skillet, fry the cashew nuts in the butter until golden brown, about 3 minutes. Drain the nuts and sprinkle the remaining ingredients over the top and toss until blended.

Serves: 4

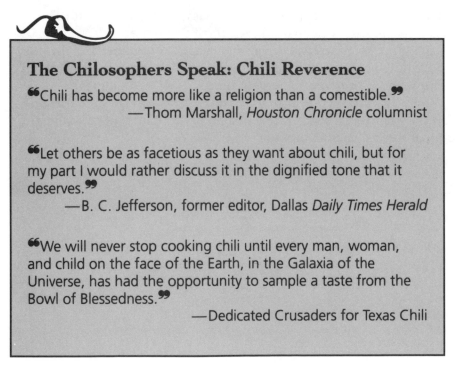

The Chilosophers Speak: Chili Reverence

❝Chili has become more like a religion than a comestible.❞
—Thom Marshall, *Houston Chronicle* columnist

❝Let others be as facetious as they want about chili, but for my part I would rather discuss it in the dignified tone that it deserves.❞
—B. C. Jefferson, former editor, Dallas *Daily Times Herald*

❝We will never stop cooking chili until every man, woman, and child on the face of the Earth, in the Galaxia of the Universe, has had the opportunity to sample a taste from the Bowl of Blessedness.❞
—Dedicated Crusaders for Texas Chili

Spicy Tortilla Spirals

The creator of this recipe, Roxanne Chan, suggests serving the spirals on a platter lined with cilantro and with a bowl of extra salsa in the middle. Roxanne submitted this recipe to the *Chile Pepper* magazine recipe contest, and we think the mix of soft and crunch and spice makes this a real appetizing appetizer.

½   cup ricotta cheese

¼   cup salsa of choice

6   6-inch fresh, soft flour tortillas

½   cup grated Cheddar cheese

½   cup cooked black beans

½   cup cooked whole corn kernels

½   cup shredded lettuce

2   jalapeños, seeds and stems removed, minced

Cilantro, for garnish on a platter

Extra salsa for dipping

In a small bowl, combine the ricotta and the salsa; spread this mixture on the tortillas. Sprinkle the Cheddar on each tortilla.

Mix the black beans, corn, lettuce, and jalapeños together and divide and spread on each tortilla. Roll up the tortillas tightly, wrap in plastic wrap, and chill for an hour or two until serving time.

To serve, cut each tortilla into 2-inch pieces and arrange on a platter lined with the cilantro garnish. Place a small bowl containing extra salsa in the middle of the arrangement.

Serves: 8

Fried Bread Puffs

These delicious puffs seem to have a counterpart in many cuisines: They are called *puris* in East Indian cookery and even have a cousin in this country— Native American fry bread. These could be used as a hot appetizer or even served in a basket to accompany a fine chili meal.

2   cups sifted all-purpose flour

1   teaspoon salt

½   teaspoon cumin (optional)

1   teaspoon ground New Mexican red chile (optional)

¼   cup butter or margarine

6   tablespoons water

Canola oil for frying

Sift together the flour, salt, cumin, and chile into a large mixing bowl.

Melt the butter and mix well with the flour. Stir in the water, mixing thoroughly with your hands.

Knead the dough for 5 to 7 minutes, pressing down hard until the dough has a satiny appearance.

Roll out the dough on a floured board until it is very thin, ⅛ to ¼ inch thick. Cut the dough into 1½-inch circles.

Heat the oil in a large frying pan or a deep-fat fryer and drop in a few dough pieces, taking care not to crowd. As soon as the dough begins to puff (about 30 seconds), press the dough down lightly with a perforated pancake turner. Turn the dough to brown lighly on the other side, about 30 seconds. Drain on paper towels.

Yield: About 32 puffs

Curried Cheese Spread

This curry spread is a palate teaser; it is good to serve before a spicy chili dinner, as the curry offers a slight bite along with the spicy chutney. It can be prepared ahead and then served with the Spicy Cashews (p. 213) for a predinner snack.

6 ounces cream cheese, softened
¾ cup sharp Cheddar cheese, shredded
½ teaspoon cayenne

1 teaspoon prepared curry powder
½ cup mango chutney, finely chopped

Garnish: thinly sliced green onions

Combine the cheeses, cayenne, and curry powder and mix thoroughly. Mound the mixture on a small serving plate, shape it into a layer about ¾ inch thick, and chill several hours until firm.

Before serving, spread the chutney over the top and sprinkle with the chopped green onions.

Serve with crisp mini-bagel rounds or any crisp cracker.

Serves: 6 to 8

Hot Chili Dip

This dip takes only a few minutes to prepare and can be made ahead of time, refrigerated, and then microwaved to reheat. It's a perfect starter while everyone is waiting for the main course to be served.

¾ pound lean ground beef or
    ground turkey

¾ cup finely chopped onion

2 cloves garlic, minced

¾ cup tomato paste

2 jalapeño or serrano chiles, seeds
   and stems removed, finely
   chopped

½ teaspoon ground cumin

Salt and ground black pepper to
    taste

½ cup shredded sharp Cheddar
    cheese

Brown the beef (or turkey); add the onion and garlic and sauté for 1 minute. Add the remaining ingredients, except the cheese, and stir to mix thoroughly.

Sprinkle the cheese over the top and heat until the cheese melts. Carefully spoon the mixture into a heated serving bowl and serve with tortilla chips, toasted mini-bagels, or toasted pita bread quarters.

Serves: 6

Armadillo Eggs

This unusual recipe is the first one listed in the *Chilympiad Cookbook,* a submission by Barbara Fox of Houston. She particularly likes this recipe because it stretches. "Because it is basically hot, a little goes a long way," says Barbara. "Besides, leftover sausage mix can be rolled into tiny balls and baked as a backup appetizer." It was also published in *Chile Pepper* magazine.

8	ounces Monterey Jack cheese, grated	2	cans whole jalapeños
1	pound pork sausage	2	eggs
1½	cups Bisquick	2	packages Oven Fry Coating Mix (pork flavor)

Preheat the oven to 325°F. Mix 6 ounces of the cheese with the sausage and Bisquick. Knead this mixture well and set aside. Slit and scrape the seeds from each jalapeño, leaving on the stems. Rinse the jalapeños and stuff with the remaining cheese. Separate the dough into patties and form around the stuffed pods. Make sure the ends are closed and only the stems are showing.

    Beat the eggs in a small bowl and set aside. Spread the coating mix on a plate. Dip each covered pepper into egg and roll in coating mix. Bake on a cookie sheet for 30 minutes, turning each one over after 15 minutes.

Serves: 6

Spicy Yogurt Dip

This tasty no-fat dip can be served with warm pita bread, warm taco-flavored tortilla chips, or fresh, crunchy vegetables such as jicama, turnip spears, broccoli, red bell pepper strips—the list is endless. Use the best of what your produce counter has to offer; just remember to combine different textures and colors for variety.

1	cup lowfat plain yogurt	1	teaspoon dry mustard
2	tablespoons minced onion	1	teaspoon commercial chili powder
1	tablespoon minced green bell pepper	¼	teaspoon ground cumin
2	tablespoons tomato paste	1	teaspoon minced Italian parsley

Combine all the ingredients and mix until well blended. Refrigerate for several hours to meld the flavors. Allow the dip to stand at room temperature for 15 to 20 minutes to remove the chill.

Serves: 4 to 5

Breaking the Gender Barrier

Because H. Allen Smith believed that "no one should be permitted to cook chili while then and there being a female person," women under the age of ninety were banned from most early chili cookoffs. But chili changed with the times when Allegani Jani Schofield and some friends created the Hell Hath No Fury Chili Society and held the women-only Susan B. Anthony Memorial Cook-In in Luckenbach. Allegani Jani went on to win at Terlingua in 1974 with her famous Hot Pants Chili.

Party Pâté

An easy blender recipe, this party pâté can be made in minutes. It will give guests or family something healthy to munch on while you deal with the "what's for dinner" syndrome. What's for dinner? Spicy, hot chili, of course!

½ cup cold V-8 juice

2 tablespoons unflavored gelatin

1 cup boiling V-8 juice

2 cups of lowfat sour cream or sour cream substitute

¼ cup chopped New Mexican green chiles

½ teaspoon Worcestershire sauce

1 tablespoon dill

7 ounces canned tuna in water, drained and flaked

Garnishes: thin slices of lime and sprigs of cilantro

In a blender, pour in the cold juice and gelatin and blend on low speed until the gelatin is soft. Add the hot juice and blend at high speed until the gelatin dissolves.

Add the remaining ingredients, except the tuna, and blend until smooth. Add the tuna and use the "stir" setting just to blend the tuna, about 5 seconds.

Pour the mixture into an oiled 5- to 6-cup mold and chill for several hours until set. Unmold onto a small platter and garnish with thin slices of lime and sprigs of cilantro.

Use as a spread on mini-bagel slices.

Serves: 10 to 12

Cheese Puffs

These "puffs" are an unusual accompaniment to chili, but the taste is complementary and the texture adds crunch. The cheese should be of the very best quality, otherwise the puffs won't have a good texture and the Swiss bite.

1 cup milk	½ teaspoon hot sauce of choice
¼ cup butter	1 cup unsifted white flour
½ teaspoon salt	4 eggs
¼ teaspoon freshly ground black pepper	1 cup shredded Swiss cheese

Heat the milk and butter in a 2-quart saucepan and add the salt, pepper, and hot sauce. Bring to a full boil and add the flour all at once, stirring over medium heat for about 2 minutes, or until the mixture leaves the sides of the pan and forms a ball.

Remove the pan from the heat and beat in the eggs by hand, one at a time, until the mixture is smooth and well blended.

Beat in half of the cheese.

Using an ice-cream scoop or a large spoon, make 8 equal mounds of dough in a circle on a greased baking sheet. Each ball of dough should just touch the adjacent ones.

Sprinkle the remaining cheese over the dough mounds.

Bake at 375°F on the center rack for 55 minutes, or until the puffs are lightly browned and crisp. Serve hot.

Serves: 8

Schrader's Brisket

Traditionally, brisket accompanies chili because it is often prepared at cookoffs. Dave and Barbara Schrader helped to produce the very first National Fiery Foods Show in El Paso in 1988. They also produce some great food in their kitchen; this brisket is one of Dave's favorites—he has to fight off their two cats, Bonnie and Clyde, in order to carve it! It's great for sandwiches; slice very thinly on the crossgrain of the meat and drizzle with the remaining juices and add some hot sauce.

1	5-pound beef brisket
¼	cup Worcestershire sauce
¼	cup teriyaki sauce
3	tablespoons lemon-pepper marinade

1	large red onion, sliced
1	can beer

Place the brisket in a small roasting pan (that has a cover that fits tightly) and sprinkle the Worcestershire and teriyaki sauces over the top. Sprinkle with the lemon-pepper marinade and arrange the red onion slices over the top. Drizzle the beer over the top of the roast and into the roasting pan.

Bake at 225°F for 8 hours, covered tightly, and check periodically for moisture. Add some water, or more beer, if the roast starts to dry out.

Serves: 1 hungry Doberman, 4 hungry cats, or 6 to 8 humans

Garlic Yogurt Dressing

This multipurpose dressing can be used over almost everything—from a salad of winter greens to a diced, fresh vegetable salad. It could also be used as a dip for spicy chips or vegetables.

½ cup plain yogurt

1 avocado, peeled

1 garlic clove, mashed

1 teaspoon fresh lemon juice

½ teaspoon dried dill, thyme, or savory

Salt and ground black pepper to taste

Hot sauce to taste (optional)

Combine all of the ingredients and beat until thick and creamy. If the dressing seems too thick, add a little more yogurt and beat it in.

Yield: ¾ cup

Note: If the dressing has more of a bite than you like, add a few grains of sugar to the dressing.

Mixed Bean Salad

If you're making chili with only a few beans, or no beans at all, try this chilled bean salad as a side dish. The herb-and-garlic dressing, plus a little marinade from the artichokes, adds a nice contrast to the chili.

1   16-ounce can yellow wax beans, or use fresh—cut into 1-inch lengths, steamed, and chilled—about 1½ cups

1½ cups fresh or frozen green beans, steamed, chilled, and cut into 1-inch lengths

1   16-ounce can kidney beans, drained and rinsed

½   cup coarsely chopped black olives

1   tablespoon capers, drained

1   jar marinated artichoke hearts, drained, and reserve marinade

½   cup of your favorite herb-and-garlic dressing

Mix all of the ingredients and chill thoroughly. Before serving, toss the vegetables to distribute the salad dressing.

Serves: 8 to 10

Spinach Salad

Of all the spinach salads we've ever had, this one is definitely our favorite. It has zip and bite—and you can make it even zippier with the addition of more Tabasco or any other hot sauce. This is not a salad for the faint-hearted —the bacon and the fat add a rich flavor as well as monumental calories, but it is *sooooo* good!

¼ pound bacon, cut into small pieces

3 tablespoons bacon fat, reserved from the fried bacon, or substitute vegetable oil

Juice of ½ lemon

Big dash Worcestershire sauce

Several dashes of Tabasco sauce (more or less to taste)

2 to 3 tablespoons cider vinegar

2 tablespoons Dijon-style mustard

¼ teaspoon freshly ground black pepper

1 tablespoon brown sugar

1 large bunch fresh spinach, cleaned and torn into bite-sized pieces

Sauté the bacon in a medium skillet until crisp and well done. Remove the bacon and drain on a paper towel, reserving 3 tablespoons of the bacon fat (or drain the fat from the skillet and substitute the vegetable oil).

Heat the fat/oil in the skillet and add all of the remaining ingredients, except the spinach, stirring until the mixture is hot and well blended.

Place the spinach into a large bowl and sprinkle with the drained bacon. Pour the hot mixture over the top, toss quickly, and serve immediately.

Serves: 4 to 5

The Cool-Down Salad

This is perfect to serve with a particularly hot chili!

2   fresh peaches, peeled and diced
     into ½-inch cubes

2   heads Bibb lettuce, torn into
     bite-sized pieces

¼   pound prosciutto ham, diced

¼   pound white button
     mushrooms, cleaned and sliced

Vinaigrette dressing or your
favorite oil-and-vinegar
dressing

Combine the salad ingredients and chill. Just before serving, dress the salad with the vinaigrette and serve.

Yield: 4 large salads or 6 medium salads

The Chilosophers Speak: Exaltations

"We thought for years that if there's such a thing as a national American dish, it isn't apple pie, it's chili con carne. . . . In one form or another, chili in America knows no regional boundaries. North, South, East, and West, almost every man, woman, and child has a favorite recipe.**"**

—Craig Claiborne

"Chili. A standard item of diet in the Texas cornucopia of succulent comestibles . . . the most glorious concoction that ever soothed the inward man, put the glow of health in his cheeks, and calmed his baser instincts, like throwing a meat cleaver at the cook for burning the toast, or shooting the hostess for putting sugar in the cornbread.**"**

—Abilene *Reporter News*

Galveston Gazpacho Salad

Serve this salad along with the chili, or serve it as a separate course as the chili pops and sputters on the stove. The fresh ingredients will prepare your mouth for the hot and spicy feast to come. Serve one of our delicious hot breads or muffins from this chapter along with the salad.

2   medium cucumbers, peeled and thinly sliced

1   teaspoon salt

⅔   cup good quality olive oil

⅓   cup wine vinegar

1   garlic clove, minced

1   teaspoon dried basil

1   teaspoon dried savory

A few grains of sugar

½   teaspoon salt

½   teaspoon freshly ground black pepper

10   white button mushrooms, cleaned and sliced

4   scallions, thinly sliced

½   cup minced parsley (Italian parsley preferred)

3   large tomatoes, peeled and chopped

1   medium green bell pepper, chopped

Place the cucumber slices in a bowl and sprinkle with the 1 teaspoon salt and allow to stand for 30 minutes.

In a 1½-cup jar, combine the olive oil, vinegar, garlic, basil, savory, sugar, salt, and pepper. Shake vigorously and pour into a large bowl. Add the mushrooms and scallions and stir.

Rinse the cucumbers under cold water and pat dry. Add to the mushroom mixture. Then add the parsley and mix.

Spoon the tomatoes over the top and spread them evenly and top with the bell pepper. Cover the bowl and chill for at least 4 hours.

Just before serving, gently toss the salad and serve on chilled salad plates.

Serves: 8

Low-key Lime Citrus Salad

A little bit of citrus in the dressing of this salad gives it a nice bite to contrast the taste of the chili. It's refreshing, crunchy, and a perfect partner for dinner. Besides, all that citrus juice is good for you.

Dressing

¾ cup canola oil

¼ cup fresh orange juice

¼ cup freshly squeezed lime juice

2 tablespoons granulated sugar

2 tablespoons white wine vinegar

¼ teaspoon salt

½ teaspoon paprika

3 tablespoons chopped fresh mint or 2 tablespoons dried mint

1 garlic clove, mashed

Combine all the ingredients in a jar and shake vigorously. Refrigerate the dressing until ready to use. Shake well before using.

Salad

Jicama, cubed

Red onion, sliced

Button mushrooms, raw

Radiccio

Belgian endive

Prepare equal portions (or your preferred ratio) of salad ingredients, and generously drizzle with the dressing immediately before serving.

Yield: 1¼ cups

Jicama and Orange Salad

This interesting combination comes from Pat Irvine of Seguin, Texas. "It's a cool and refreshing salad," says Pat. "I also like the different textures of the ingredients." Pat has served on the board of the Chili Appreciation Society International. This recipe first appeared in *Chile Pepper* magazine.

1	head romaine lettuce	½	cup olive oil
½	pound jicama, peeled and sliced paper thin	6	tablespoons lime juice
		3	tablespoons red wine vinegar
6	seedless oranges, peeled and sectioned	1	teaspoon salt
		3	tablespoons orange marmalade
2	red onions, sliced		Freshly ground pepper

Line a shallow bowl with the romaine. Alternate overlapping circles of jicama and oranges on the romaine. Cover and refrigerate (it can be prepared 3 hours ahead). Combine the remaining ingredients in a jar and shake well. Pour the dressing over the salad and serve immediately.

Serves: 4 to 6

Green Chile Coleslaw

This recipe is from *Chile Pepper* food editor Nancy Gerlach, who remarks: "The texture of this crispy cabbage salad goes well with chili con carne. Mix the salad and make the dressing ahead of time to blend the flavors, but combine the two just before serving to prevent the salad from becoming soggy."

Slaw

6   New Mexican green chiles, roasted and peeled, seeds and stems removed, chopped

½   head green cabbage, shredded

½   head red cabbage, shredded

1   small onion, finely chopped

Cilantro

Combine all the ingredients and let sit refrigerated for 2 hours.

Dressing

⅛   teaspoon cayenne

½   cup mayonnaise

1   tablespoon sugar

1   tablespoon white vinegar

½   teaspoon celery seed

⅛   teaspoon white pepper

Salt to taste

Combine all the ingredients and let sit refrigerated for 2 hours.

Before serving, combine the dressing with the salad and garnish with fresh cilantro.

Serves: 6 to 8

Real Corn and Corn Muffins

These are rich muffins because of the addition of the creamed corn. If you want some variations, we suggest adding some ground red chile to the dry ingredients or some chopped green chile, but make sure the green chile has had all of the excess liquid blotted out of it.

½ cup all-purpose flour	1 can good quality cream-style corn
¼ teaspoon baking powder	
1 teaspoon salt	⅔ cup milk
1 tablespoon sugar	1 egg, beaten
1 cup cornmeal	2 tablespoons melted margarine

Sift the dry ingredients, add the cornmeal, and mix together. Add the corn, milk, egg, and margarine and mix well.

Pour the mixture into 12 greased muffin tins or nonstick pans and bake at 450°F for 20 minutes or until golden brown.

Yield: 12 muffins

Jalapeño Cornbread

Here's another recipe from Nancy Gerlach, who notes: "You can vary the heat of this bread by decreasing the amount of jalapeño or by substituting peeled and chopped green chiles. Use blue cornmeal in place of the yellow for a real northern New Mexican speciality."

1 cup cornmeal	1½ cups buttermilk
1 cup flour	2 tablespoons minced jalapeños
2 teaspoons sugar	1 cup minced onion
1 teaspoon baking soda	2 eggs, beaten
1 teaspoon baking powder	1 cup Cheddar cheese, grated
1 teaspoon salt	3 tablespoons bacon drippings or
¼ teaspoon garlic powder	shortening

Combine all the dry ingredients in a large bowl.

Heat the buttermilk with the jalapeños and onion and let cool. Combine the eggs and cheese. Add the milk, eggs, and cheese to the dry ingredients and blend until smooth.

Pour into a greased 9-inch square pan and bake at 425°F for 40 to 50 minutes or until the cornbread is golden brown.

Serves: 6

Casserole Bread

This is a fast and easy bread to make while your pot of chili is simmering on the stove. Serve the bread warm and listen to the raves. The recipe can be varied by adding red chile powder, minced onion, or chopped green chile that has had all the excess moisture squeezed out with paper towels.

1	cup milk	1	cup warm water
3	tablespoons sugar	2	packages yeast (4 teaspoons)
1	tablespoon salt	4½	cups unbleached white flour
1½	tablespoons shortening		

Scald the milk and stir in the sugar, salt, and shortening. Cool the mixture to lukewarm.

Pour the warm water into a large bowl and sprinkle with the yeast. Stir until the yeast is dissolved. Stir in the cooled milk mixture.

Add the flour and stir until well blended, about 2 minutes.

Cover and let the mixture rise in a warm place until more than doubled in bulk, about 40 minutes.

Stir the batter down and beat for 30 seconds. Pour the batter into a greased 1½-quart casserole.

Bake at 375°F for 50 to 60 minutes.

Yield: 1 loaf

Ann's Pita Bread

Even though pita bread is readily available almost everywhere, our friend Ann's recipe is superb as well as easy to make. Besides, there's nothing like the smell of bread baking to whet the appetite for the pot of chili cooking on top of the stove—the perfect antidote for a cold winter night.

½	cup warm water	3	tablespoons olive oil
2	packages yeast (4 teaspoons)	2	teaspoons salt
¼	teaspoon sugar	2	cups warm water
6	cups unbleached white flour		

Combine the ½ cup water with the yeast and sugar. Stir until the yeast is dissolved and begins to bubble a little. Let the mixture sit for 5 minutes.

Sift the flour into a large bowl; add the olive oil, salt, and warm water and stir well. Beat in the yeast mixture until thoroughly blended.

Knead the dough for 10 minutes on a floured board. Oil a bowl and turn dough in the bowl to coat it on all sides. Cover the bowl and let the dough rise 2 hours or until doubled.

Punch the dough down and knead it for 3 minutes. Then roll the dough and stretch out into a thick sausage-like roll 15 inches long and 3 inches wide.

Cut the roll into 15 equal pieces and pat each piece into a ball. Roll the balls into circles about 6 inches in diameter and ⅛ inch thick.

Place the circles on foil and let stand for 1 hour until the dough rises again.

Preheat the oven to 500°F. Leave the dough circles on the foil and put directly into the hot oven on the lowest shelf. Bake 3 to 5 minutes until the bread puffs up and browns.

Serve warm with a bowl of chili.

Yield: 15 pita breads

Margarita Pie

What a great finale for a chili dinner! This one is tart and light and really fills your mouth with flavor. The jury is still out on the crust—we prefer a pretzel crust (included here), but many of our friends insist that a graham cracker crust is the way to go. Make your choice.

¾ cup pretzel crumbs

5 tablespoons melted butter or margarine

2 tablespoons sugar

1 envelope plain gelatin

½ cup fresh lime juice (or use half lime juice and half lemon juice)

4 eggs, separated

1 cup sugar

1 teaspoon grated lime zest

¼ cup Jose Cuervo Gold tequila

3 tablespoons Cointreau or Triple Sec

Combine the crumbs, butter, and sugar and press the mixture into a 9-inch pie plate. Chill.

Sprinkle the gelatin over the lime juice and let the mixture set for a few minutes until it is soft.

Beat the egg yolks in the top of a double boiler and add ½ cup of the sugar and the lime zest and continue beating. Add the gelatin and continue cooking over the boiling water, stirring constantly until the mixture is slightly thickened. Pour this mixture into a bowl and blend in the tequila and Cointreau. Chill this mixture for 20 to 30 minutes.

Beat the egg whites until frothy and foamy and gradually add the remaining ½ cup of sugar; continue beating until stiff peaks form. Fold the whipped whites into the chilled, cooked mixture and pour into the crust and chill until set, 4 to 5 hours.

Serves: 8

San Antonio Strawberry Pie

San Antonio was probably the home of chili, so it's appropriate to serve a pie from that Riverwalk city.

1 9-inch prepared pie pan with a graham cracker crust	1 tablespoon fresh lemon juice
	Dash salt
10 ounces frozen strawberries	½ cup whipping cream, whipped
1 cup sugar	1 teaspoon vanilla or almond extract
2 egg whites	

Thaw the strawberries in a colander, and when they reach room temperature combine them in a big mixing bowl with the sugar, egg whites, lemon juice, and dash of salt. Beat this mixture until very stiff, about 15 to 20 minutes.

Fold the whipped cream and vanilla extract into the beaten berry mixture and pour into the prepared pie crust. Freeze the dessert for 2 to 3 hours, or until very firm.

Serves: 8

Watermelon Ice

This is an unusual and tasty dessert because the ice ends up resembling a soft sherbet. It's cooling to the taste buds and will perk them up after all that blazing chili.

6	cups watermelon, cut into ½-inch cubes, seeds removed	¾	cup sugar
		¼	cup fresh lemon juice

Place 2 cups of the watermelon cubes in a blender and blend at high speed for about 15 seconds, or until the watermelon is pureed. Pour into a bowl and repeat with the remaining cubes.

Stir the sugar and lemon juice into the pureed watermelon until the mixture is well blended.

Pour into sherbet glasses and freeze for 1½ to 2 hours or until the mixture is almost firm but still easily spoonable. Serve immediately.

Serves: 6 to 8

Chimayo Chocolate Cake

This is not just any chocolate cake—it is rich and creamy, with the unusual addition of sour cream to the frosting to cut through some of the sweetness and cool the palate. It is also impressive to serve; after it is cut and frosted, it stands high and mighty.

¾ cup semisweet chocolate chips
½ cup walnuts
3 eggs
½ cup granulated sugar
½ cup light brown sugar
2 tablespoons butter
2½ teaspoons cinnamon
1 cup buttermilk
1 teaspoon vanilla

2 cups sifted flour
1½ teaspoons baking powder
½ teaspoon baking soda
¼ teaspoon salt
1 6-ounce package semisweet chocolate chips
1 cup sour cream
½ teaspoon ground cinnamon

Preheat the oven to 350°F and grease a 10-inch tube pan.

Chop the ¾ cup of chocolate chips and the walnuts together in a blender.

In a large bowl, beat the eggs and add the sugars and butter and beat well. Fold in the chopped chocolate and walnuts, and then add the cinnamon, buttermilk, and vanilla.

Gently fold in the flour, baking powder, soda, and salt until the dry ingredients are well blended. Pour the mixture into the greased tube pan and bake at 350°F for 45 to 60 minutes.

Cool the cake in the pan on a wire rack for several minutes until the pan is cool enough to handle. Turn the cake out on the wire rack to finish cooling completely and then slice it horizontally into 3 layers.

Melt the 6 ounces of chocolate chips in the top of a double boiler and then remove the chocolate and let it cool slightly. Stir in the sour cream and cinnamon. If the mixture seems a little runny, refrigerate it for a minute, then test the consistency.

Spread the frosting between the layers and on the outside of the cake.

Serves: 12 to 14

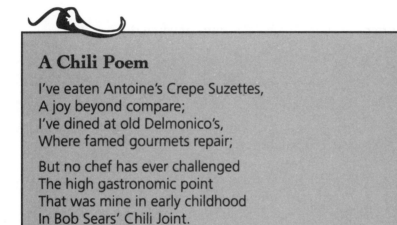

A Chili Poem

I've eaten Antoine's Crepe Suzettes,
A joy beyond compare;
I've dined at old Delmonico's,
Where famed gourmets repair;

But no chef has ever challenged
The high gastronomic point
That was mine in early childhood
In Bob Sears' Chili Joint.
                    —Carlos Ashley, Sr., Texas Poet Laureate, 1949–51

Sour Cream Apple Bake

A fruit dessert is always a good choice to serve after a hot and spicy bowl of chili. This one can be served hot or cold, and the sour cream and lemon really do seem to refresh your mouth.

3	tablespoons butter	4	eggs, separated
4	large, tart cooking apples, peeled and sliced	1	teaspoon grated lemon zest
		1	teaspoon vanilla
1	cup granulated sugar	½	cup sour cream
2	tablespoons fresh lemon juice		

Optional garnishes: powdered sugar and whipped cream

Melt the butter in a large skillet and add the apples, ⅔ cup of the sugar, and the lemon juice and cook over medium heat, turning the apple slices until they are tender and glazed and most of the juices have dissipated.

Place half of the glazed apples in a 7-by-12-inch baking pan or in an ovenproof 10½-inch frying pan. Reserve the remaining apple slices for the topping.

Beat the egg whites until soft peaks form and then gradually add the remaining sugar, beating until the whites are stiff. In another bowl, beat the egg yolks until thick and then mix in the lemon zest, vanilla, and sour cream; fold into the beaten egg whites.

Spoon the egg mixture over the apples in the pan and arrange the remaining slices over the top.

Bake at 350°F for 25 minutes, or until the soufflé is puffed and lightly browned. Dust with powdered sugar.

Serve hot or cold. Add a dollop of whipping cream if desired.

Serves: 6 to 8

Fresh Apple Pastry Squares

This easy, make-ahead dessert is perfect to serve after you've been slaving over a hot pot of chili all day. The baked apples and the spices blend "tastefully" with the tender, flaky crust.

2½ cups unsifted all-purpose flour

1 teaspoon salt

1 cup plus 2 tablespoons butter or margarine

1 egg yolk

Milk

1 cup crushed corn flakes cereal

8 cups tart apples, peeled, cored, and sliced

⅔ cup sugar

½ teaspoon ground ginger

½ teaspoon ground nutmeg

½ teaspoon ground cinnamon

1 egg white, stiffly beaten

½ cup sifted powdered sugar

Preheat the oven to 400°F. Place the flour and salt in a large bowl and cut in the butter with a pastry blender until it is crumbly and well blended.

In a measuring cup, beat the egg yolk lightly and add enough milk to make ⅔ cup. Stir the egg mixture into the flour and mix with a fork to blend, stirring until the mixture holds together and cleans the side of the bowl.

Divide the dough into two equal parts. Roll one part of the dough to line a 15½-by-10½-inch low-side pan. Place the dough in the pan, pressing down lightly. This dough will be the bottom crust of the dessert.

Sprinkle the bottom crust with the corn flakes.

In a large bowl, mix the apples, sugar, and spices. Spread the mixture evenly over the bottom crust.

Roll out the remaining dough and place on top of the apple mixture. Pinch the edges of the dough together to seal it. Brush the beaten egg white over the top for a glaze.

Bake at 400°F for 50 to 60 minutes, or until the pastry is golden brown. Let the pastry cool slightly and then sprinkle with the sifted powdered sugar. Cut into squares and serve warm or at room temperature.

Serves: 12 to 14

Frozen Waldorf Dessert

Traditionally, this dish is served as a salad, but we've added the whipped cream and dressed it up—suitable for a dessert and maybe too rich for a salad. It's fruity and cold and the perfect finale for a chili dinner.

2   eggs, slightly beaten
½   cup granulated sugar
½   cup pineapple juice
¼   cup fresh lemon juice
⅛   teaspoon salt
½   cup diced celery

½   cup drained crushed pineapple (in natural juices)
2   medium apples, peeled and diced
½   cup coarsely chopped walnuts
1   cup whipping cream, whipped

In a double boiler, combine the eggs, sugar, pineapple juice, lemon juice, and salt. Cook over low heat, stirring constantly until the mixture is thick. Set aside to cool.

When the mixture is cooled, stir in the celery, pineapple, apples, and walnuts. Then gently fold in the whipped cream and pour the mixture into an 8-inch square pan, cover tightly with foil, and freeze for several hours.

To serve, cut into squares, according to each diner's appetite. Serve on small, chilled dessert plates.

Serves: 6 to 9

Mexican Fruit Cake

This luscious, rich, crunchy cake is for those of you who have a serious sweet tooth. It's easy to make and easy to frost. We like it after chili because of the fruit and the crunch; it's a good textural contrast.

1   20-ounce can crushed pineapple, with juice

2   cups flour

1   cup chopped walnuts or pecans

2   teaspoons baking soda

2   cups granulated sugar

2   eggs

1   8-ounce package cream cheese, softened

2   cups powdered sugar

1   stick melted butter or margarine

1   teaspoon vanilla

In a large bowl, pour in the pineapple, flour, nuts, baking soda, sugar, and eggs and beat thoroughly with an electric mixer. Pour into a 13-by-9-inch pan and bake at 350°F for 45 minutes (35 minutes if a glass pan is used). Place the cake (in the pan) on a cooling rack while you make the frosting. Have everything ready because the cake needs to be frosted while it is still hot.

In a large bowl, whip the cream cheese, powdered sugar, melted butter, and vanilla. Spread the frosting on the hot cake.

Serves: 4 to 8, depending on the sweet-tooth contingent

Fried Fresh Cherries

This dessert is particularly good when those sweet, red cherries are readily available. It's best served warm from the pan and sprinkled with sugar and cinnamon.

1   cup flour
¼   cup granulated sugar
¼   teaspoon salt
⅓   cup milk
½   cup dry white wine
3   eggs, slightly beaten

1   pound ripe red cherries, stems intact
½   cup powdered sugar
1   teaspoon cinnamon
Canola oil for frying

Mix together the flour, sugar, salt, milk, and wine and stir in the eggs. Continue stirring until the batter is smooth.

Dip a small cluster of cherries (3 to 5) into the batter, making sure they are well coated. Quickly drop them into the hot canola oil and fry until the batter is lightly browned.

Remove the cherries quickly and drain on paper towels. Sprinkle the cherries with a mixture of the powdered sugar and cinnamon.

Continue dipping and frying the remaining cherries and sprinkle with the sugar mixture. Serve immediately.

Serves: 6

Mocha Spice Delight

This recipe has many variations, as it is a very popular dessert in eastern Mediterranean countries, where ultra-rich sweets and candies are part of the cultures. It works well as a dessert accompanying a spicy chili dinner.

2   cups brown sugar

2   cups sifted all-purpose flour

½   cup butter

¼   teaspoon salt

1   teaspoon grated orange zest

2   tablespoons Espresso-style instant coffee

1   teaspoon ground cinnamon

¼   teaspoon ground nutmeg

1   teaspoon baking soda

1   cup sour cream

1   egg, beaten with a fork

½   cup chopped nuts

Preheat oven to 350°F. Combine the sugar, flour, butter, salt, zest, coffee, cinnamon, and nutmeg in a medium mixing bowl and blend well with a pastry blender until the mixture is crumbly.

Grease a 9-inch square cake pan and spoon in half of the spiced crumb mixture.

Stir the baking soda into the sour cream and add this to the remaining crumb mixture, then add the egg, and stir to mix. Pour this mixture over the crumbs in the pan and sprinkle with the chopped nuts.

Bake for 40 to 45 minutes or until a toothpick comes out clean.

Serve warm, plain or topped with orange-flavored whipped cream. It is just as delicious when served at room temperature, topped with mocha or cinnamon ice cream.

Serves: 9

Chocoholic Delight

Even though this dessert is on the extremely rich side, it is still delicious and satisfying to sink your teeth into. Perhaps it's the sweetness and the coldness combined, but whatever the reason, treat your taste buds because this dessert is definitely a splurge!

2	cups pecans	16	ounces semisweet chocolate
¾	cup granulated sugar	1	egg yolk
¼	cup butter, melted	2	cups whipping cream

Preheat the oven to 375°F. Place the pecans, sugar, and melted butter in a food processor or blender and pulverize. Transfer to a 9- or 10-inch springform or tart pan and press the mixture firmly on the bottom of the pan and about ½ inch up the sides.

Bake the crust for 10 minutes, or until golden brown. Remove the shell from the oven and set on a wire rack to cool.

Melt the chocolate in a double boiler and then beat the egg yolk into the chocolate.

In a second double boiler, heat the cream until it is scalding. Gradually beat the hot cream into the melted chocolate mixture.

Pour this mixture into the prepared crust and chill in the refrigerator for at least 2 hours, or until cool and firm.

Serves: 6 to 8

Elegant Poached Pears

Prepare this ahead of time; then all it needs is a quick reheating and a topping of coffee ice cream. It is another cool-down for overtaxed chili taste buds.

3   pears, cored, peeled, and halved
½   teaspoon whole anise seed
½   cup dry white wine
½   cup granulated sugar

⅓   cup water
2   ounces brandy
Coffee ice cream

Place the pears in a large nonreactive saucepan, sprinkle with the anise seed, and pour the white wine over the top.

In a small saucepan, heat the sugar and water and stir until the sugar has dissolved. Pour this mixture over the pears in the large saucepan. Heat the mixture and simmer for 15 minutes. Remove the pan from the heat and let stand until cool.

To serve, reheat, add the brandy, and stir in the liquid, being careful not to mash the pears.

Place 2 drained pear halves on each dessert plate and top with coffee ice cream. Serve immediately.

Serves: 3

Cinnamon Peach Bake

This dessert is special to us because we make it only when we get our annual fresh peach pack from our good friend and grower Jeff Campbell of Stonewall, Texas. Jeff's peaches are "to die for." They are the biggest, juiciest critters that we have ever come across, and we just know we are going to get flak from the state of Georgia on this one!

3   medium fresh peaches (if using Jeff's, 2 peaches will do!)
¼   cup frozen orange juice concentrate
1½ cups flour
½   cup plus 3 tablespoons sugar
2   teaspoons baking powder

1   teaspoon grated orange zest
½   teaspoon grated lemon zest
½   teaspoon salt
2   eggs, beaten
¼   cup butter, melted
½   teaspoon cinnamon

Peel and quarter the peaches and place them in a small bowl. Toss the peaches with the orange juice concentrate and place in a colander over a bowl to drain for an hour or so; reserve the drained juice. The orange juice keeps the peaches from turning brown and also adds flavor to the "drippings."

Combine the flour, the ½ cup sugar, the baking powder, orange zest, lemon zest, and salt, then set aside.

Mix the eggs with 2 tablespoons of the drained juice and the melted butter. Pour this into the dry ingredients and stir just to blend slightly. Spread this batter into a greased tart, quiche, or springform pan with removable sides, 8½ inches in diameter and at least 1 inch deep.

Using paper towels, dry off the peach pieces as thoroughly as you can. Place the peaches evenly, cut side down, on the batter. Sprinkle with the remaining sugar and the cinnamon.

Bake at 400°F for 25 minutes, or until a toothpick inserted into the center comes out clean. Place on a wire rack to cool. Remove from the pan and serve.

Serves: 5 to 6

Cheese Tarts

We thank our friend Dick Fosco for this recipe. He gave it to us years ago, and we are still making his cheese tarts! They are easy to make, freeze well, and can be topped with fresh berries. It is a light and tangy cool-down after a ferocious chili dinner.

20 vanilla wafer cookies	¾ cup sugar
20 cupcake papers	1 tablespoon fresh lemon juice
16 ounces softened cream cheese	1 teaspoon vanilla extract
2 eggs	

Place a vanilla wafer on the bottom of each cupcake paper and put the papers into muffin tins.

Whip the remaining ingredients together for a minute or two. Fill each cupcake paper half to two-thirds full.

Bake at 375°F for about 20 minutes. Cool for 5 minutes.

Serve warm or chilled, with or without a fresh fruit topping.

Yield: 20 tarts

Note: The recipe can be doubled, and the remainders freeze very well.

Creamy Lemon Pudding

Creamy and totally fulfilling, this dessert would almost make you want to skip dinner! It's rich and lemony, but if you live in an area where limes are abundant, they are a wonderful alternative. Fresh berries can also be added. This pudding could be served in glass dessert bowls or in puff pastry containers. A big boon to the chef—the pudding actually tastes best if it's left in the refrigerator overnight.

4	egg yolks	2	teaspoons grated lemon rind
½	cup sugar	1	cup whipping cream, whipped
3	tablespoons fresh lemon juice		

Beat the egg yolks until they are thick and creamy. Then gradually beat in the sugar and add the juice and the rind.

Cook this mixture in a double boiler over hot water for 5 to 8 minutes, stirring constantly, until thick. Remove the mixture from the heat and chill in the refrigerator until cool. Then fold in the whipped cream and chill for several hours or overnight.

Serves: 4 to 5

Broiled Grapefruit

Often, the simplest dessert is the best, especiallly after a belly-scorching bowl of chili. We prefer citrus recipes, as they are not only simple, but refreshing as well. This one takes just minutes to prepare.

2   large fresh grapefruits, sliced in half   8   tablespoons grenadine syrup

Spoon 2 tablespoons of the grenadine over each grapefruit half.

Place the halves under the broiler for a minute or two and then serve. Garnish with a fresh mint sprig, if desired.

Serves: 4

Variation: Use Campari for a different taste or use an almond-flavored liqueur for a sweeter taste.

The Chilosophers Speak: Visuals

"A true Texas bowl of red is a stunning vision, reminiscent of a Technicolor sunset created in a Hollywood studio: opaque currents of molten mahogany, lustrous orange, and cordovan are flecked with grains of spice and swirled with rivulets of limpid grease.**"**

—Jane and Michael Stern

Frozen Almond Crème

The dessert is simple, rich, and high in calories, but it sure is good!

1   cup whipping cream
1   pint vanilla ice cream
¼   cup almond-flavored liqueur

⅓   cup almonds, toasted and
    chopped

Whip the cream until stiff peaks form, then soften the ice cream with the same beater.

Combine the cream, ice cream, and liqueur. Pour the mixture into cupcake papers set in muffin tins.

Sprinkle with the chopped almonds and freeze until firm.

Serves: 6

Almond Peach Soufflé

Don't let the title intimidate you; this soufflé is simple to prepare and the only special item needed is a soufflé dish. Most people have one or two lying around. If you don't, buy one—they are also great for serving summer fruit salads and potato salads.

1½ cups fresh peach slices	5 egg whites
¾ cup macaroon crumbs	½ cup butter or margarine
3 tablespoons almond-flavored liqueur	½ cup granulated sugar
	4 egg yolks

Crush the peaches and combine with the macaroon crumbs and liqueur. Set aside.

Beat the egg whites until stiff and set aside.

Cream the butter and sugar, adding the egg yolks, one at a time, and beating thoroughly after each addition.

Combine the peach mixture and the egg yolk mixture, and then fold in the beaten egg whites.

Pour the mixture into a buttered and sugared soufflé dish. Bake at 350°F for 35 minutes, or until it is well puffed.

Serve while warm and still puffed (it will sink just a little as it cools).

Serves: 6 to 8

Poached Oranges

Once again, here's a dessert that is easy, can be prepared ahead of time, and gives a citrus kick to those chili taste buds. This one is quite basic, but it gets nods of approval after a feisty chili dinner.

6   large navel oranges   ¾   cup water
1½ cups sugar

Carefully peel the oranges and remove the white membrane.

Julienne enough of the rind to make 6 tablespoons of slivers.

In a nonreactive metal or enamel pot, combine the slivers with the sugar and water. Cook over moderate heat without stirring for 8 minutes, or until the syrup thickens slightly.

Place the whole, peeled oranges in a nonreactive skillet and pour the syrup over them.

Cook over low heat, basting the oranges constantly for 5 minutes.

Remove the oranges from the heat and chill, basting occasionally with the syrup.

Serve very cold on small dessert plates.

Serves: 6

Strawberry-Pear Sorbet

Here is another delicious and light dessert to cool those flaming taste buds.

3	medium ripe pears	2	fresh egg whites
⅓	cup fresh lemon juice		
2	cups fresh strawberries, cleaned, with stems removed		

Garnishes: whole strawberries and sliced pears

Peel, core, and cut up the pears. Puree with the lemon juice to make 2 cups.

Puree enough strawberries to make 1¾ cups and then pour the pureed berries through a sieve, pressing down with a wooden spoon.

Combine the two purees and pour into metal freezer trays, cover with foil, and freeze until the mixture is almost firm.

Beat the egg whites until they form soft peaks. Gradually beat in the firm puree mixture and pour this into 2 metal freezer trays and freeze until firm.

Spoon the mixture into small dessert bowls and garnish with whole berries and pear slices.

Serves: 4 to 6

Old-fashioned Sugar Cookies with Lemon Zest

Practically nobody makes homemade cookies these days, and they are *soooooo* good! Our busy schedules sometimes don't allow us to prepare these great treats, but do make these cookies—bake, cool, and freeze them. Nothing gets lost in the process, and the recipe can even be doubled. Mary Jane has been making these for years, since she was in the seventh grade, as a matter of fact!

½	cup margarine	2	cups sifted unbleached white flour
½	teaspoon salt		
¾	teaspoon grated lemon zest	1	teaspoon baking powder
½	teaspoon nutmeg	½	teaspoon baking soda
1	cup granulated sugar	2	tablespoons milk
2	eggs		

Combine the first six ingredients in a bowl and beat until smooth.

Sift the flour with the baking powder and soda, and add to the first mixture; add the milk and mix until well blended.

Drop level tablespoons of the dough on a greased cookie sheet. Flatten each cookie by stamping with a flat-bottomed glass covered with a damp cloth. Then, sprinkle each cookie with granulated sugar.

Bake at 375°F for 10 to 12 minutes. Cool on a wire rack and store in an airtight container, or put in freezer bags and freeze for future munching.

Serve with chocolate frozen yogurt or chocolate-mint ice cream.

Yield: About 3 dozen cookies

Ginger Cookies

This cookie is another old-fashioned favorite of ours. It takes only a little time to prepare and can be frozen for future use. The ginger taste refreshes your mouth, and, when served with vanilla yogurt or ice cream, the taste buds really tingle. Cookies and ice cream—what a simple but classic dessert, especially when you go the extra mile with homemade cookies. When was the last time you had a good homemade cookie?

¾	cup shortening	2	cups unbleached white flour
1	cup granulated sugar	1	teaspoon ground ginger
1	egg	1	teaspoon ground cinnamon
¼	cup molasses	¼	teaspoon salt
2	teaspoons baking soda		

Cream the shortening, sugar, egg, and molasses until light.

Sift the remaining ingredients together and add to the creamed mixture and mix thoroughly.

Roll the dough into 1-inch balls, dip the balls into granulated sugar, and place on a lightly greased cookie sheet.

Bake at 350°F for 13 to 15 minutes.

Cool on a wire rack.

Yield: About 3½ dozen cookies

Easy Crème Brûlée

Many cuisines claim this dessert as their own—in France, it's called Crème Brûlée; in Spain it is called flan. It's a delicious, creamy, and refreshing finale to any dinner, especially one that has been spiked with a few chiles.

12	vanilla caramels (Kraft preferred)	2	cups milk
¼	cup milk	⅓	cup sugar
4	eggs	¼	teaspoon salt

Heat the caramels and milk in a double boiler, stirring occasionally, until the caramels are melted. Pour into a 1½-quart baking dish or divide into six 6-ounce custard cups.

Beat together the milk, eggs, sugar, and salt until light and fluffy.

Carefully pour the milk mixture over the sauce in the baking dish or custard cups.

Place the prepared dishes into a larger pan; fill the larger pan with hot water to a 1-inch depth.

Bake at 350°F for 30 to 40 minutes, or until the center is nearly set. Serve warm or cold.

Serves: 6

Microwave Pralines

After all this good chili, some people might skip dessert—but not if it's Microwave Pralines by Jean Dillard! This recipe was originally published in *Chile Pepper* magazine.

1   box light brown sugar
½   pint whipping cream
1½ teaspoons vanilla

½   stick margarine
2   cups pecan halves

Mix the brown sugar and whipping cream in a large, microwave-safe bowl. Cook in the microwave on high for 12 minutes. Stir and add the vanilla and margarine. Microwave 2 minutes more. Add the pecans, stir, and microwave 2 minutes more. Spoon-drop on greased aluminum foil quickly and allow to cool.

Serves: 8

Appendix: Publications, Associations, and Cookoffs

There are literally hundreds of chili cookoffs held each year, and space requirements prevent us from listing them all—and they change from year to year anyway. The chili publications are the best source of information on the cookoffs.

Publications

- *Goat Gap Gazette,* 5110 Bayard Lane #2, Houston, TX 77006
- *International Chili Society Publication,* P.O. Box 2966, Newport Beach, CA 92663, (714) 631-1780

Associations and Cookoffs

- Chili Appreciation Society, International (CASI), 1307 Smiley, Amarillo, TX 79106, (806) 352-8783. Hut Brown, Executive Director
- The Original Viva Terlingua International Frank X. Tolbert–Wick Fowler Memorial Championship Chili Cookoff, also called "Behind the Store," is held the first weekend in November each year. For more information write: Viva Terlingua, P.O. Box 617, Corsicana, TX 75110
- The International Chili Society (ICS) World's Championship Chili Cookoff moves around from year to year and has recently been held in Reno, Nevada, and Scottsdale, Arizona. For more information, write: International Chili Society, P.O. Box 2966, Newport Beach, CA 92663, (714) 631-1780

Mail-Order Sources
for Chili Supplies

- Casados Farms, P.O. Box 1269, San Juan Pueblo, NM 87566, (505) 852-2433
- Colorado Spice Co., 5030 Nome St. Unit A, Denver, CO 80239, (303) 373-0141
- Don Alfonso Foods, P.O. Box 201988, Austin, TX 78720, (800) 456-6100
- Fredericksburg Herb Farm, P.O. Drawer 927, Fredericksburg, TX 78624, (800) 284-0525
- Frieda's, Inc., P.O. Box 58488, Los Angeles, CA 90058, (800) 241-1771
- Gunpowder Foods, P.O. Box 293, Texas, MD 21030, (800) PEPPERS
- Hi-Co Western Products, 1806 E. Main, Mesa, AZ 85203, (602) 834-0149
- Hobson Gardens, Rt. 2, 3656 E. Hobson Road, Roswell, NM 88201, (800) 488-7298
- Los Chileros, P.O. Box 6215, Santa Fe, NM 87502, (505) 471-6967
- Old Southwest Trading Company, P.O. Box 7545, Albuquerque, NM 87194, (505) 836-0168
- Pendery's Spices, 304 E. Belknap, Fort Worth, TX 76102, (800) 533-1870
- Santa Cruz Chili & Spice Co., Box 177, Tumacacori, AZ 85640, (602) 398-2591
- Southwestern Flavor Company, P.O. Box 315, Red River, NM 87558, (505) 754-2221
- Stonewall Chile Pepper Company, P.O. Box 241, Stonewall, TX 78671, (800) 232-2995

Bibliography

Associated Press. "State Accepts Chile Challenge." *Las Cruces Sun-News* (March 12, 1993): A-1.

———. "Chile or Chili?" *Albuquerque Tribune* (June 14, 1985).

Baldwin, Pat. "Texans All Hot Over Illinois' 'Chilli'-State Claim." *The Dallas Morning News* (November 2, 1993): 8D.

Bianco, Marie. "Chile Cultists Keep Contests on the Front Burner." *Albuquerque Journal* (March 14, 1991): B-1.

Booth, George C. *The Food and Drink of Mexico*. Menlo Park, Calif.: The Ward Ritchie Press, 1964.

Bridges, Bill. *The Great American Chili Book*. New York: Rawson, Wade Publishers, 1981.

Brittin, Phil, and Joseph Daniel. *Texas on the Halfshell*. Garden City, N.Y.: Doubleday & Co., 1982.

Brooks, William T. *Chili, Chile, Chilli, Chille*. Cornville, Ariz.: CBK Productions, n.d.

Butel, Jane. *Chili Madness*. New York: Workman, 1980.

Calhoun, Ray. *Pretty Faire Eats*. Richardson, Tex.: Ray Calhoun, 1991.

Caldwell, Red. *Pit, Pot & Skillet*. San Antonio: Corona Publishing, 1990.

Carlisle, R. F. "A Systems Engineering Analysis of a Process: How to Cook Winning Chili." Unpublished ms., 1986.

Chili. 1979–. P.O. Box 2966, Newport Beach, CA 92663. Official Publication of the International Chili Society. Jim West, ed.

Chili Appreciation Society, International. *Official CASI Rules*. Dallas: CASI, Inc., 1992.

Cogan, Floyd J., and Bessie D. Cogan. *The Devil's Sourcebook of Chili and Other Hellish Things*. Waterville, Ohio: Floyd J. Cogan Enterprises, 1980.

Cooper, Joe. *With or Without Beans*. Dallas: William S. Henson, Inc., 1952.

Cox News Service. "Wimberly Family Cooking Up Texas Chili Dynasty." *San Antonio Express-News* (January 27, 1993): 5B.

Crum, John K. "A Small Dissertation Upon Chili con Carne." Washington, D.C.: American Chemical Society, 1987.

DeWald, Louise. *Arizona Highways Heritage Cookbook*. Phoenix: Arizona Department of Highways, 1988.

DeWitt, Dave, and Nancy Gerlach. "The Evolution of Chili con Carne." *The Whole Chile Pepper* (Winter 1989): 14.

Domenici, Peter. "The Correct Way to Spell Chile." *The Congressional Record*, vol. 129, no. 149 (November 3, 1983).

Earl, Johnrae, and James McCormick. *The Chili Cookbook*. Los Angeles: Price/Stern/Sloan, 1972.

Eckhardt, Linda West. *The Only Texas Cookbook*. New York: Grammercy Publishing Co., 1985.

Evans, George W. B. *Mexican Gold Trail, The Journey of a Forty-Niner*. San Marino, Calif.: The Huntington Library, 1945.

Fischer, Al, and Mildred Fischer. *Chili Lovers' Cook Book*. Phoenix: Golden West Publishers, 1984.

Freelander, Douglas. "Chili Cook-Off Draws Record Crowd." *Houston Post* (January 24, 1993): A-23.

Geltner, Herb, and Chris Geltner. *Chilimania! The Chilihead's Handbook*. Merrit Island, Fla.: GSC Books, 1992.

Goat Gap Gazette. 1985–. 5110 Bayard Ln. #2, Houston, TX 77006. Judy Wimberly, pub.; Jo Ann Horton, ed.

Gomez, Bill. Interview. December 2, 1993.

Herter, George Leonard, and Berthe E. Herter. *Bull Cook and Authentic Historical Recipes and Practices*. Waseca, Minn.: Herter's, Inc., 1960.

Heywood, Jim. "Chili: The All-American Dish." *Taste,* Culinary Insitute of America, vol. 21, no. 1 (Spring/Summer 1993): 22–23.

Horton, Jo Ann. "The Chili Appreciation Society, International—A History, Sorta." *The Whole Chile Pepper* (Winter 1989): 22.

———. "Not By Chili Alone: What Chiliheads Cook When They're Not Cookin' Chili." *Chile Pepper* (September–October 1990): 28.

Housholder, Andy. *How to Make a Championship Chili and Win!* Mesa, Ariz.: Hi-Co Western Products, 1990.

Hudgins, Sharon. "Red Dust: Powdered Chiles & Chili Powder." Oxford, England: Oxford Symposium on Food & Cooking, 1992.

Huebner, Jeff. "United for Chili." *Chicago Tribune* (November 7, 1991).

Jamison, Cheryl Alters, and Bill Jamison. *Texas Home Cooking.* Boston: Harvard Common Press, 1993.

Kolpas, Norman. *The Chili Cookbook.* Los Angeles: HP Books/Price, Stern, Sloan, 1991.

Linck, Ernestine Sewell, and Joyce Gibson Roach. *Eats: A Folk History of Texas Foods.* Fort Worth: Texas Christian University Press, 1989.

Logan, Paul. "Chile Cook's Efforts Spiced with Taste of Success." *Albuquerque Journal Business Outlook* (February 8, 1988): 17.

Marshall, Thom. "Consumed by Bowls of Red." *Houston Chronicle* (June 7, 1991): A-25.

McGee, Harold. *On Food and Cooking.* New York: Charles Scribner's Sons, 1984.

———. *The Curious Cook.* San Francisco: North Point Press, 1990.

McNeil, Blanche, and Edna McNeil. *First Foods of America.* Los Angeles: Suttonhouse Ltd., 1936.

Miller, Mark. "Chile Flavor Descriptors." Flyer from his lecture at Santa Fe Wine and Chile Festival (September 1993).

Morton, Julia. *Herbs and Spices.* New York: Golden Press, 1976.

Neely, Martina, and William Neely. *The International Chili Society Official Chili Cookbook*. New York: St. Martin's Press, 1981.

Ortiz, Elisabeth Lambert. *The Complete Book of Mexican Cooking*. New York: M. Evans, 1967; Bantam, 1976.

————. *The Encyclopedia of Herbs, Spices & Flavorings*. New York: Dorling Kindersley, 1992.

Patoski, Joe Nick. "Chili Relations." *Texas Monthly* (November 1992): 60.

Pendergrast, Sam. *Zen Chili*. Abilene, Tex.: Little Red Hen Press, 1983.

————."Requiem for Texas Chili." *The Whole Chile Pepper* (Winter 1989): 28.

Pickard, Nancy, and Virginia Rich. *The 27-Ingredient Chili con Carne Murders*. New York: Delacorte Press, 1993.

Potts, Richard L. "Pardon My Emission: Our Most Explosive Article Yet." *Chile Pepper* (May–June 1993): 46.

Preston, Mark. *California Mission Cookery*. Albuquerque: Border Books, 1993.

Robinson, Randy. "A View from the Top." *Official Publication of the International Chili Society* (June–August 1992): 15.

Rosenblatt, Richard. "Chili Bill Hottest Topic in Congress." *Albuquerque Journal* (September 13, 1993): A-1.

Ruark, Lou Ann. "When Not Lobbying for Chili, He's Eating or Judging It." *Tulsa World* (September 9, 1989).

Schad, Tom. "The Spicy History of Chili." Kansas City, Mo.: Gilbert & Christopher, 1993. (Press Release)

Smith, H. Allen. "Nobody Knows More About Chili Than I Do." *Holiday Magazine* (August 1967).

————. *The Great Chili Confrontation*. New York: Trident Press, 1969.

St. Ann's Society. *Mission Cookbook*. Tucson: St. Ann's Society, 1909.

Stern, Jane, and Michael Stern. *Way Out West*. New York: HarperCollins, 1993.

Stiger, Susan. "Rival Cities Pepper Mexican Cook-Off." *Albuquerque Journal* (December 10, 1987): D-1.

———. "Santa Fe Wins Chile Challenge." *Albuquerque Journal* (November 11, 1988): F-7.

Stock, Melissa T. "Viva Terlingua!" *Chile Pepper* (September–October 1993): 18.

Thompson, Chuck. *Chuck Thompson's Canned Chili Report*. Houston: Chuck Thompson, 1992.

Thorne, John. *Just Another Bowl of Texas Red*. Boston: The Jackdaw Press, 1985.

———. "Just Another Bowl of Texas Red." *Chile Pepper* (September–October 1990): 37.

Tipton, Alice Stevens. *The Original New Mexico Cookery*. Santa Fe: New Mexico State Land Office, 1916.

Tolbert, Frank X. *A Bowl of Red*. New York: Doubleday, 1966.

Valentine, Tom. "How to Get the Most Out of a Chili Cookoff 'Happening.'" *Chili*, (1985): 22.

West, Jim, and Ormly Gumfudgin. "The International Chili Society—History, Maybe." *The Whole Chile Pepper* (Winter 1989): 25.

Whelpley, Keith. "Chile Event Aims at Texas. *Las Cruces Sun-News* (December 16, 1992): A-1.

Wood, C. V., Jr. "How to Judge a Chili Cookoff." *Chili Magazine*, vol. 1, no. 1 (1980).

York, A. Vann. Personal correspondence. October 12, 1993.

Zumwalt, Betty. *Ketchup, Pickles, Sauces: 19th Century Food in Glass*. Sandpoint, Idaho: Mark West Publishers, 1980.

Index

International Conversion Chart

These are not exact equivalents; they've been slightly rounded to make measuring easier.

Cup Measurements

American	Imperial	Metric	Australian
1/4 cup (2 oz)	2 fl oz	60 ml	2 tablespoons
1/3 cup (3 oz)	3 fl oz	84 ml	1/4 cup
1/2 cup (4 oz)	4 fl oz	125 ml	1/3 cup
2/3 cup (5 oz)	5 fl oz	170 ml	1/2 cup
3/4 cup (6 oz)	6 fl oz	185 ml	2/3 cup
1 cup (8 oz)	8 fl oz	250 ml	3/4 cup

Spoon Measurements

American	Metric
1/4 teaspoon	1 ml
1/2 teaspoon	2 ml
1 teaspoon	5 ml
1 tablespoon	15 ml

Oven Temperatures

Farenheit	Centigrade
250	120
300	150
325	160
350	180
375	190
400	200
450	230